UNSOLVED

UNSOLVED

True Canadian Cold Cases

Robert J. Hoshowsky

DUNDURN
TORONTO

Editor: Cheryl Hawley
Design: Courtney Horner

Library and Archives Canada Cataloguing in Publication

Hoshowsky, Robert J.
          Unsolved : true Canadian cold cases / by Robert J. Hoshowsky.

ISBN 978-1-55488-739-2

          1. Cold cases (Criminal investigation)--Canada. 2. Murder--Canada.

I. Title.

HV6535.C3H68 2010   364.152'30971   C2009-907476-1

1   2   3   4   5   14   13   12   11   10

We acknowledge the support of the **Canada Council for the Arts** and the **Ontario Arts Council** for our publishing program. We also acknowledge the financial support of the **Government of Canada** through the **Book Publishing Industry Development Program** and **The Association for the Export of Canadian Books,** and the **Government of Ontario** through the **Ontario Book Publishers Tax Credit program,** and the **Ontario Media Development Corporation.**

Care has been taken to trace the ownership of copyright material used in this book. The author and the publisher welcome any information enabling them to rectify any references or credits in subsequent editions.

J. Kirk Howard, President

Published by The Dundurn Group

www.dundurn.com

Dundurn Press
3 Church Street, Suite 500
Toronto, Ontario, Canada
M5E 1M2

Gazelle Book Services Limited
White Cross Mills
High Town, Lancaster, England
LA1 4XS

Dundurn Press
2250 Military Road
Tonawanda, NY
U.S.A. 14150

Contents

Acknowledgements

WRITING IS A SOLITARY PURSUIT; research is not. A book like *Unsolved: True Canadian Cold Cases* is not possible without conducting numerous interviews, expanding upon the crimes themselves through additional details, and clarifying or correcting information which originally appeared in stories published in newspapers and magazines at the time of the murder or disappearance in question.

Works of true crime often require material from a variety of sources beyond archival stories, and documents from various police agencies. *Unsolved* is largely based on original interviews with individuals who were directly affected by the crimes, such as surviving family members and friends of victims. Without exception, all those I spoke to who have lost a family member to homicide, or whose relatives vanished without a trace and have never been found, have a great interest in seeing the cases solved, and the guilty parties brought to justice. I thank them all for their enthusiasm, courage, and willingness to share their feelings about crimes that, in some cases, took place forty years ago.

Attempting to solve cold crimes is a lengthy process involving police officers and professionals from many other areas. For *Unsolved* I interviewed detectives and other individuals directly involved in the process, past and present, including retired officers and auxiliary police who were part of the original investigation, lawyers, forensic artists, representatives from missing persons agencies, victims rights advocates, private investigators, and television producers. My gratitude goes out to everyone who was willing to participate in this project.

They are: Sonja Bata (founding chairman, Bata Shoe Museum), Brent Bauer, David Boothby, Jim Bunting, Norina D'Agostini (Toronto Police Museum), Jacqueline de Croÿ (Fondation Princesses De Croÿ), Trish Derby (former executive director, Child Find Ontario), Christopher M. Downer (investigator/professional speaker, the C.D. Group), Angela Ellis (media representative, the Doe Network), Tim Gore (detective, Homicide and Missing Persons Bureau — Cold Case Unit, York Regional Police), Edward Greenspan (Greenspan Partners), Ann Greenwalt (technical records specialist, Central Records, Idaho Department of Correction), Gary Grinton (detective sergeant, Toronto Police Service), Linda Harris, David Johnson (president, Innotech Rehabilitation Products Inc.), Teresa Jones (administrative support manager, Idaho Department of Correction), Cherilyn Lafferty, Brian J. Lawrie (founder, POINTTS), Mark Mendelson (Mark Mendelson Consulting Corporation), Irwin Patterson, Alexa Phillips [name changed by request], Reg Pitts (detective sergeant, Toronto Police Service Homicide Squad, Cold Case/Special Projects), Bruce Priestman (Metropolitan Toronto Police Pensioners Association), David Quigley (detective inspector, Ontario Provincial Police), Nikki Randall (sergeant, Caledon Ontario Provincial Police), Brian Raybould (staff inspector, Toronto Police Service Homicide Squad), Peter Thompson (master corporal, Canadian Forces National Investigation Service), Diana P. Trepkov (forensic artist), Todd B. White (Greenspan Partners), Robert Wilkinson (detective, Toronto Police Service), and Ray Zarb (detective sergeant, Toronto Police Service Homicide Squad).

I especially wish to thank everyone I mentioned for their time, understanding, patience, and candor. Some generously provided me with original research materials, photos, and other documents that greatly benefitted my writing and understanding of the crimes themselves.

While researching this book I was especially touched by the honesty and openness of family members who have lost loved ones to murder

Acknowledgements

or abduction. I cannot imagine anything more personal than sharing your feelings about how someone you cared for was brutally stolen, in some cases at a very young age. For the families of many victims, the loss affected their lives in ways many of us can never — and hopefully will never — know. In several chapters of *Unsolved*, I have incorporated the effects these murders have had on surviving family members, taking care not to victimize the families all over again. Likewise, while researching and writing this book, I have developed an even greater respect for members of many missing children organizations, and those who fight one of the greatest dangers facing children today: online predators. All of these people are dedicated volunteers who work with little or no funding and cannot be acknowledged enough for their hard work.

In addition, I would like to thank all the staff at Dundurn for their support, in particular president and publisher Kirk Howard, editorial director Michael Carroll, Tony Hawke, and assistant editor Cheryl Hawley. This book would not be possible without their assistance, and the generosity of the Ontario Arts Council.

My heartfelt thanks also to all staff working in branches of the Toronto Public Library. This book, and much of my work over the past twenty years, has benefitted from your knowledge, patience, and valuable assistance.

On a personal note, my deepest gratitude goes out to my wife, Elizabeth, for her unwavering support and tolerance of my absenteeism, sometimes for months at a time, while working on *Unsolved*.

Thanks always to Peter C. Newman for his encouragement and words of wisdom, and to the spirit of my mother, Ann Hoshowsky, for always watching over my shoulder.

It is my sincere wish, for the families and victims of the dead and disappeared in this book, that the guilty parties be brought to justice, and that their unsolved cases can finally be closed.

This book is dedicated with love and respect to my father, Morris Hoshowsky, the most honourable and decent man I will ever know.

Introduction

We are each of us responsible for the evil we might have prevented.
— James Martineau

WRITING A BOOK ABOUT UNSOLVED crimes — as I have found
out — is a physically, spiritually, and emotionally unsettling experience.
Over the course of researching and writing *Unsolved: True Canadian Cold
Cases* my thoughts kept going back to a well-known character from Greek
mythology by the name of Sisyphus. Condemned by Zeus to Tartarus —
a monstrous place deep below the underworld — his punishment was to
roll an enormous boulder up a hill, only to have it tumble back down the
steep slope time and time again, for all eternity. The task was maddening,
repetitive, unforgiving, and without end. For families of the murdered and
the missing whose crimes remain unsolved, every re-examination of their
case, every anniversary marking the death or disappearance of their loved
one, every tip or clue that starts out promising but eventually leads nowhere,
keeps bringing them back to the very same spot they started years before.

When someone is murdered or vanishes, never to be found, a void
is left behind that never completely closes. There is something especially
cruel about unsolved crimes and the pain that comes from not knowing
who took the life of someone you love, why they were killed, and what

happened to their remains. For the parents and surviving siblings, life the way it was before the crime comes to a sudden stop and can never be the same again. Even years later, the slim hope that their missing youngster is alive and might still be reunited with their family keeps coming back, as do the thoughts that they are likely dead, and that their bodies may never be recovered.

Sometimes, families of victims learn about new developments in their case when a piece of evidence is uncovered, forensic facial reconstructions unveiled, hidden genetic information revealed through DNA tests, or long-silent witnesses come forward to tell their story. Identifying skeletal remains after many decades, as in the case of Richard "Dickie" Hovey and Eric Jones, may bring families some satisfaction, but never closure. Reuniting missing family members and burying them alongside other relatives fills in large pieces of the puzzle but not the whole picture, especially if the person who took their life remains unapprehended and unpunished. In some instances, families talk to cold case detectives every few years about their case, resurrecting every single painful detail over and over again. *Did they have any enemies? Were they involved with drugs, or gangs? Was there anyone who paid your child too much unwanted attention? Did they have any unpaid debts, or gambling problems? Can you think of anyone who would want them dead?*

The families portrayed in *Unsolved* have given countless interviews to the media — often on the anniversary of their brother, sister, mother, father, or child's death or disappearance — and remain cautious, even guarded, about their emotions, never allowing themselves to become *too* excited about potential "new breakthroughs" or "exciting developments" in the crimes. Being hopeful is one thing, and being realistic is something else entirely. If tips come forward in their cold case it's easy to get caught up in the anticipation that the guilty will be brought to trial, and after so many years justice will finally be served. If the information leads nowhere, as often happens, and there is no resolution, the boulder rolls back downhill to the foot of the mountain, families gather the pieces of their soul, and the rebuilding process starts all over again.

When someone's life comes to a violent, abrupt end, the mourning process for the family members is fractured and incomplete. There is nothing natural or normal about murder. Losing a family member slowly over time allows grief to come in stages, not all at once, as those left behind struggle to prepare themselves for the inevitability of death. A loved one lost to homicide often creates overwhelming feelings of anger, grief, and guilt that can consume people for the rest of their lives. The shock is sometimes too much to bear, and no two people experience emotions the same way or for the same amount of time. Just as there is no statute of limitations on murder, there are no rules for how long someone will feel the pain, frustration, fear, and fault when someone they care about is killed. Some take solace in their faith, believing in a higher power and the thought that they will eventually be reunited in the afterlife. For others, friends and family endlessly repeat overused phrases like, "It is God's will," and, "Time heals all wounds," are of little comfort, as many question why a supreme being, if one exists, would allow someone they love to die such a brutal death.

Fortunately, there are numerous victims' rights groups that provide assistance to grieving families of murder victims. Some, like the Toronto Police Victim Services Department, offer material on resources, support groups, and the police investigative process. For many families the officer in charge (OIC) becomes their lifeline, the person they can call upon to find out where the investigation into the homicide of their family member stands. While some simply want to know when the person who took their relative's life is caught, others want to be as much a part of the entire criminal process as possible, from investigation to arrest, and trial to sentencing.

Those left behind to mourn are sometimes called homicide survivors. They are the other victims of crime, the living relatives of the dead whose rights have, for many years, been forgotten by society or ignored altogether. The Canadian Resource Centre for Victims of Crime poignantly states the realities facing families of murder victims: "No amount of counselling, prayer, justice, restitution or compassion can ever bring a loved one back." The emotional reactions some of these survivors have — including shock, guilt, anger, and depression — can lead to adverse physical symptoms, such as nausea, nightmares, increased blood pressure, and loss of appetite. Dealing with other family members, friends, and co-workers can become difficult, sometimes impossible. If these symptoms last a month or more following the murder, it is possible to be diagnosed with post-traumatic stress disorder (PTSD).

The number of families that fall apart after the death or disappearance of a loved one cannot be calculated. Some will stay together for months, even years, while others — especially parents of murdered children — blame their partner or surviving sons or daughters for not "being there for them," and not protecting the victimized child from a violent predator. Many couples divorce and surviving children sometimes become estranged from one another, as attention focuses on the dead instead of the living.

Wherever possible, I conducted interviews with family and friends of missing persons and murder victims for *Unsolved*. Very early on I was amazed at how many were not just willing but eager to talk, sharing not only their memories but their feelings, often of guilt, anger, and remorse. This often meant resurrecting painful details about how their loved ones died. The reason for many of them: to keep the stories of the dead and missing alive and let the world know they are not forgotten — and neither are their killers.

Following a homicide many people become involved in the process. There are the families of the victim, friends, witnesses, and police who investigate the crime. There are the detectives, the searchers, volunteers, and the media, who often play a large part in disseminating details about the crime and the possible suspects. Trying to catch a killer is a complicated process involving police working on many levels. There are the uniformed officers who are often the first to arrive and cordon off areas to protect the integrity of the crime scene, which can be as small as a room or as large as several city blocks. There are the detectives who come in and direct officers to search here and there, or go door-to-door to find witnesses, anyone who heard or saw anything that could help in the investigation. In the case of a missing child, there are the officers who go wherever the search takes them, from police divers in the muddy waters of an old gravel pit to abandoned buildings, dense forests to rundown rooming houses. Depending on the case there are often countless people involved in trying to catch a killer, including forensic artists, private investigators, ballistics experts, child find and missing persons agencies, and pathologists.

Writing a book about unsolved cases brings with it a host of challenges. There is the need to ask the cold, dispassionate, and often grisly specific questions: *How long did it take them to die? What type of weapon was used? What was the exact cause of death? Was the weapon recovered? Were they sexually assaulted?* These types of questions were best left to police officers, veteran detectives, private investigators, and others possessing first-hand knowledge of the crime. Family and friends of murdered and missing persons were better able to fill in details about their loved ones and his or her personality traits, likes, dislikes, successes, failures, goals, and aspirations.

The genesis of *Unsolved* was in conversations I had with some of the talented editors at Dundurn, namely Michael Carroll and Tony Hawke. After the publication of my first book, *The Last to Die: Ronald Turpin, Arthur Lucas, and the end of Capital Punishment in Canada*, in 2007, I had a number of ideas for my next project. Several outlines were written, and a number of ideas were tossed back and forth. One of them was suggested by Tony: "Why not write a book about unsolved crimes?" Tony is perhaps one of the most knowledgeable people I've ever met when it comes to the subject of Canadian mysteries, having overseen and edited countless books on strange goings-on in Canada. He possesses not only genuine warmth of character but an almost childlike enthusiasm and eagerness for potential projects. A number of older cases were mentioned, such as the unusual circumstances surrounding the 1917 death of artist Tom Thomson, the unexplained disappearance of Toronto theatre magnate Ambrose Small in 1919, and the mysterious murder of millionaire Sir Harry Oakes in his Bahamas mansion in 1943. All were mesmerizing cases about larger than life figures who have become an integral part of the Canadian consciousness over the decades, and a collection of these old stories would surely become a valuable reference book.

At the time my feelings were mixed. Having a familiarity with all of these cases, I know that all of them have been the subject of numerous books published over the years, along with documentaries, movies, plays, even entire websites devoted to a single case. I was reluctant to write a book about these and other older crimes unless I could bring something new to the reader, as I had with my first book, such as previously unknown letters, hidden or suppressed government documents, never before published photographs, or interviews with individuals who had not spoken to the media in decades, if at all.

My interest as a writer has always been bringing together stories from the past with interviews from the present. After several weeks of searching through my own memory, missing persons websites, true crime blogs, police cold case websites, newspaper files, books, magazines, archives, and talking to friends, I began working on an outline for a book on Canadian crimes, which eventually became *Unsolved.*

All writers, from first-timers to professionals, need guidelines and structure, or their work is likely to float off into the heavens like an untethered balloon. To satisfy my needs, I came up with a number of parameters for all of the cases. It didn't matter if the victims were male or female, rich or poor, known or unknown, or if their deaths or disappearances were widely covered in the press at the time or have been forgotten. The words *still solvable* kept echoing through my head as I was researching and writing this book, and I settled on a timeline: no case could be more than approximately forty years old. The rationale behind this? Even if a case is decades old, there is still a chance the killer — even if he or she is now a senior citizen — can still be caught and convicted. Assuming a murder or disappearance took place back in the late sixties, there could still be people who remembered the victim or victims, as was the case with Richard "Dickie" Hovey and Eric Jones, who recalled seeing these young men getting into a car with a stranger, most likely their killer. All the murders and disappearances in this book are still open, and in many cases, leads continue to trickle in to the police years later.

Unsolved is unlike many other true crime books. There are many things it is, and many things it is not. It was never my intention to create an "encyclopedia" of unsolved Canadian crimes, since such an endeavour for one writer — let alone a team of writers, researchers, editors, proofreaders, photographers, and fact checkers with years to spare and an unlimited budget for resources — is simply not possible. Across the country, there are literally thousands of cold cases waiting, pleading to be solved, some of them going back decades.

Many major police departments in Canada have websites devoted to unsolved cases and murder suspects, including the Royal Canadian Mounted Police. In Toronto, the Homicide Squad Unsolved Cold Cases website (*www.torontopolice.on.ca/homicide/unsolvedcold.php*), which went online in 2008, currently features dozens of cases along with summaries of the crimes, photos, maps, videos, applicable reward and contact information, and other related materials. It is their intention to post hundreds of other unsolved murders on the site, estimated between three hundred and 350, going back to 1957, the year Toronto Police Service was formed. The number of hours required by police, computer technicians, web designers, and others to write the summaries, scan and post the photos, update, and maintain the website is tremendous. The Resolve Initiative, a website created by the Ontario Provincial Police (*www.missing-u.ca*), works in partnership with the Office of the Chief Coroner. Featuring hundreds of cases, divided into missing persons and unidentified bodies/remains, the site went online in 2006 and receives thousands of hits per month. These sites, regularly updated and maintained, provide up-to-the-minute accounts of cold cases that cannot possibly be covered in one book.

Likewise, *Unsolved* is not a traditional "anthology" that true crime aficionados are accustomed to reading. Unlike the majority of compilations, which assemble dozens of short, previously published articles, usually culled from newspapers or magazines, into book form, all the cases presented here are original, researched and written expressly for this book, and have never been published in any other form — book, magazine, or on any websites — until now. During the course of researching and writing this book every effort has been made to paint as complete a picture as possible, from the time the crimes took place to the present day. In a number of cases new information was made available shortly before the book was published and has been incorporated into

Unsolved. This need to include information that is as up-to-date as possible resulted in several unavoidable delays, and I am grateful to my publisher, Dundurn, for realizing the importance of presenting this material in the book.

Books based solely on repackaging old stories are informative — and heaven knows my shelves are full of them — yet they all suffer from one serious drawback: the author rarely, if ever, updates the material, in effect leaving the reader with an incomplete snapshot rather than a full portrait. In my opinion, this does a tremendous disservice to the reader, the victim, and his or her family. *All* cold cases going back forty years can be updated, even if tips are few and far between. Over time, police will often release information that wasn't made available years earlier in the interest of generating more coverage about a particular cold case, such as the disappearance and murder of Veronica Kaye in 1980. A significant piece of evidence, a small metallic button found underneath her skeletal remains in 1981, was not released to the public until almost thirty years later, in 2009. In the case of Hovey and Jones, their unidentified skeletal remains sat in boxes at the office of the coroner for almost four decades, until the Ontario Provincial Police retained the services of a forensic artist, Master Corporal Peter Thompson, from the Canadian Forces National Investigation Service. Over the course of several weeks Thompson painstakingly applied depth markers, clay, and false eyes to the skulls until they became faces once again. As a result, the remains of both young men were soon reunited with their families, yet their murderer remains at large.

Readers may remember some widely publicized stories, such as the brutal 1983 rape and murder of nine-year-old Sharin' Morningstar Keenan. The only suspect in her murder, Dennis Melvyn Howe, remains at large. The search for Howe was one of the largest in Canadian history, taking police to remote locations across North America, from mining camps to a cemetery in Sudbury, Ontario, to exhume the remains of a man believed to be Sharin's killer. Although Howe has not been caught, his face is etched into the minds of many Canadians through wanted posters and news coverage, and Toronto Police continue to receive tips about the case to this very day.

Introduction

Some cases, such as the unexplained disappearances of fourteen-year-old Ingrid Bauer in 1972 and eight-year-old Nicole Louise Morin in 1985, remain unsolved despite massive searches by police and volunteers, age-enhanced photos and illustrations depicting what they would look like as adults, rewards, and the distribution of thousands of missing persons posters. At the time they disappeared the Internet was many years away. Today, their names and the details of their cases are being kept alive through video re-enactments on YouTube, and information posted on police websites, the Doe Network, and Child Find, to name a few.

One of the greatest challenges in writing a book about unsolved crimes is deciding which cases to include. And what happens if a case you're writing about is solved? As someone with a keen interest in true crime since childhood, I grew up reading about a number of the crimes in this book and have wanted to write about them for a long time. Others were suggested by police officers and representatives from missing persons organizations. I also received numerous emails from friends and families of murdered and missing persons who heard about my upcoming book via the Internet, and have tried to include these cases where possible.

A number of cases I originally intended to include in *Unsolved* were, in fact, solved during the time I was researching and writing, most notably the May 2007 murder of multi-millionaire and philanthropist Glen Davis. I originally intended to contrast the Davis homicide with another case, the unsolved 1998 murder of businessman and Obus Forme founder, Frank Roberts. Both men were enormously wealthy but came by their millions in entirely different ways. Davis was the son of Argus Corporation chairman Nelson M. Davis and inherited a vast fortune when his father died in the pool at his Arizona home in 1979. Roberts was a self-made man who, following a tennis injury, invented a unique back support that found its way into thousands of homes and offices across Canada.

Both Davis, sixty-six, and Roberts, sixty-seven at the time of his death, were enormously rich but had completely opposite public personas. While Roberts embraced the limelight, Davis eschewed it completely, except on those rare occasions when it helped to promote awareness of his favourite environmental charities, like the Sierra Club and the World Wildlife Fund. The thrice-married Roberts was the father of two sons, a daughter, and had thirteen grandchildren; Davis was married to the same woman for years, and had no children. Tragically, the larger than life Roberts and the shy, unassuming Davis both met their ends violently. Roberts was gunned down in the West Toronto parking lot of his factory, while Davis was shot to death in a North Toronto underground parking lot. Immediately, the lives of both men were plastered across newspaper headlines and stories were a muddied mixture of fact, rumour, and innuendo. *Were the murderers dissatisfied business associates from the past? Did a jealous husband order the hit? Were large corporations, whose very existence depended on logging, mining, and other activities that destroy wildlife behind the slaying of Glen Davis?*

In both cases, the line between fact and fantasy quickly became blurred in the media and online, as reporters exposed the professional and personal lives of Davis and Roberts. In many ways, Davis was the world's luckiest man. Left with an empire worth $100 million, he cheated death. The first time was in 1983, when he survived an airplane fire that claimed twenty-three lives, including Canadian folk musician Stan Rogers. The second was in 2005, when he was savagely attacked outside his Toronto office by a man wielding a baseball bat. The third occasion, in the parking garage on the afternoon of Friday May 18, 2007, Davis's luck ran out. As a youngster I knew Davis — albeit not very well — and remember speaking to him at length soon after he survived the fire that broke out aboard Air Canada flight 797. Davis was a soft-spoken and decent individual, and as of this writing several men, including Davis's first cousin once removed, have been charged in connection with his senseless homicide. In the end, it appears the motive for his murder had nothing to do with conspiracy theories about big businesses versus environmentalists, but money, which he willingly gave away in the millions to help causes to benefit humanity.

Unsolved crimes present us with a kaleidoscope of emotions. Intriguing and infuriating, I believe that some of the cases in *Unsolved* still have a chance of being solved, even years after the murder or disappearance took place. Time and technology can sometimes be an advantage in cold cases. As the years pass, witnesses may recall details that seemed unimportant at the time or feel more comfortable approaching police with information because they no longer fear reprisal. Scientific advances, such as DNA technology, have given new life and renewed hope to solving many cold cases, as seen in the case of Susan O'Hara Tice and Erin Harrison Gilmour. In life, Tice and Gilmour never knew one another and had very little in common. A recently divorced mother of four children, Tice moved back to Toronto from western Canada in the summer of 1983, and was brutally murdered soon after. Just a few months later, attractive, single socialite Erin Harrison Gilmour, just twenty-two, was murdered in her Yorkville apartment. Both women were raped and semen recovered from the crime scenes was subjected to DNA testing seventeen years later in 2000, revealing the same man was responsible for killing both women. The murders of Tice and Gilmour remain unsolved, yet their killer's genetic fingerprint is on file.

Technology has dramatically advanced the way police search for suspects, going far beyond the days of wanted posters papering the walls of police stations and post offices. Just as criminals have kept pace with technology, so have police agencies, which frequently use the latest tools to apprehend criminals. It is not uncommon for police to incorporate social networking websites like YouTube and Twitter to inform the public and the media about murder or bank robbery suspects, or help locate missing children. As technology progresses, friends and families of murder victims also pay tribute to their lost loved ones through websites like MySpace and Facebook.

This book has been an emotional experience from the beginning, and I cannot say "from beginning to end," since there is no end, at least not yet. Unsolved crimes don't reach their conclusion with the death or disappearance of a loved one, they reach their end with the perpetrators being caught. Even in cases like the murder of Sharin' Morningstar Keenan where there is only one suspect: Dennis Melvyn

Howe. For many people, the case will never be closed until he is located, alive or dead.

My intention with this book is to keep the names of the murdered and the disappeared alive, and possibly resurrect memories from someone, anyone, who has information in whoever committed these crimes so that they can be brought to justice.

Every effort has been made to paint as complete a picture as possible, from the times the crimes took place to the present day. In a number of cases new information was made available shortly before the book was published and has been incorporated. All the cases in this book should be here and deserve to be solved, not just for the victims but for the families left behind.

One final note: Some of the cases in this book have been the subject of numerous theories; a few of these theories are plausible, while others are highly unlikely. *Unsolved* is based on facts made available to the author up to the time of publication. In order to create as accurate a picture of the crime(s) and subsequent investigation(s) as possible, a number of these theories are included in the book. They are clearly stated as "theories" or "speculation" in the text and are *not* the belief of the author or the publisher. They have been included to provide the reader with the greatest amount of knowledge possible about each case.

Visit Robert J. Hoshowsky's website at *www.truecrimecanada.com.*

Chapter 1

Richard "Dickie" Hovey and Eric Jones (1967)

BACK IN 1967, THE WORLD WAS A vastly different place than it is today. While every generation can stake a claim to a decade as their own, anyone coming of age in the sixties remembers it as a period of unprecedented social change. In the United States, citizens were challenging not only themselves but their government and its policies as race riots were sweeping throughout the county, and fifty thousand men and women protested against the war in Vietnam at Washington's Lincoln Memorial. In Canada, the country united in celebrating its centennial at Expo 67 in Montreal — and threatened to divide when French President Charles de Gaulle proclaimed "Vive le Québec libre!" ("Long live free Quebec!"), enraging English Canadians and sowing the seeds of separatism. Shouts of equal rights for all were heard as legions of young women, blacks, gays, and lesbians took to the streets, demanding respect. The generation gap was widening, as legions of bewildered parents realized that the expression "Don't trust anyone over thirty" was not intended for someone else, but for them. Sons and daughters, wearing suits and dresses only a few years before, were discarding their sensible, conservative clothes for tie-dyed T-shirts, ripped jeans, sandals, and scraggly hair. It truly seemed as though the planet had changed overnight, leaving legions of exasperated parents and rebellious teenagers in its wake.

Across America a new age had dawned, and the cosmic epicentre was San Francisco's Haight-Ashbury district. Named after the intersection of the two streets, the Haight was the perfect place to rent a cheap apartment in one of the area's massive, old wooden houses. A popular gathering place for students, poets, writers, musicians, and philosophers, the Haight soon became the beating heart of the counterculture movement in America. "Make Love, Not War!" was the chant of the young, as thousands of idealistic, wide-eyed teenagers converged on the area, lured by the promise of free love, cheap drugs, the right to free speech, and music many of them never imagined could even exist. Just a few years earlier, kids and their parents were listening to vinyl records by moral and non-threatening artists like Neil Sedaka, Connie Francis, Pat Boone, and Bobby Vinton. By the mid-sixties these acts were seen as antiquated and boring. A new musical tide was rising, led by reactionary musicians like the Grateful Dead, Janis Joplin, and the Doors, fronted by the sexually hypnotic and deeply disturbed singer-songwriter, Jim Morrison.

In the late sixties, rock 'n' roll was still king but a new monarch was coming to court. Her name was Grace Slick, and her band was Jefferson Airplane. The release of the group's innovative 1967 album *Surrealistic Pillow* was nothing less than a psychedelic sonic overload. Regarded today as one of the finest acid rock records ever recorded, *Surrealistic Pillow* spawned the hits "Somebody to Love" and "White Rabbit," a two minute and thirty-two second aural experience referencing many of the otherworldly characters in Lewis Carroll's book *Alice's Adventures in Wonderland*, such as the dormouse and the hookah-smoking caterpillar. The song became an anthem, if not *the* anthem, for the hippie generation. Back then, no one could predict that Jefferson Airplane would morph into Jefferson Starship before finally landing on the airways as Starship almost twenty years later with their pop hit, "We Built This City," arguably one of the most reviled songs of all time. San Francisco, once the centre of the psychedelic universe, became, with breathless exclaim, "The city that rocks, the city that never stops!"

Back then it seemed as though the new ideals would last forever. It was a defining period in history, an age of sexual liberation that became known as the Summer of Love. For some Canadians, the year would be known not as a time of peace, love, and understanding, but for things dark, terrifying, and murderous. Over forty years later, many would come to remember Canada's summer of 1967 as the Summer of Death.

Slender, energetic, and still just a boy at seventeen years of age, Richard James Hovey — "Dickie" to his friends — was one of the many thousands of young men and women who flocked to Toronto in 1967. America may have had San Francisco as its counterculture oasis, but Canada claimed its own musical Mecca in the streets of downtown Toronto. The States had bands like Jefferson Airplane and the Quicksilver Messenger Service, but Canada boasted plenty of its own talent, including future legends like Neil Young and Joni Mitchell, many of them playing live in Toronto's Yorkville area. Hovey came from out east for the

Richard "Dickie" Hovey, lead guitarist for Teddy and the Royals, with his prized guitar, an inexpensive Sears model that he painted white and modified to look like an expensive Fender. Hovey's skeletal remains were not identified for almost forty years

(Ontario Provincial Police)

25

musical experience; others were hippies looking for a place to stay, or draft dodgers from the United States, who came because they didn't believe in the war in Vietnam. Whatever the reason, Yorkville was the place to be that year.

Today, the area's narrow, boutique-lined streets bear little resemblance to the Yorkville of forty years ago. The borders remain the same, decades after the sonic and cultural revolution of the sixties: Bloor Street to the south, Avenue Road to the west, and Yonge Street and Davenport Road to the east and north. The section near downtown is the home to a number of luxury hotels, condominiums, and countless famous designer shops like Vuitton, Boss, and Chanel, exclusive places where money is no object, and if you need to ask the price you should be buying somewhere else. One of the world's top shopping destinations, rents in Yorkville are among the highest in North America today, averaging a minimum of several hundred dollars per square foot, depending on what side of the street you're on.

In 1967, Yorkville wasn't about expensive handbags, salons, and shoes, it was about the music. It was the place where countless Canadian artists got their start, like Murray McLauchlan and Neil Young. "You could walk down Yorkville Avenue and see Joni Mitchell on her front doorstep playing guitar,"[1] said David Clayton-Thomas, lead singer for Blood, Sweat & Tears. Back then, Yorkville was a place without pretension, where you could go to any of the local European-style coffee houses or bars and sit for hours on end, listening to one great folk or rock artist after another. Yorkville was a veritable who's who of music, where the country's finest congregated: Young, Mitchell, Gordon Lightfoot, and Bruce Cockburn to name a few. Many American artists also flocked to play at one of Yorkville's many clubs and cafes, like future funk legend Rick "Super Freak" James, Blues singer and guitarist Buddy Guy, and folk musician Mike Seeger.

The names of clubs soon became as legendary as the musical acts they hosted. There was the Riverboat, a coffee house featuring a mix of established and up-and-coming Canadian bands. Nearby were the Mousehole and the Purple Onion. One of the most famous was the Mynah Bird, known in equal parts for the calibre of the musical talent and the eccentricity of the surroundings. Yorkville had a lot of great clubs where you could catch the latest groups, but the Mynah Bird was the only one featuring a real talking bird, barely dressed go-go dancers grooving to the music, and live grass literally growing up the walls. The Mynah Bird was the place to see and be seen. It was also where Richard Hovey played his guitar for a few weeks back in 1967. Hovey's style of dress was decidedly more mod than hippie. He kept his dark blond hair swept forward, and favoured turtlenecks, expensive-looking jackets, and narrow trousers over long, unwashed hair and sloppy clothes. When "Dickie" dressed in his royal blue jacket, his look resembled one of the early British Invasion bands that landed on the shores of North America a few years earlier, like the Kinks, the Beatles, or the Moody Blues.

Like many boys in their teens, Hovey's face — with its high, arched eyebrows, turned-up nose, triangular jaw, smooth skin, and compact mouth — was still very delicate, almost feminine. As the Kinks song goes, he was a dandy, a handsome young man concerned with his appearance, and why not? At just five and a half feet tall, Hovey was not much larger than many of the girls who clamoured after him as he played guitar in Yorkville or back home in Marysville, a suburb of Fredericton, New Brunswick. Out east, Hovey had been playing lead guitar in a band called Teddy and the Royals since he was fifteen and still attending school. The group was popular, playing dances for local kids. They were named after Teddy Brown, the band's eighteen-year-old vocalist; the "Royals" part of their name came from the clothing the five members wore onstage, sharp-looking royal blue jackets. The band was profiled a number of times in the local papers, complete with photos and references to one of their influences, Johnny Rivers, famous for his song Secret Agent Man.

For Richard Hovey, Marysville was home, the place where his family, friends, and bandmates lived, but Toronto's emerging music scene was calling. When he left New Brunswick in 1967, Hovey hitchhiked his way to Ontario, taking few possessions except for a couple of dollars and his prized electric guitar. He was passionate about music and making it big, and if it was going to happen it was going to be in Yorkville. In time, the name Richard Hovey might have been mentioned in same venerated breath as Neil Young or Gordon Lightfoot, except that at some point in 1967, soon after arriving in Toronto, the young musician literally disappeared without a trace.

Most of Hovey's friends from Marysville knew he'd gone to Toronto, and didn't think it was strange when they didn't hear from him, at least not for awhile. It was the sixties, after all, and travelling across the country for weeks at a time wasn't all that unusual back then. Still, some of his family and friends became concerned when the weeks turned into months without a word, not even a letter, a long-distance collect call, or even a hastily-scribbled postcard. Some assumed Hovey settled down and was living a normal life in Ontario, but his parents, Melvin and Phyllis, weren't so sure. Melvin took his concerns about Richard to the local branch of the Royal Canadian Mounted Police, but for reasons unknown the information was never properly filed as a missing persons report. His parents knew their teenaged son made it to Toronto, guitar in hand, but what became of him? Years went by, turning into decades of uncertainty over the young man's fate. Melvin passed away in 1991, followed by Phyllis in 2003. Both parents went to their graves never knowing what happened to their son. It would be almost forty years before young Richard Hovey's fate, and name, would be revealed.

On May 15, 1968, a farmer was plowing his field in Tecumseth Township near Schomberg, about twenty-five miles north of Toronto. It was an isolated area, surrounded by tall grass, dense brush, and overgrown trees, certainly not a place you'd go to unless you had a very good reason. Troubled by a foul smell he thought was coming from his septic tank, the farmer went to investigate and saw something that would haunt him forever. Near a rusty wire fence in a hedgerow were the rotting remains of a young man. The naked body, reduced by decay, insects, and animals to a skeleton, was laying face down in the earth. A few pieces of dried, blackened skin could still be seen here and there, and some hair still remained on the scalp. Although almost all the flesh was missing, a white shoelace remained intact, tying the hands of the body behind its back. With no signs of clothing present and the hands restrained, this clearly was no accidental death.

As disturbing as the discovery was, it was part of a larger problem: this was the *second* body found in a remote area, in a similar advanced state of decay. On December 17, 1967, less than six months prior to the remains being discovered by a farmer near Schomberg, the skeletal remains of another male were uncovered in a lonely, wooded area of Balsam Lake Provincial Park, about ninety miles north of Toronto, south of Highway 48, near Coboconk, Ontario. In time, Ontario Provincial Police would refer to this body as the "Balsam Lake Victim." Forensic tests revealed the remains were those of a young man, likely fifteen to eighteen years old, twenty-two at most. It was believed the remains had lain in the same spot for about six months. A forensic examination revealed that the teeth were in exceptionally good condition, and had recent fillings in the left and right lower first molars. Remaining hair on the head was straight, light brown, and of medium length. Unlike the discovery near Schomberg, this skeleton displayed a number of unusual characteristics. Instead of twelve thoracic vertebrae, this body had a thirteenth vertebra, and an additional thirteenth rib on the right side. If these physical anomalies were known to the victim's family or friends, it could help identify the remains.

Like the body found near Schomberg, this young man was also naked. No clothing was found except for a pair of white, low-cut, size seven, tennis-style shoes made in Czechoslovakia. The hands were tied together, just like the other victim. Instead of binding the hands with a shoelace, however, they were tied with an eleven-foot length of twine. The remains were those of a small man, no more than five feet three inches tall. Police did not know the identity of either of these nameless young victims, yet they were united in many ways, like brothers in death.

"The bodies were linked by victimology," said David Quigley, a deputy inspector with the Ontario Provincial Police and lead investigator in the cases. Details about both young men, along with those of many other cases, are online as part of the OPP Resolve Initiative, a website created in 2006. In partnership with the Office of the Chief Coroner, the site features hundreds of cases, divided into missing persons and unidentified bodies/remains. In just a few years, the Resolve Initiative has become a successful example of the powers of the Internet, generating hundreds of tips from the public, and receiving between four and six thousand hits per month.

From time to time, the OPP reviews cold cases, such as the unidentified remains found near Schomberg and the skeleton discovered close to Coboconk. For almost four decades, the unclaimed bodies of these two young men sat on a shelf in numbered boxes at the coroner's office in Toronto. Both victims had much in common: they were male, small, likely still in their teens, and found in secluded areas within the same general time period, late 1967 to mid-1968. The hands of both victims were bound, and since no clothing was found except for a pair of tennis shoes in the area of the Schomberg victim, the murders appeared sexual in nature. As part of the resurrected investigation, Quigley and other officers revisited the places where the bodies were found, armed with metal detectors and original crime scene photos. The hedgerow near the farmer's field had grown over in the decades since the first body was discovered, but it was recognizable, and looked about the same way it did back in the sixties — still isolated, and not a place likely to attract much attention.

The Ontario Provincial Police soon presented details of the crimes to the media, along with the faces of the deceased victims. Using the actual skulls, a forensic artist carefully placed tissue depth markers and layers of clay to reconstruct the faces, which were displayed at an OPP press conference in late 2006, almost forty years after the two sets of remains were found. The heads and neck were visible, and both wore simple white dress shirts, one with stripes, the other checks. The faces were young and boyish looking underneath brown wigs that sat atop the heads of both victims, their expressions wide-eyed and not quite human, almost frozen with terror.

A major crimes investigator and forensic artist with the Canadian Forces National Investigation Service, Master-Corporal Peter Thompson spent hour after hour applying clay to the skulls of the deceased, rebuilding the faces in the hope that someone could identify them and finally give them back their names. Thompson was known to the OPP for some time for his composite drawings, many of them based on witness descriptions of bank robbers and kidnappers. Although he was accustomed to creating sketches of criminal suspects this was the first time in his career that Thompson did three-dimensional reconstructions.[2] Before he could begin working for the OPP, Thompson had to receive permission from his superiors at the Canadian Forces. Once the chain of command gave their approval, Thompson met with the OPP, who presented him with photographs of the skulls and old crime scene photos of the remains. These were essential to providing the artist with a sense of the tools he would require — and the many challenges he would face — recreating the faces of the dead.

"With three-dimensional reconstruction, skulls have to be in good condition, and be able to bear the weight of the clay," said Thompson, who painstakingly examined, measured, sketched, photographed, and catalogued the remains from the moment he received them. If the skulls were damaged he likely would have created a drawing instead, a two-dimensional reconstruction of the faces. Fortunately, the remains were stable enough to tolerate handling and the application of depth markers and clay.

Thompson was thoroughly prepared to recreate the faces of the two dead boys. He is quick to credit the forensic techniques taught to him by two of his key instructors when he was learning his craft at "the Academy," the Federal Bureau of Investigation in Quantico, Virginia. A fast learner, Thompson was fortunate enough to study under artists widely considered legends in the field of forensics: Betty Pat Gatliff and Karen T. Taylor. Gatliff, a retired medical illustrator, teaches forensic art workshops on facial reconstruction using actual human skulls, and operates her own studio, Skullpture Lab, in Norman, Oklahoma. Among her many credits, Gatliff did clay reconstructions of some of the decomposed victims of John Wayne Gacy, one of America's most notorious serial killers. Her work allowed a number of families to give their dead sons proper burials.

Taylor's background is no less impressive than that of her fellow instructor. Credited with coining the term "forensic art" in the 1980s, her qualifications include working as a portrait sculptor at Madame Tussauds Wax Museum, and as an instructor at the FBI Academy for over twenty years. The classes Peter Thompson took with Taylor and Gatliff were his only formal art instruction, and he said his natural ability to draw came from his father.

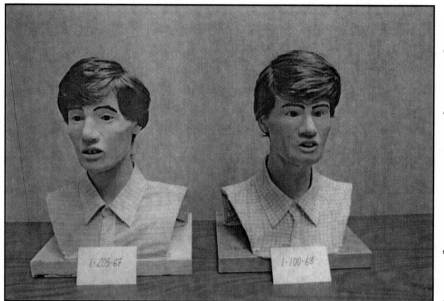

(Master Corporal Peter Thompson, Canadian Forces National Investigation Service)

Forensic facial reconstructions of two young men who were recognized years later as Eric Jones (left) and Richard "Dickie" Hovey. The actual skulls are beneath the layers of clay.

The forensic reconstruction process, said Thompson, is a cooperative one between the police, the coroner's office, and the artist. Meeting with the coroner in Toronto where the skeletal remains of both young men were housed, Thompson performed intensive assessments on the bodies. Although he had the training to identify bones as being male or female, an anthropologist measured the bones as they lay on a table, and compared the measurements to photos taken in the sixties.

Remaining true to his FBI training, Thompson avoided putting any "ego" into his work. He omitted any details or embellishments that could mislead anyone viewing the completed reconstructions, keeping them as simple as possible. Before applying any clay to the skulls he did a detailed preliminary examination, noticing both victims had an overbite of the bottom teeth. This detail was crucial, and the faces were deliberately created with the mouths slightly open, "So that people who would view the reconstructions would be able to see the teeth, and perhaps that would trigger some recognition." Once the faces were completed the two victims looked like brothers, young men united in death.

The skull of Richard "Dickie" Hovey with depth markers attached. His skeletal remains were found in an isolated area of Tecumseth Township near Schomberg, about twenty-five miles north of Toronto, on May 15, 1968.

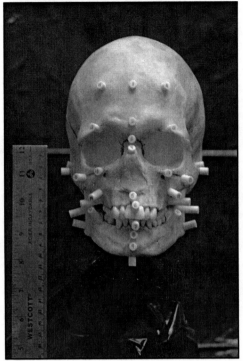

(Master Corporal Peter Thompson, Canadian Forces National Investigation Service)

After finishing his work, Thompson remembers hoping to God that someone would recognize the young men, and be able to give a name to the mysterious remains that sat shelved in boxes for almost forty years. His silent prayer was answered when a friend and a family member, independent of one another, viewed media coverage of the reconstructions and contacted the OPP. One of the clay-covered skull photographs seemed hauntingly familiar, resembling a long-lost relative and friend who left home for Toronto back in 1967. Members of the OPP travelled to New Brunswick and, after obtaining blood samples from family members, confirmed that one set of remains were those of Richard Hovey, the handsome young guitarist missing for almost forty years. A name could finally be placed to the "Schomberg" remains found in May 1968, just one day after what would have been Hovey's eighteenth birthday.

Although the positive identification of the body provided some degree of consolation to Hovey's family and the police, many questions remained unanswered. What was the identity of the other young male found in the desolate forest of Balsam Lake Provincial Park? How did these young men arrive at their final destinations? When were they killed, and how? What happened to Hovey and the other male during the last hours of their lives? Were there other known victims, living or dead? Most important of all: who killed them?

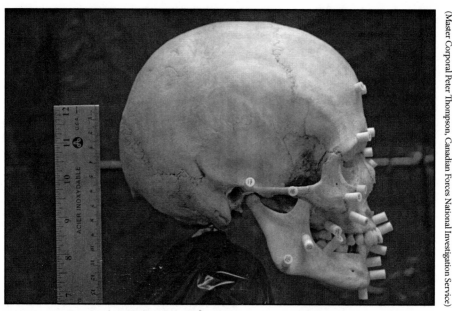

(Master Corporal Peter Thompson, Canadian Forces National Investigation Service)

A profile view of the skull of Richard "Dickie" Hovey with depth markers attached.

Although police will not confirm any specific suspect or suspects in the murders, it is known that young men were targeted by a serial sexual predator in the Church and Wellesley area of Toronto back in 1967. Just as Yorkville was a haven for musicians in the sixties, so was the downtown Church/Wellesley section the heart of the city's growing gay village. Today, the area is an immensely popular tourist destination for gays, lesbians, the transgendered, drag queens, and the merely curious. Regarded as "the Gay Mecca of Canada," the place was not nearly as open or friendly in the sixties. Back then, the area was frequented by young men who feared the police morality squad and gangs of gay bashing teenagers more than being picked up by an overly aggressive sexual partner. Yellowed, old newspapers of the time reveal articles about one man who frequented the area, and remains the most likely suspect in the murders.

Now in his early seventies, James Henry Greenidge fits the pattern of murders in an eerily perfect way. Presently behind bars in a British Columbia prison, Greenidge — who has since changed his name to James Gordon Henry — is by all accounts a model prisoner with a surprisingly high IQ. During his many years in prison, Greenidge hasn't touched drugs or gotten himself into trouble. He has completed the Intensive Sexual Offender Program, and is known to be helpful and cooperative with staff. Reportedly, he has spent much of his time tutoring other inmates, yet it remains uncertain how many of them, if any, are aware of the staggering, unimaginable brutality he committed in the past.

The crimes perpetrated by Greenidge are not just disturbing, they are truly horrifying — rivalling those committed by the character Jame Gumb, better known as "Buffalo Bill," in the book and film, *The Silence of the Lambs*. At least there is some solace to be had in the knowledge that Gumb is fictional; Greenidge is all too real, and considered to be Canada's first serial killer. His early life — like that of many youngsters who grew up to become pattern killers — was rife with abuse, abandonment, neglect, and a barely contained temper that unexpectedly rose to a boil. At the age of five, Greenidge developed tuberculosis and was sent to a sanatorium, where he was forced to clean toilets. Soon after, he began a pattern of running away and stealing. At one point, he was raised by a strict aunt whose child rearing skills included physical and mental torment. The young Greenidge frequently fled his so-called home, and was sexually abused at reform school.

Over the years, Greenidge's body grew, and so did his uncontrollable fury. By the age of sixteen he was working as a "hustler," a male prostitute, and began to demonstrate incredibly violent sexual tendencies. In time, he would blame much of his behaviour on his aunt, who allegedly told him of the dangers of being a male Negro in society, and of the lynchings of young black men that took place in the American South. According to parole records, Greenidge viewed himself as a lonely and isolated individual, a victim of racism — or so he said — and someone who needed to protect himself at any cost. The biggest threats to his life, his aunt told him, came from associating with "white women or homosexuals." Tragically, Greenidge took her words seriously. In his teens, he was exhibiting a high degree of narcissism and sexual sadism, which he inflicted on girls and boys alike, all of them white. Although still young, his violent, sadistic streak was far from satiated — it was just beginning.

In 1955, Greenidge, then eighteen years old, was sentenced to ten years for viciously attacking and raping a fourteen-year-old girl in Toronto. Examined by psychiatrists at the time, the teenage Greenidge demonstrated a "defect in personality," was deemed irresponsible, and showed no sign of wanting to reform. A hospital laundry worker, Greenidge was arrested a mere twenty-one hours after the attack, following the announcement of a reward. At the trial, the jury took only one hour and fifteen minutes to reach their verdict of guilty. The pronouncement was not surprising, considering the brutal circumstances of the attack.

In what would amount to the greatest understatement of the judge's career, Greenidge was told, "I don't think you are safe to have around." The young black man showed no signs of remorse, or wanting to reform. The teenaged girl was walking home with a bag of groceries when Greenidge grabbed her, dragging her kicking and screaming down an alleyway. He then proceeded to sexually assault her, choking her at the same time, almost to the point of death. Even veteran police officers, men who had witnessed all kinds of depravity, were thoroughly repulsed by the viciousness of the attack on the helpless girl. All her clothes, right down to her shoes, were ripped from her body, which was left beaten, bloodied, and desecrated. Fortunately, the girl was able to give a remarkably detailed description of her attacker, "a husky Negro," about five feet eight inches tall, eighteen years of age. At his trial, Greenidge, the one-time art student and church choirboy, complained the confession was beaten out of him at a police station. No one cared to listen.

Tragically, the rape was only the start of Greenidge's life as a sexual predator and unstoppable violent offender. After his parole in 1960 he was unable to control his rage and continued his pattern of becoming violent in mere moments. In 1965 Greenidge nearly choked a man to death, believing he was responsible for helping to put him behind bars. Characteristic of the viciousness of his attacks, Greenidge beat the man, dragging him one hundred feet into a laneway to continue the assault. He had his hands around the man's throat when neighbours saw the horrific assault taking place and called the police. In a sickening twist, he almost pummelled the wrong man to death. The mistaken identity assault landed Greenidge in a reformatory for six months, while his victim was

Undated photo of convicted killer James Greenidge, who later changed his name to James Gordon Henry. He was first convicted of violent crimes in the fifties, and is presently behind bars in British Columbia for the horrific murder of a young woman in 1981.

sent to hospital to recover from his serious injuries.

Although just in his twenties, Greenidge had spent years of his life in jail and was rarely out on the streets for long before being sent back behind bars. In 1967 he was sentenced to seventeen years for a number of horrific crimes. He nearly killed one man he'd picked up in Toronto's gay village. Another victim, seventeen-year-old Robert Wayne Mortimore, wasn't so lucky. Mortimore's naked, tattooed body was found in a field northeast of Markham, Ontario. The young insurance clerk was reported missing on July 11 by his brother, and his decomposing remains — missing in the heat of summer for over a week — had to be identified through fingerprints and part of a birth certificate found in Greenidge's car. One of Mortimore's tattoos said "Born to raise hell," while another was a dagger, dripping blood. A number of items were missing from the body, including a silver ring with the initials R.M., a second ring with a black stone, a chain with a gold cross, and a pair of blue and white mod-style trousers.

At the time of Mortimore's murder, Greenidge was already serving time for the attempted murder of a twenty-one-year-old man who he left beaten, naked, and bleeding in a field. The pair, said Greenidge, met at a movie theatre known as a gay pickup place and drove out to the country on a gravel stretch of road to a farmer's field north of Barrie, Ontario. The man then made the mistake of asking Greenidge for twenty bucks, allegedly for sex. This threw him into a rage. Pouncing on his victim, Greenidge began punching, kicking, and stabbing the man repeatedly in the throat and chest with a penknife. He then bound the man and left him naked, alone, and bleeding to death. Police said that if the man had not been found within a few hours, he surely would have died.

When he was released from prison in 1978, Greenidge changed his name to James Gordon Henry. His name was different, but his sexual rage remained as strong as ever. In Winnipeg he was charged with sodomizing a thirteen-year-old boy, who he then tried to strangle to death with a blanket. The charges against Greenidge were stayed. While out of jail, Greenidge killed his last known victim in 1981. He was sentenced to life in prison for the brutal rape and murder of Elizabeth Fells, a twenty-four-year-old prostitute. Picking up the woman, Greenidge drove her to an isolated spot in the woods north of Vancouver and flew into a rage. Raping the woman, he then stabbed her over and over again, slashing her throat and leaving her barely alive in an isolated area, repeating his unremitting pattern of violence. Somehow, Fells managed to crawl to the side of the Squamish Highway and flagged down a passing car. She died in hospital eight days after her horrifying attack, but lived long enough to give police a detailed description of her attacker: James Henry Greenidge. Her statement helped police capture Greenidge, who was arrested and charged with her murder.

Over the years, many people fell victim to Greenidge's rage: women, men, and children. They all have one thing in common: they were white, like Richard Hovey and the young man found at Balsam Lake. The lives of these young men were cut tragically short and no one, save for their killer or killers, knows what the last moments of their lives were like, dying naked in an isolated area with no one there to save their lives.

Thanks to the skills of forensic artist Master Corporal Peter Thompson, the remains formerly known as the Balsam Lake Victim finally have a name. On March 9, 2009, police revealed his identity. The skeletal remains found near Coboconk, Ontario — with the extra thoracic vertebra and rib — were those of Eric Jones from Noelville, Ontario. The original forensic estimate of his age was accurate: Jones was just

For Public Display
Pour affichage

GHQ Special Circular 09-03
First Issue 06-18

Circulaire spéciale QG 09-03
Première publication 06-18

ONTARIO PROVINCIAL POLICE
POLICE PROVINCIALE DE L'ONTARIO

Victim – La victime :
Eric JONES

$ 50,000 REWARD
RÉCOMPENSE DE 50 000 $

The Government of the Province of Ontario is offering a total reward of fifty thousand dollars ($50,000) for information leading to the arrest and conviction of the person(s) responsible for the murder of Eric JONES.

On December 17, 1967, skeletal remains were found in a wooded area of Balsam Lake Provincial Park, south of Highway 48, near COBOCONK, Ontario. There was no clothing present with the exception of a pair of low cut, white tennis style shoes, size 7, made in Czechoslovakia. An eleven-foot length of twine was found with the skeleton. This piece of twine had a knotted loop immediately adjacent to the hand and wrist bones.

It has been estimated that the remains may have been at this location since late spring to early summer, 1967. The cause of death is not known. These remains were identified in 2009 to be those of Eric JONES.

JONES was last seen by family members in April of 1967. At the time of his death he was 18 years old and living in the City of Toronto.

Any person with information regarding the person(s) responsible for this murder should communicate immediately with the Director of the Criminal Investigation Branch, Ontario Provincial Police at 1-888-310-1122 or (705) 329-6111, their nearest police authority, or Crime Stoppers.

This reward will be apportioned as deemed just by the Minister of Community Safety and Correctional Services for the Province of Ontario and the Commissioner of the Ontario Provincial Police.
CIB File# 955-10-1968-030

Le gouvernement de la province de l'Ontario offre une récompense de cinquante mille dollars (50 000 $) pour tout renseignement pertinent qui conduira à l'arrestation et à la condamnation de la ou des personnes responsables du meurtre d'Eric JONES.

Le 17 décembre 1967, des restes humains ont été découverts dans une région boisée du parc provincial Balsam Lake, au sud de la route 48, près de Coboconk (Ontario). Il n'y avait aucun vêtement aux alentours, à l'exception d'une paire de chaussures de sport, coupe basse (style chaussures de tennis), blanches, taille 7, fabriquées en Tchécoslovaquie. Avec le squelette se trouvait une corde qui comportait une boucle nouée immédiatement adjacente aux os de la main et du poignet.

Il a été estimé que ces restes humains se trouvaient à cet endroit depuis la fin du printemps ou le début de l'été 1967. La cause de la mort est inconnue. En 2009, ces restes humains ont été identifiés comme étant ceux d'Eric JONES.

Eric JONES avait été vu pour la dernière fois par des membres de sa famille en avril 1967. Il était alors âgé de 18 ans et vivait à Toronto.

Il est demandé à quiconque en possession de renseignements sur la ou les personnes responsables de ce meurtre de communiquer immédiatement avec le directeur des enquêtes criminelles de la Police provinciale de l'Ontario, au 1 888 310-1122 ou au 705 329-6111, avec le poste de police le plus proche ou avec Échec au crime.

Le partage de la récompense s'effectuera de la manière jugée équitable par le ministre de la Sécurité communautaire et des Services correctionnels de la province de l'Ontario et le commissaire de la Police provinciale de l'Ontario.
Dossier n° 955.10.1968-030

Ontario Provincial Police reward circular for Eric Jones, whose skeletonized remains were found in a wooded area of Balsam Lake Provincial Park on December 17, 1967.

eighteen when he died. Once the identification was made, police were able to create a profile of the young man and the circumstances that may have led to his death. If it were not for one of Jones's sisters watching a television program she rarely viewed, her brother's body would likely have remained unidentified forever.

In February 2009, *W-Five* aired a special about Richard Hovey and the other unidentified remains. Pauline Latendresse, one of Eric's sisters, happened to turn on the television program that day and immediately recognized the clay reconstruction of her long-lost brother's face. Excited, she began phoning her siblings, telling them to "watch it, watch it right now." The next day, police came by and collected DNA samples from family members. Tests soon confirmed the remains were those of the missing Eric, son of the late Napoleon and Alexina Jones.

Through interviews with surviving family members, police were able to reconstruct the life and final days of Eric Jones, who came from a large family of eleven children. An older brother, Oscar, remembered the last time he saw Eric. It was at a wedding for one of their sisters in April 1967. By this time, Eric had moved to Toronto to live with an aunt and look for work as a dishwasher, returning for his sister's wedding. The brothers argued about Eric quitting school and moving away from home. Tragically, it would be the last time Oscar saw his brother alive.

Described by his family as a bit of a shy kid and a loner, Eric wrote letters back and forth to his sister Pauline for about six weeks after he arrived in Toronto. One day, the letters she mailed to her brother came back unopened and unread, marked "No such address." The aunt Eric was living with in Toronto had moved to Montreal, taking his belongings with her. Since she had not seen or heard from the eighteen-year-old, she assumed he moved back to Noelville. The missing man's sister contacted police agencies across the province and was led to believe that Eric, a solitary sort, probably didn't want to be in contact with his family. His sister never believed her brother would want to estrange himself from the family and hoped to see Eric alive again some day. That day never came, and once the remains were released, Eric Jones was buried next to his parents.

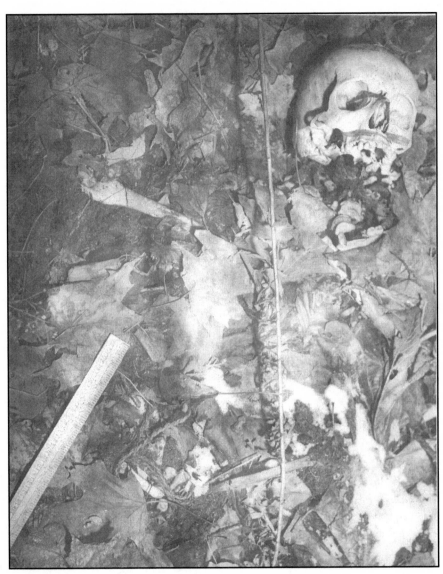

(Ontario Provincial Police)

The skeleton of the Balsam Lake victim, estimated to be about fifteen to twenty-two years of age at the time of death. For years, police hoped the remains would be identified due to some unusual physical anomalies, such as an additional thoracic vertebrae and a thirteenth rib on the right side.

Since reopening the cases of Hovey and Jones, the OPP have aggressively investigated leads in the decades-old cases. A $50,000 reward has been announced for information leading to an arrest of the person or persons who murdered Jones and Hovey. Police believe the dead teenagers are only two of five young men who were abducted, bound, sexually assaulted, and slaughtered.

Back in 2006, OPP investigators spoke to Prime Timers — a gay social seniors group — at a special meeting in Toronto. Displaying Thompson's forensic reconstructions of the two then-unidentified young men, police hoped viewing the faces might help someone remember who they were, and where and when they were last seen. Since that time, police have determined that Richard Hovey — whose remains were found near Schomberg — was last seen alive in Yorkville, in 1967, getting into a light blue Corvair driven by "a muscular black man." It is believed Jones also got a ride with the man in the same model car.

Convicted sex killer James Henry Greenidge drove a light-coloured Corvair, which was used to identify him by a surviving victim, the twenty-one-year-old who Greenidge beat, stabbed, and left for dead in a farmer's field north of Barrie. Ironically, the car driven by Greenidge was deadly in more ways than one. The Corvair remains one of the most dangerous vehicles ever made, with a tendency to oversteer, overheat, skid wildly out of control, lift, or worse, flip over. The car was so dangerous it became the first chapter of the book by lawyer and consumer advocate Ralph Nader, *Unsafe at Any Speed*. More than merely hazardous, driving the car could be fatal, leading Nader to call its design, "One of the greatest acts of industrial irresponsibility in the present century."[3] For Greenidge, the car suited his personality: fast, powerful, unstable, and potentially deadly.

The similarities between the murders and Greenidge's *modus operandi* are too many to ignore. The FBI classifies three types of serial killers: organized, disorganized, and mixed. Organized killers are methodical, and often have an above average IQ. Disorganized killers have a lower than average IQ, and rarely take the time to cover their tracks or dispose of a body. The disorganized killer is unlikely to have his own vehicle, usually relying on other forms to transportation, like public transit or walking. If he does have a car it is likely to be messy and not in good working order. Organized offenders usually have their own means of transportation, keeping it in top condition. Perhaps most telling is the way organized killers operate. Unlike the disorganized offender, the organized killer takes along their own restraints, such as a rope and handcuffs, during their hunt for their next victim.

In many ways, criminologist and noted FBI serial killer tracker, Robert K. Ressler, might have been writing about the killer of Hovey and Jones when he wrote his book, *Whoever Fights Monsters*:

> Taking one's own car, or a victim's car, is part of a conscious attempt to obliterate evidence of the crime. Similarly, too, the organized offender brings his own weapon to the crime and takes it away once he is finished. He knows that there are fingerprints on the weapon, or the ballistic evidence may connect him to the murder, so he takes it away from the scene. He may wipe away fingerprints from the entire scene of the crime, wash away blood, and do many other things to prevent identification either of the victim or of himself. The longer a victim remains unidentified, of course, the greater the likelihood that the crime will not be tracked back to its perpetrator. Usually the police find the victims of an organized killer to be nude; without clothing, they are less easily identified.[4]

Police are investigating Greenidge in connection to yet another unsolved murder of a victim who has yet to be named. On July 16, 1980, a motorist pulled his car off the side of a rural road in the town of Markham, Ontario, ostensibly to relieve himself. It was around 8:30 p.m. and getting dark. The area around the Eleventh Concession north of Steeles Avenue was much like it is today, semi-rural, full of woods and dense brush, and sparsely populated with farms and houses. The man walked about seventy-five feet from the road into the woods when he made an unnerving discovery. On the ground were the skeletal remains of a human body. Unlike the bodies of Hovey and Jones, found decades earlier, this time police found a significant amount of clothing lying on the earth next to the skeleton. But considering that the bones turned out to be those of a male, the items were not quite what police expected to uncover.

All the garments and accessories were women's clothing. Police discovered a red blouse, a pair of size thirty women's blue jeans, a pair of red and pink high-heeled shoes, short white frilly socks, and a woman's powder compact complete with a mirror. All the items led investigators to believe that the remains were those of a transgendered male or a cross-dresser, someone who likes to wear clothing from members of the opposite sex.

Although the body had been reduced to a skeleton and disturbed, likely by animals, forensic examiners were soon able to determine that they belonged to a small male about five feet three inches to five feet five inches tall. Even without flesh a great deal can be revealed about someone from their skeletal remains, such as approximate age, sex, physical stature, and race, known as "the big four" to forensic anthropologists. Our bones and teeth reveal vast amounts of information about our age through the epiphysis, caps on the ends of long bones that fuse completely once we leave our teens. Epiphysis on bones in other parts of the body, such as the clavicle, fuse later in life, around age thirty. From then on, signs of bone loss, deterioration, and work-related injuries become more evident. Someone who lays bricks or pours concrete for a living will have a much different bone structure and density than another person who works as a personal assistant in an office.

Tests of the bones revealed that the Markham victim was white, and about twenty-five to forty years of age. In life, the man would have been small with an extremely light build — somewhere between one hundred and 120 pounds at the most — and a thin, even gaunt, face. Considering the weathered condition of the boney remains, the body and clothing would likely have been in the woods for about two years by the time they were found, placing the time of the man's death at around 1978. The time frame coincided with a period when Greenidge was out of jail.

It is believed the victim wore the items found around him at one point, but was not wearing them at the time he died. Later testing revealed there were no signs of decay inside the clothes, such as the socks and pants, which

A museum quality facial reconstruction of the face of the Markham victim, unveiled in December 2009. Found off the side of a rural road in the Town of Markham, Ontario, on July 16, 1980, it is estimated that the body remained undiscovered for two to three years. The victim, a male twenty-five to forty years old, is believed to have been transgendered or a cross-dresser and has yet to be identified.

(York Regional Police)

a skeleton, investigators at the tim[...] cause of death. Police say the rema[...] weapons being used or blunt force[...] have been strangled, as was the [...] victims? Police aren't saying.

Adding to the mystery is the question of what became of the remains of the Markham victim? Unlike the bodies of Richard "Dickie" Hovey and Eric Jones, which sat properly stored in numbered boxes at the office of the coroner in Toronto for decades, the unidentified male discovered in the woods was, for some unknown reason, buried in a pauper's grave at Toronto's Mount Pleasant Cemetery on Christmas Eve 1983, along with the clothes. The reasons for interring the remains *and* the female garments found near the body have not been revealed.

In 2007 the cold case of the mysterious Markham victim was resurrected by York Regional Police and the skeletal remains — which had been buried in the cemetery for years — were disinterred and reexamined using the latest available technologies. "We felt that it was necessary to exhume the body," said Douglas Clarke, a homicide detective-constable with York Region. "We had photographs but we didn't have the actual items."[5]

The initial belief by police at the time the body was discovered was not that this was the body of someone who was murdered, but a young male who wandered into the brush and died, or the unfortunate victim of a car accident. The original coroner's report is confusing, and allegedly states the man was possibly struck by a car, sailing over the road and into the trees, where his body remained for several years until it was found in 1980. The notion has since been revised, since it doesn't take the obvious question into consideration: why would the victim of a hit and run be found naked in the woods, with clothing near his body? It is not unusual for the victim of an auto accident to literally be knocked out of their shoes by the tremendous force of the impact, but to suggest that the rest of the clothing — jeans, socks, and blouse — would also be wrenched off is absurd, and makes one question the professionalism of anyone foolish enough to suggest such a ridiculous scenario, or allow the clothing to be buried with an unidentified body. York Regional Police have revised the earlier notion that these are the remains of an accident victim, and now believe the young man met his demise as a result of foul play.

Following the exhumation of the remains, police were able to obtain something not available to them at the time the bones were discovered in 1980: DNA. Even though the technology exists, there was still no guarantee that precious DNA would be recoverable. The body had been in the woods for at least two years by the time it was found, and subjected to insect activity, animals, wind, rain, the blistering heat of summer, and the ice and snow of winter. Conditions following burial at Mount Pleasant Cemetery would have been better, but only slightly, since the skeleton would still face the cold and damp conditions of the grave.

Fortunately it was possible to extract DNA from the disinterred bones and teeth, which was collected and compared with missing persons reports across the province. York Regional Police recently had a close call with the family of a missing gay man from Montreal. The physical description was very close and the man disappeared around 1978, approximately the same time as the male victim died in the Markham woods. Hoping for a break in the cold case, Detective-Constable Clarke drove to Montreal and obtained a blood sample — unfortunately, it wasn't a match to the remains. Police are hopeful that the DNA sample they now have on file can be used to compare the Markham victim's remains to those of a living relative, and that one day a match will be made.

Like Hovey and Jones, the victim found in 1980 recently had a clay

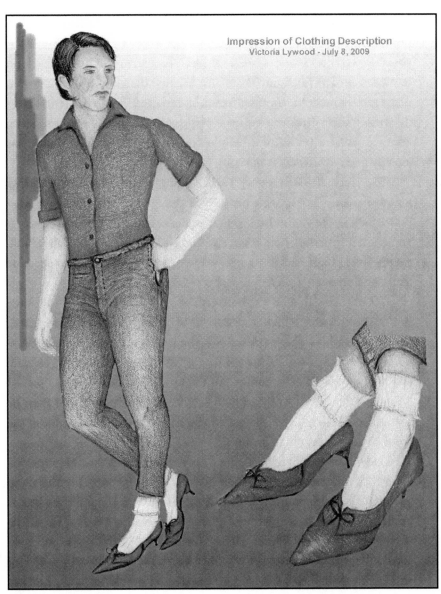

Impression of Clothing Description
Victoria Lywood - July 8, 2009

A recent artist impression of the male Markham victim, based on clothing found near the body in 1980. In life, the man was no more than 120 pounds and five and a half feet tall. A red blouse, women's blue jeans, red and pink high-heeled shoes, frilly, white socks, and a woman's powder compact led police to believe the body was that of a male cross-dresser.

bust recreation made of his face, which was unveiled to the media and posted online at the York Regional Police website in December 2009. Considering the actual skull that the reconstruction was based on had been buried for many years and became damaged and misshapen due to extreme cold, the final result is remarkably lifelike. The three-dimensional clay portrait was sculpted by an artist after the skull was scanned using a brand new technology, and is so accurate that it has already been described as museum quality.

"We hope it looks pretty close to this and that someone comes forward," said Clarke, who unveiled a drawing to the media of what police believe the victim looked like in life: a slender, effeminate-looking young man with dark hair about four inches long, wearing red and pink, pointy-toed, high-heeled shoes, white frilly socks, form-fitting blue jeans, and an open-collared, red, short-sleeved blouse.

"It's my belief that he was transgender, possibly in the sex trade down in the Toronto area which … was a bit of a haven, in the 70s, for gays," said Clarke, who also speculated that the young man may have come to Toronto years ago to live his life as part of the city's large gay, lesbian, and transgendered community. "In my opinion, I think he was picked up in the city, taken to [Markham], endeavours occurred and then he was killed and left there," repeated the detective-constable, calling the wooded area "a dumping ground."[6]

Considering the viciousness of his earlier crimes and his repeated pattern of picking up young men in downtown Toronto, driving them to remote areas, assaulting and choking them, then leaving their naked bodies to rot in the wilderness, all eyes are looking once again at the seventy-two-year-old James Henry Greenidge. Currently serving his time at a prison in British Columbia for the horrific 1981 murder of young Elizabeth Fells, Greenidge was denied parole in 2007, but has another shot at freedom in 2010. Some may feel Greenidge is an old man who has served his time; others, especially police, victims' rights groups, and Toronto's gay community, would rather see the muscular man who preyed upon and brutalized so many smaller and weaker individuals than himself leave prison not in a cab, but a body bag.

"This is just one of at least three cold cases involving victims with ties to Toronto's gay communities," stated *Xtra!* following the unveiling of the clay reconstruction of the face of the Markham victim. "In two other cases, forensic sculptures, like the one of the Markham man, have led police to identify long-nameless victims."[7] As one of Canada's leading gay and lesbian newspapers, *Xtra!* has published a number of stories over the years into the investigations of the murders of Hovey and Jones, and any possible connection to James Henry Greenidge, and the attacks on other young gay men in Toronto in the sixties and seventies.[8]

Back in 1977, Greenidge was transferred to a minimum security institution in Ontario. During that time, he went on numerous, unescorted weekend passes, presumably to visit a friend in Toronto. It is believed Greenidge only visited his friend one time, leaving many other weekends during that year unaccounted for.

Over the years, Greenidge, the model prisoner, has come up for parole a number of times. Although considerably older than he was in the late sixties during the Summer of Love, many police officers consider him as dangerous as ever if he is released back into society. Although police have re-interviewed Greenidge, he is unlikely to admit any involvement in the murders that occurred while he was free and out on the streets. If he killed these young men it will remain a secret, one he will take to his grave.

Back in 1967, Richard Hovey was just one of thousands who made the migration to Yorkville's music scene. Some old-timers still remember him, the sharp-looking kid full of talent and musical promise. Back east, his former bandmates from Teddy and the Royals kept a reel-to-reel tape of their band practice from the mid-sixties. The reel was tucked away in an attic for decades and has made the technological transference over the years from reel-to-reel to cassette tape, then onto CD. It contains several original songs by members of the group, with titles like "I Love You So" and "You Say That You Love Me." They were recorded over forty years ago, alongside cover versions of songs like "19th Nervous Breakdown" and "Satisfaction" by The Rolling Stones, "Nowhere Man" by the Beatles, and "Heart Full of Soul" by the Yardbirds.

In an old black and white photo, Hovey is pictured standing alongside his bandmates holding his prized guitar in his right hand. The instrument was his pride and joy. Although it was just a plain-looking electric guitar he'd bought at Sears, Hovey painted it white and modified it to look like an expensive Fender. Left hand in his pocket, he is pictured wearing a dark suit and white turtleneck, his hair is combed forward in a mod style. He has the wide-eyed look of a boy trying to be a man, someone whose life was full of promise. Friends suspected that dream would never come true when he failed to pick up his guitar from the Mynah Bird back in 1967. The people who knew him realized he would leave just about anything behind, but not his guitar, not even if his life depended on it.

While reconstructing the faces of these two dead boys, forensic artist Peter Thompson remained clinical and dispassionate. For him, Hovey finally became real when he listened to the CD of old some songs by Teddy and the Royals, recorded in mono, which have a haunted, otherworldly sound to them. "And that's when I went, 'Oh my God,' because you're hearing this man, Mr. Hovey, actually do something in the past. The hairs stood up on the back of my neck, and at no other time did I feel that way, until I heard him playing his guitar."

After Hovey's remains were identified, Thompson spent four hours — "from 9 a.m. to 1 p.m." according to his notes — carefully removing all the clay and hair from the skulls of the two young men he had so painstakingly applied, the boys who would later be identified as Richard "Dickie" Hovey and Eric Jones. Bit by bit, the clay and depth markers came off, until nothing remained but two whitish skulls, smiling up at him. By the time Thompson was finished, the remains looked exactly the way they did when he received them. The process of giving these teenagers their faces back had been meticulously documented on paper and in numerous photographs, from the moment they arrived at his office in boxes sealed with police tape to the moment of completion. It simply wasn't necessary leave the clay in place any longer. Thompson worked on the two reconstructions for about a month while working on another major case, and now his job had come to an end. One thing was certain: he could not give these young men their lives back, but after forty years he helped give them their names. The skull and bones were no longer those of strangers, but two teenaged boys brutally murdered sometime during the Summer of Love.

Hovey's remains were carefully packed into a box, sent back to his family in New Brunswick, and buried next to his mother and father. His killer remains at large, but at least now Richard James Hovey is home again.

Chapter 2

Catherine Edith Potter and Lee Rita Kirk (1971)

ALL MURDERS ARE MONSTROUS, yet it is especially disturbing when the lives of children are taken, the reason — if there possibly *can* be one — for killing them is left unanswered. Cold cases remain open in police files, but solving them often proves to be far more difficult than many of today's television shows and movies would have us believe. Forensic technology has made tremendous advancements over the years, but the detectives who relentlessly pursued the original investigations retire, leads evaporate, and police are faced with the urgency of solving recent homicides. Older cases may not be entirely forgotten, but unless there are some new developments murders that took place decades ago continue to languish in cardboard boxes in police storage units, silently waiting for new information to come along.

Back in 1971 two teenagers — Catherine Edith Potter and Lee Rita Kirk — were found murdered in a gravel pit in Pickering, Ontario, the motives for their deaths unknown. The girls were young; Potter was just thirteen, while Kirk was fifteen. The media has a habit of playing up where a victim was found, and soon Potter and Kirk became known not by their names but where their battered bodies were discovered. The mystery of the Gravel Pit Murders was born.

As with any investigation, police needed to retrace the steps that could possibly lead these two youngsters to where their remains were

Just fifteen at the time of her murder, Lee Rita Kirk was found next to her friend Catherine Edith Potter in a Pickering, Ontario, gravel pit on October 3, 1971. She had been beaten and strangled.

(Ontario Provincial Police)

dumped; a shallow, weed-filled pit about three miles north of the Highway 401–Liverpool Road cloverleaf. Detectives quickly learned both Catherine and Lee were wards of the Children's Aid Society, and had been living in a group home on Rochelle Crescent in Toronto. The couple supervising the girls, Mr. and Mrs. Robert McMaster, said they were good kids who caused no problems while in the home, where they lived along with four other youngsters. Both girls were in school, Catherine in grade eight at Woodbine Junior High School, and Lee in grade nine at Georges Vanier Secondary School. Both were described as carefree, and got along well with others in class.

The evening of Friday October 1, 1971, the pair ate a spaghetti dinner at the home of their foster family. Leaving the house around 6:30, the girls got a ride with their foster father and were dropped off at the corner of Yonge Street and Finch Avenue in the north end of Toronto. All the residents in the group home were free to come and go, but they were expected to say where they were heading and what time they'd be back. The girls had made plans to visit Kirk's biological father in Richmond Hill that evening, and said they would return home no later than 11 p.m. It was an exceptionally warm night for October, 76°F, and the pair were going to take a bus the rest of the distance. When McMaster said goodbye to the two, there was no way he could imagine it was the last time he would see them alive.

Catherine Edith Potter, thirteen, was found murdered alongside her friend Lee Rita Kirk.

When the girls hadn't come back to the group home by 1 a.m., McMaster contacted a social worker. When there was still no sign of them an hour later the police were notified. It wasn't like Catherine and Lee to not be home on time, or call. Police were concerned about the missing girls: for the past few years, a growing number of young women had been hitchhiking around the Toronto area and several of them had been robbed, beaten, or sexually assaulted. It was estimated in 1971 alone the number of Toronto-area rapes had increased by 10 percent from the previous year.

Shortly before Midnight on Sunday October 3, friends Albert and Vincent were walking in the area of Pickering Township's Valley Farm Road, between the third and forth concessions. It was a popular spot for teenagers to hang out and drink, fool around, or ride their motorcycles and dune buggies. The two were on their way to watch some motorcyclists race on the trails when they cut through the gravel pit and found the missing girls, their bodies laying side by side behind some sumac bushes. Moving closer, they saw blood on the grass and a nearby concrete block. Catherine and Lee were dead. As soon as police were contacted the area was cordoned off. The apparent positioning of the bodies troubled police, because it looked as though the girls were killed somewhere else and dumped in the gravel pit next to one another.

After the bodies were taken to Oshawa General Hospital, they were sent to the Centre for Forensic Sciences in Toronto. When they were found, both girls were still dressed in their corduroy slacks and squall jackets, and there were no signs they had been sexually assaulted. Autopsies revealed one of the girls had been badly beaten. The official cause of death for both was asphyxia by means of ligature strangulation, meaning they had been strangled to death with something other than bare hands, possibly a rope, wire, or cord. There were no signs of drugs in their systems and tests of their stomach contents revealed the two had been killed approximately three hours after eating, placing the time of their deaths at around 9:30 p.m.

Further forensic examinations performed on the girls revealed some strange findings. The clothes of both Catherine and Lee had flecks of paint on them, in not just one or two hues but many different colours. Paint found on Catherine's clothing was mainly the metallic kind popular on customized cars and motorcycles, including yellow, orange, red, and pale green. The same colours were discovered on Lee's garments, along with dark green and dark blue metallic paint.

Under a microscope, investigators took samples from the sole of Catherine's shoes, and found traces of silicon, aluminum, iron, and titanium. There were small silvery globs — the kind that drop to the floor when using a welding machine — clinging to the remains. Smudges of motor grease and light engine oil were found on the clothes and hands of both girls, along with a few grey wavy hairs. Bloodstains on the girls flowed from head to foot, indicating they were standing when beaten. To police, the evidence pointed to Potter and Kirk being murdered somewhere other than the Pickering gravel pit, probably an autobody shop or a garage. Considering the grease, oil, and paint particles, their bodies could have also been moved from the scene of their murder in a van or the trunk of a car. Soil stains on their clothes indicated the girls may have been dragged before being dumped into the gravel pit. Chemical analysts attempted to link the samples from the clothing to dozens of local garages and motorcycle repair shops, but were unable to find a match.

The question remained: how did the girls get from the north end of Toronto to a gravel pit in Pickering? Police believed that the two spent their bus fare on cigarettes — a new package of Export As was found in

Lee's pocket, with four cigarettes missing. They then hitchhiked and were picked up by the person or persons who killed them.

Within weeks, a $5,000 reward was posted by the Attorney General's department for information leading to whoever killed Potter and Kirk. Police investigated one hundred tips from people who swore they remembered seeing the girls getting into cars not just in Toronto, but places like Port Perry and Whitby. Neighbours in the area of the gravel pit remembered seeing a later-model car parked with its lights on about a half mile from where the bodies were found. For some reason, their dogs seemed upset at that time, but since it was dark the residents weren't able to gather any more information about the car.

At the time of their murders, police had difficulty locating the next of kin for both girls. The policy of the Metro Children's Aid Society was to advise police — not the biological mother and father — when wards of the society were missing from foster homes. As a result, the biological parents of both girls were not told their daughters failed to return to the group home. Catherine's mother discovered her daughter was dead when she heard about the murders on the radio. There was no money to pay for her young daughter's funeral. She applied for and subsequently received $902 under the Compensation for Victims of Crime Act. The money was just more than enough to pay the funeral home, with $804 towards arrangements paid by the girl's grandfather and $98 for other expenses.

In 1976, five years after the murders, police were still no closer to finding their killers, despite taking two thousand statements and interviewing 225 Toronto-area, known sexual offenders.

After almost four decades, the murders of Catherine Edith Potter and Lee Rita Kirk remain unsolved. A number of theories — ranging from the girls being killed as part of a motorcycle gang initiation to them dying at the hands of sexual perverts — don't hold up. There were no signs of sexual assault on either girl, and motorcycle gangs are extremely unlikely to target two young girls for no reason whatsoever. Today, there is a $50,000 reward for information leading to the arrest and conviction of the person, or persons responsible for the deaths of these two young girls. Even after all these years, police believe there is still some hope of solving the Gravel Pit Murders.

Chapter 3

Ingrid Bauer (1972)

THOUSANDS OF PEOPLE GO MISSING across Canada every year. Fortunately, the majority are found safe within a very short time. Some are children who wander off on their own, others are senior citizens, recent immigrants unfamiliar with their surroundings, or physically or mentally impaired people who are unable to find their way back home. Many so-called "disappearances" are deliberate, often the result of someone dodging the police, bill collectors or late alimony payments, leaving town with a lover, or simply fed up with their home life and making a dramatic change by leaving it all behind. It isn't unheard of for teenagers doing poorly in school to choose to run away from home instead of facing the repercussions from their parents when the report card arrives. However, it is extremely rare for someone to leave without taking any money or personal belongings with them. In cases where police suspect abduction there are often personal belongings left behind, or a witness who can place the individual at a specific location.

Back in the early seventies, Ingrid Bauer became one of the few persons to disappear in Canada without leaving a single piece of physical evidence behind. When Bauer went missing from the area close to her home in Kleinburg, Ontario, the circumstances surrounding her disappearance were extremely rare: soon after leaving her parents' home

When fourteen-year-old Ingrid Bauer vanished shortly after leaving her family home in Kleinburg, Ontario, on August 16, 1972, she became one of the few known people to disappear in Ontario without a trace — no clothing or personal effects have ever been found.

on the evening of August 16, 1972, Bauer vanished without leaving any physical evidence (such as a wallet, purse, makeup, or clothing) behind. There was absolutely nothing that could help police locate the missing fourteen-year-old girl. Many people go missing, but very few evaporate without a trace. In fact, the number of people who vanished without leaving any clues could literally be counted on one hand. Ingrid was one of the few.

"The police didn't find one blasted thing," said Brent Bauer, Ingrid's older brother, who saw his sister minutes before she vanished. He remembers Ingrid as being a bright girl, a bit straitlaced. She was a lot like her boyfriend, Larry. She didn't smoke cigarettes and had no interest in alcohol. A solid student, her lowest grade was a "B." She got along well with her family and was taking modelling courses. Ingrid Bauer was not a girl who had a reason to run away from home.

Prior to Ingrid's disappearance, there were only two other known similar cases in Ontario, both occurring many years before. The most recent was the case of Mabel Crumback, who was last seen at her parents' Toronto home on May 28, 1950. A quiet, well-behaved, nineteen-year-old girl who didn't smoke or drink, Crumback was employed in the office of a steel company, active in her church community, and sang in the choir. Crumback was small, just five foot one inch tall, with dark hair and a fair complexion. The girl's parents were out of town that May weekend, and her younger brother woke to find Mabel had disappeared from the family's Willard Avenue home. Police were unable to find any reason for her to simply get up and leave, and there was no sign of a struggle. To police, it appeared Mabel's bed had been slept in that night, and for some reason her pyjama bottoms were found folded underneath her pillow, but her pyjama top was missing and never recovered. All her personal effects were left in her room, along with her purse and cash. Almost fifty years after she disappeared, when the excavation of a building in the area uncovered a human skull, many long-time residents were convinced it was Mabel. The skull turned out to be several centuries old, and to this day Mabel is still missing.

Prior to Crumback's odd disappearance, Toronto was swept up in the missing person case of millionaire Ambrose Small. A tremendously successful theatre owner, Small allegedly left his downtown Toronto office on the evening of December 2, 1919, and was never seen again. A slight man, about five-and-a-half-feet tall and 140 pounds, Small had no reason to disappear of his own accord. Earlier on that cold December day, the mustachioed fifty-six-year-old Small signed a deal to sell his theatre chain for a staggering $1.7 million, an enormous amount of money at the time. Small deposited a cheque for $1 million, with the rest of the money to be paid in installments over the next five years. He would never again have to work a single day in his life.

Police simply could not find a motive for Small's vanishing act. All of the millionaire's fortune was intact, there were no signs of kidnapping, and no ransom note was ever found. Although married, Small was a notorious womanizer, and his disappearance remains the subject of much speculation. Rumors that his body was hidden in one of his many Ontario theatres led police to tear up floorboards and sift through furnace ashes for charred, boney remains. None were ever found. Some believed Small was a victim of amnesia, while others thought he simply left life in Canada behind and fled to a foreign land. Decades after his disappearance, people swore they saw the missing theatre magnate in countries all over the world. Although Toronto Police officially closed the investigation into Small's death in 1960, they continued to receive letters and tips for years, and searched for a possible grave in the city's Rosedale Valley area in 1965.

The circumstances leading up to Bauer's disappearance are no more unusual than those of Small and Crumback. On Friday August 11, 1972, Ingrid's father, Oscar, drove from his job as a manager of purchasing for Kodak Canada Limited to the family cottage in Thornbury, Ontario. Other members of his family, including his wife, youngest son Kevin, and Ingrid were already at the cottage, and had been there since the last week of July. The weather turned out to be rainy and less pleasant than expected over the next few days, so Oscar said it was time to head back. On Wednesday August 16, Oscar told his family he was driving back home to Kleinburg. Ingrid decided to drive back with her father, and thought it would be nice to surprise her boyfriend, Larry, who lived in Pine Grove, less than five miles away from the Bauer household.

As soon as Oscar returned home, he decided to do some laundry and headed downstairs. Ingrid carried her suitcase inside, putting it on her bed. It was around 9:30 p.m., and she said she was going to visit Larry. Ingrid didn't plan on being away for long and left the house without taking makeup or money. She said she'd be returning home around 10:30 that night.

"That's when she vanished off the face of the planet," said older brother, Brent, who remembers his sister leaving the house in bare feet. There wasn't anything out of the ordinary, and absolutely nothing to indicate she wouldn't be back soon.

Back in the seventies, the Kleinburg area was still semi-rural, and had a large agricultural component. There was no public transit, and if you didn't get a ride with your mother or father there was always hitchhiking. "People in the community would see you walking, and offer you a ride," said Bauer. "It was just the way kids got around back then, if you didn't have wheels. You walked, bicycled, hitchhiked, or got a ride. Nobody thought it was unusual — it was rural Ontario." Bauer remembers his father driving the family in their Volkswagen Beetle, and the kids moving over to make room for a soldier hitchhiking his way back to Camp Borden.

Soon after Ingrid left, Brent walked up the street to the local store to buy some cigarettes. He remembers seeing Ingrid near the intersection of Pennon Road and Islington Avenue. He also saw a police cruiser parked

An age-enhanced pencil drawing of what Ingrid Bauer might look like today. Since it is not possible to determine what a missing person's hair looks like, forensic artist Diana P. Trepkov sometimes parts hair in the middle, and depicts the subject with two different hairstyles.

(Diana P. Trepkov)

nearby. Brent went into the store, bought his cigarettes, and by the time he was back outside Ingrid was gone. Brent began walking and was back home around 10:10 p.m. Soon after, Ingrid's boyfriend Larry called the house, asking for her. Confusion turned to worry as the family realized that if Ingrid wasn't at Larry's, and she wasn't at home, then where was she? Oscar Bauer immediately drove to Larry's to check for himself. On the way back, he checked the ditches by the side of the road, to make sure his daughter hadn't been hit by a car. Unable to find her, he contacted police and was told he would have to wait a number of hours before Ingrid could be reported missing. He said no. Ingrid was a responsible teenager, if she was missing it wasn't because she ran away. The police listened and the intensive search for Ingrid Bauer began the evening she vanished.

Within three hours, every police force in Ontario was alerted to Ingrid's disappearance. In the days after she was last seen, a twenty-square-mile area was searched by a team of two hundred, including police officers, firemen, conservation officers, and volunteers. A helicopter was used to aid in the search. Police checked in and around the Humber River for signs of the missing girl. Scuba divers explored forty-foot deep, murky waters in some of the area's old gravel pits. They didn't find any sign of Ingrid, but brought some strange items up to the surface, including hundreds of feet of recording tape and a surveyor's transit, which police believed were likely stolen and discarded by thieves who didn't know what to do with the items.

Soon after Ingrid vanished, her description was being broadcast on police radios every hour, twenty-four hours a day. She was five feet six inches tall, one hundred pounds, medium build, long straight hair, light complexion, brown eyes, last seen wearing bellbottom slacks and a short beige sweater with a red apple and green leaf design in the pattern. One of the investigating officers, Detective Sergeant Bill Hay of York Region Police, kept a replica of the sweater hanging on a coat hook in his office, which served as a reminder. A five-man detective squad was formed under Hay, and soon interviewed hundreds of people, including inmates involved in previous abductions.

Hay and other officers continued searching all over the province for Ingrid, collecting and following-up on approximately 1,400 leads. Some sounded farfetched, while others seemed legitimate. One tipster said Ingrid was seen walking on a road near Lindsay. Another told police she was being held prisoner in a North York apartment. A third stated she was alive and well, and working as a waitress in Vancouver. None of the tips helped to reveal what happened to Ingrid, with police pursuing leads in Windsor, Ottawa, and Montreal.

By mid-October, the reward of $1,000 for information leading to Ingrid's whereabouts was increased to $3,000. When the missing girl's father added $1,000 to the amount his employer, Kodak, put in an additional $1,000. Despite the increased reward, massive searches of the Kleinburg area, and appeals for information broadcast on TV and radio stations, there was still no sign of Ingrid. In the first week of November, a unique highway billboard campaign was put in place, aimed at motorists driving on routes from Montreal all the way to Vancouver. Forty-two roadside billboard ads were installed to help find the missing girl, with the cost being absorbed by the billboard company.

Week after week went by, and Ingrid was still missing. The search was massive — one of the most publicized cases up to that point in Ontario's history. Thousands of hours, a well publicized reward, and the printing and distribution of 15,000 posters all failed to turn up one single shred of evidence. A body was found in the Halton area about a year after Ingrid disappeared. Some believed it was Ingrid, but dental records revealed it was someone else.

In the years since her disappearance, the Bauer family grew to know the officers who tried so hard to track down Ingrid. Her brother, Brent, still remembers them, saying they pursued leads "like bulldogs." In 1982, ten years after her disappearance, two of the original investigators were dead. William Hay was electrocuted in a freak accident while working on his boat that summer. Detective Wally Harkness died from cancer around the same time.

To this day, the file on Ingrid Bauer's mysterious disappearance is still open, York Region Cold Case number 1972-10461. The area where she was last seen has changed dramatically over the years, and what was once farmland and forest has been developed into large subdivisions. "They've basically paved everything over," said Brent Bauer. "If somebody put her somewhere, God knows what happened to any remains. If Ingrid was buried, there's a chance, if somebody leads us to where it was. But other than that, you can pretty much forget it that she'll ever be found."

Today, Brent Bauer doesn't hear from police very often. Almost forty years after his younger sister went missing the emotions come back full force whenever he hears about human remains being found in the area, and wonders if, one day, the family will know what happened to their beautiful fourteen-year-old daughter the night of August 16, 1972.

Chapter 4

Wendy Tedford and Donna Stearne (1973)

WHEN SOMEONE YOU KNOW and love is brutally murdered, the hackneyed expression "Time heals all wounds" somehow manages to sound even more meaningless. Capturing and convicting their killer will not bring the dead back, or erase the thoughts of what their final moments must have been like, but at the very least it assures family members that the guilty person is behind bars. Some relatives of murder victims try to push the past aside and live their lives in the present. Others, especially families of victims whose crimes remain unsolved, refuse to stop until the guilty party is brought to justice.

For the past thirty-seven years, Linda Harris has spoken to more police detectives than most of us will meet in our entire lifetimes. The unsolved double homicide of her younger sister, seventeen-year-old Wendy Tedford, and her best friend, Donna Stearne, also just seventeen, is currently the oldest case on the Toronto Police Services unsolved cold cases website. Since her sister was murdered in 1973, Harris estimates she has had contact with at least twenty to thirty different detectives over the years. Some have moved on to other positions within the Toronto Police Service, while others retired years ago, and the cardboard file boxes marked Tedford and Stearne have been passed from one detective to the next.

For many years, while information was being gathered for the Toronto Police Homicide Squad Unsolved Cold Cases website, the only murder posted online was the unsolved double murder of Donna Stearne and Wendy Tedford. It is listed as Homicide Number Five for 1973, and is first on the website, which went online in 2008.

All over the world, the Internet has become another tool used by police agencies to try and crack open cold cases, new and old. Instead of the traditional static images printed on missing persons posters, the Internet has allowed police at all levels to communicate directly with the public and the media in ways that are faster, cheaper, and extremely effective in getting the message across. Many police forces across Canada — including the Royal Canadian Mounted Police, Toronto Police Service, and the Ontario Provincial Police — use the Internet to display photos not only of crime victims, but missing persons, unsolved murders, suspected abductions, forensic facial reconstructions of unclaimed human remains, and more. There are often multiple photos of victims, video re-enactments, maps of where bodies were discovered, and pictures of weapons, vehicles, houses, streets, and buildings relevant to their investigation. Someone may not recognize a photo of a victim, but they might recall seeing or hearing something strange going on in a certain place indicated on a map.

Posting unsolved cases like the double homicide of Wendy Tedford and Donna Stearne on the Internet helps to keep the story alive in the hopes that someone, somewhere, will come forward with new information. The amount of work involved in getting these cold cases online is formidable, and includes creating a synopsis of the investigation, who the victim was, and circumstances surrounding his or her murder. If there is a reward, as there are in some cases, the amount is often posted. In the case of Tedford and Stearne, there are also aerial photos depicting where the bodies of the two were found, and an image of the .38 calibre Colt revolver used to kill the girls.

One of the officers behind the website is Toronto Police Detective-Sergeant Reg Pitts, who said they eventually hope to have three hundred to 350 unsolved murders on the site, going back to 1957, the year Toronto Police Service was formed. All cold cases are important, and it will take years to post all of them on the website. The challenge for police creating the site was deciding which cases to feature online first.

"We tend to focus more on women and children," said Pitts. "It's one of the stated goals of the police service, the protection of the most vulnerable members of society." The website also serves as a place where family and friends of victims can turn to see if there are any new developments in their particular unsolved case.

"If your mother, brother, father or sister was killed 20 years ago, you probably had a lot of contact with police back in the day, but not so much obviously as it goes on," said Pitts. The Toronto Police Service Homicide Squad is the department that relatives often call when they hope and pray additional evidence has been found, or a witness has come forward with new information. Some families ask to be called only if there are new developments, while others call homicide officers often, waiting for any news. "They want contact," said Pitts. "Families want the personal touch, and that's what we do here, to some degree."

———

Many details are known about Wendy Tedford and Donna Stearne — where they were immediately before they were shot, and the calibre of weapon used to steal their lives — but the rationale for killing two good-hearted seventeen-year-old girls remains a mystery, and to this day no one has been charged in their murders.

In the morning of Friday April 27, 1973, a student named Tony was heading to a basketball game at Downsview Secondary School when he took a shortcut through a rubble-filled lot south of Wilson Avenue near Keele Street in Toronto. It was early, about 7:30 a.m., and the young man found something he would never forget. Lying on the ground, side by side, near a chain-link fence topped with barbed wire, were the bodies of two young women. Tony was scared stiff by the horrific discovery and didn't look too closely at the remains. He quickly headed over to a nearby business on Wilson Avenue, and a truck driver for the company went over to investigate. When he got there, the man took a closer look and saw blood on the hands of one of the girls, which was in a clawing position. His heart sank: who would do such a thing to a couple of teenagers?

Police immediately went to the scene, where they found the bodies of Wendy Tedford and Donna Stearne. Wendy was face down and Donna was next to her on her back, one girl practically on top of the other. Both of them were fully clothed. Nearby, police found several empty shells from a .38 calibre revolver. Autopsies would late reveal both girls had been shot at close range. Wendy had been shot twice through the neck, while Donna suffered a single gunshot to the back of her head. For many people, the murders served as an uncomfortable reminder of another double murder involving young girls that took place just a year and a half earlier.

In October 1971, thirteen-year-old Catherine Edith Potter and Lee Rita Kirk, just fifteen, were found dead in a Pickering, Ontario, gravel pit. Although the cause of death was different than Tedford and Stearne — both girls were strangled to death, likely with a rope or cord of some sort — there were far too many similarities to ignore. Both sets of girls were young and travelling together. None of the bodies showed any signs of sexual assault, and all were fully clothed when their bodies were discovered. All the young women were killed within a short time, just a few hours from the time they were last seen. Robbery did not appear to be a motive in any of the murders. Detectives were puzzled by the unexplained deaths. There appeared to be no reason for any of these young lives to be taken so soon, and to this day the murders of Tedford and Stearne, and Potter and Kirk, remain unsolved.

The deaths of Tedford and Stearne made front page news in Toronto newspapers. The *Toronto Star* headline for Saturday April 28, 1973, "No clues, motive in shooting deaths of 2 Metro girls." At the time, police admitted they were stumped and had no leads. They were, however, able to piece together the final hours of the two best friends through reports from eyewitnesses and local residents.

On Thursday April 26, 1973, Donna left her home at 7 p.m. and arrived at Wendy's house soon after, around 7:30. The two friends had plans to go shopping, and took public transit to Yorkdale Shopping Centre at Dufferin Street and Highway 401. After spending a few hours shopping at the mall, the pair took a bus to Keele Street, north of

Wilson Avenue. Around 10:45 p.m., they were seen in the Sit 'n Eat, a local restaurant, drinking Coca-Cola. Wendy and Donna left soon after, around 11 p.m., and were not seen again until the next morning, when their bodies were discovered.

Wendy's sister, Linda Harris, remembers that awful day from almost forty years ago, when she heard that her younger sister was dead. Wendy was living with Shirley, another sister, and working in the office of Towers department store on Orfus Road. When she didn't hear from Wendy, Linda grew concerned. Wendy and Donna had a habit of staying out late, sometimes all night, but hadn't done so for a while. When Linda called Towers, they said he sister didn't come in that morning. She thought this was odd, and called Shirley, who said she hadn't seen Wendy, either. The sisters were worried: *if Wendy wasn't at work, and she wasn't at Shirley's, where was she?* Linda called police, and gave them Wendy and Donna's first and last names. "They asked how Stearne was spelled, and the police said someone would be out to see them very shortly. I knew right away something was wrong," said Linda. A police car arrived at her door within minutes with the awful news.

Almost immediately after her sister and Donna were murdered, Linda and the rest of her family had to endure not only her brutal death, but a factual error that has loomed over the case for decades. One local Toronto paper reported Linda saying the girls often smoked marijuana, and were out the night they were murdered looking to score some weed. This was not true, said Linda, and the inaccurate statement has been wildly misreported and repeated over and over again through the years.

"Wendy was out to buy a present for our sister Shirley's birthday party the next day, not drugs," said Linda, who attributes the alleged drug connection to a close friend of the family's. An older man already in his early twenties and a bit of a troublemaker, he showed up during a newspaper interview immediately after the murders, when the family was most vulnerable, and for reasons known only to himself told the reporter the girls were out buying marijuana. The effect was catastrophic, and overnight the drug rumour was published. Upset, Linda spoke to a journalist from another Toronto newspaper who came by for an interview, to set the record straight. For whatever reason, the man inexplicably showed up again during the interview, but this time the reporter told him to be quiet and mind his own business. The story published in the *Globe and Mail* attempted to clear up the alleged marijuana connection mentioned in the other Toronto newspaper, but by that time the damage was already done.

Over the years, the double homicide of Tedford and Stearne has been the subject of tremendous speculation rather than fact. At the time, the unsubstantiated drug rumors may have led police in the wrong investigative direction. Even nine years after the murders, one of the original investigators told the *Toronto Sun*, "It was initially felt that the murders were drug related and we still feel that way."[1]

To the families of the dead girls, the murders simply made no sense. Both Wendy and Donna were friendly and had no known enemies. The girls had been inseparable since they met four years earlier while attending C.W. Jefferys School. At the time of their deaths, Donna was in grade twelve at Downsview Secondary School. She loved animals and had aspirations of continuing her education and becoming a vet. A spiritual girl, she attended church and had recently applied to be a counsellor at a children's camp run by the People's Church, where she was baptized three years before she was murdered. A talented artist, Donna loved painting and was working on a landscape of a bridge at dusk for her mother, which she never got the chance to complete.

For Wendy Tedford, the past few years had been difficult ones. She dropped out of school in 1971, after her father Kenneth died from cancer. She moved from her widowed mother's home to live with her older sister, Shirley, and her young son, and got a job at the office at Towers department store. In the months before her death, things had been looking up for the seventeen-year-old. Wendy had just rented a basement apartment in a house, and was planning to move in a few days; there was even talk of Donna moving in with her. Linda went to see the apartment for herself after her sister's death, and noticed the location was close to where she was killed, a street behind a field running almost parallel to the 401 Highway overpass. She and other family members believed Wendy may have been taking Donna over the check out her new apartment the night they were shot.

Following the murders, Toronto Police appealed to the public for any tips that could help solve the case. Some officers believed marijuana was a motive, while others thought the girls were murdered by "a madman," someone so deranged that he mistook Donna and Wendy for someone else.

Compared to previous years, a significant number of young women in Southern Ontario were murdered for no apparent reason — such as sexual assault or robbery — in the early to mid-seventies. All of those murders are still unsolved.[2] There were the gravel pit murders of Potter and Kirk in 1971, Tedford and Stearne in 1973, and a number of others who were killed or possibly abducted, never to be seen again, like Ingrid Bauer. Just fourteen at the time of her disappearance in August 1972, Bauer went missing immediately after leaving her family home in Kleinburg to visit her boyfriend, who lived about five miles away. Polite, well-mannered, and mature for her age, Bauer was intelligent, didn't drink alcohol, smoke, or do drugs, and had no reason to run away from home. Despite a sizeable reward, multiple searches of the area, radio and television appeals for information, a cross-Canada billboard campaign, and thousands of posters being distributed, not a single shred of evidence has ever been found. She remains missing to this day.

At first, police did not rule out a possible link between the murders of Tedford and Stearne and that of another girl named Yvonne Leroux killed just six months earlier. Just sixteen at the time of her death, Leroux left for a youth clinic for drug therapy in Weston the night before her murder, and was found by an elderly caretaker on the morning of Thursday November 30, 1972. Partially clad in her white blouse, blue top coat, and knee-high boots, the young woman was discovered face down on a frozen road in King Township, her purse still beside her, blue bell-bottom jeans clutched in her hand. Police were unspecific whether or not the teenager had been raped. Three months before her death, the pretty, dark-haired high school student feared for her life, and asked Metro Toronto Police for protection. Tragically, she had become involved with drug dealers months earlier, and they asked her to do something for them. Leroux was told by dealers to participate in a drug ring drop-off operation, where she was supposed to leave drugs in specific spots for others to pick up later. She refused, and was found brutally beaten to death by an assailant or assailants wielding a blunt object with such force that her skull was cracked and her brain lacerated.[3]

The dead girl's father, Gerard Leroux, was still dealing with the shock and grief of Yvonne's death when he attended the funeral service for Wendy and Donna on May 1, 1973. Nearly one thousand people came for the requiem at the People's Church, where Donna sang in the choir. The dismal weather — dark, drizzling, and gloomy — reflected the mood of everyone in attendance. The two girls, close in life and in death, were both laid to rest at Beechwood Cemetery.

A year after the murders, there were still no solid leads, despite police interviewing about five hundred people and the posting of a $5,000 reward for information leading to the killer or killers. Donna's father, Jack Stearne, gave an interview to the *Toronto Star* and said he believed his daughter was killed because she was hitchhiking, and got a ride with the wrong person. He warned his daughter many times about the perils of hitchhiking, "but they don't listen," said Stearne. "The police tell them about the risks they run, there are stories in the paper about hitchhikers raped or killed … and yet you see them every day, sensible kids in every other way until it comes to climbing into a car with a stranger."[4] Stearne said he refused to pick up hitchhikers and wouldn't let his two other daughters accept rides from strangers. Mel Lastman, the mayor of North York at the time, tried to get hitchhiking outlawed all over Metropolitan Toronto.

Although many youngsters stuck out their thumbs and got a free ride here and there, fears over the growing number of violent attacks on unsuspecting hitchhikers were not exaggerated. In 1973, the year Donna and Wendy were murdered, there were 102 documented cases of rape and indecent assault associated with hitchhiking in the city. Years ago, Toronto was not the same city it is today. Public transit was limited, especially in outlying areas, and hitchhiking was a common practice among teenagers at the time. Toronto Police Detective Robert Wilkinson has handled the Tedford and Stearne files for a number of years, and heard the numerous theories surrounding the murders.

"Back in the seventies, there weren't that many places to go for a burger at night in North York," said Wilkinson. "The Sit 'n Eat restaurant was probably one of half a dozen places open in Toronto at night, so for the girls to go there wasn't that strange, because it was the only place within a bus ride where you could go if you wanted a coffee. Back in the seventies, there was virtually no place that was open at night. Unless you knew of its existence, you wouldn't get off the highway and go there for a late-night coffee."

Some believe the girls were picked up hitchhiking after leaving the Sit 'n Eat restaurant, and murdered soon after. An eighteen-year-old witness, Michael Armstrong, remembered seeing the two at the restaurant at 10:35 p.m. on Thursday April 26, 1973. He recognized Wendy and Donna from school. They were on the quiet side, especially Donna, who he remembered blushing whenever he said hi to her in the halls. He said hello to the two in the restaurant and went on his way to buy a couple of takeout coffees to go, one for him and one for his brother, who was working at a nearby Becker's Milk Store. Armstrong and his bother were standing outside Becker's for about five minutes, drinking their coffees and talking to friends, when he went back towards the Sit 'n Eat. "I looked in and both girls were gone. That was about five minutes later." Armstrong's tip — which he reported after seeing photos in the newspapers of the slain girls — was the most significant breakthrough for police in several days. A public appeal was issued for anyone who might have seen the two girls get into a car.

However, there were a number of accounts conflicting with Armstrong's statement to police. The owner of the Sit 'n Eat didn't remember seeing either girl there the night they were killed, while a young woman told police she saw Wendy and Donna get on the Keele Street bus at 10:45 p.m. — around the same time Armstrong said he saw them in the Sit 'n Eat, drinking Cokes.

At the time of the murders, police believed the girls were driven to the empty lot, forced to stand side by side, then shot at close range. When they were found, the two were fully dressed in the same clothes they were wearing when they were last seen alive. Wendy, at five feet six inches and 114 pounds, with medium brown hair that fell just below her shoulders, was wearing black shoes, blue jeans, a three-quarter-length grey jacket with belt and black buttons, and an off-white blouse. Donna, five feet three inches tall and 123 pounds, with dark brown hair, was still dressed in brown shoes, blue jeans, beige coat with brown knitted material at the collar, cuffs, and waist, and a multicoloured, plain blouse.

Some neighbours recalled hearing unusual sounds around midnight, dull thuds, "like something hitting the ground." Another young woman living nearby remembered hearing "loud bangs" around midnight, and told her parents about what she had heard over breakfast the next morning — by that time, the bodies had been discovered.

Over the years, there has been a great amount of speculation about the positions in which the bodies were found, lying side by side and head to foot, and if they were killed as part of a motorcycle gang initiation. Both theories are unlikely. Bikers are not likely to kill young women as part of an "initiation," especially anyone unknown to them. As for allegations that the girls were killed and "positioned" head to foot as a sign, there is a much greater likelihood they just happened to fall the way they did after they were shot. Today, Toronto Police say there is nothing to lead them in the direction that the two were killed as part of a motorcycle gang initiation and that the theory is overblown.

"When bikers kill, they kill for a reason," said Toronto Police Detective-Sergeant Gary Grinton. "They are mercenary, and do everything for a reason." If anything, bikers have been known to "initiate" young women who are known to the gang or hangers-on by ordering them to perform sexual favours, not by killing them.

Since the girls were murdered in 1973 there have been a number of leads in the case. In an unrelated investigation, a gun was recovered by the Ontario Provincial Police in Windsor, Ontario, and sent to the Firearms Section of the Centre of Forensic Sciences. The weapon was positively identified as the gun that killed both Tedford and Stearne. Police were able to determine the gun — a six-shot .38 calibre Colt revolver with a six-inch long barrel — had been stolen from a Windsor area home during a break and enter a few months before the murders. Police ran the weapon through IBIS, the Integrated Ballistics Identification System, in the hopes of connecting it to other crimes. Despite a lengthy investigation, police were unable to find any new information regarding the murders, and the Colt revolver has not been linked to any other crimes.

Another piece of information not published at the time of the murders was the presence of semen found at the scene. Both Wendy and Donna had broken up with their boyfriends, and the semen wasn't a match to either one of them. "Semen in itself is a wonderful thing, in its existence at the crime scene," said Detective Wilkinson, "but it tells you absolutely nothing, because there's no date stamp on it."

––––––––––––

To this day, Linda Harris remembers a conversation she had with her Wendy not long before she was murdered. Their mother had been in a terrible car accident and Wendy was so terrified of hospitals that she never went in to see her. At one point it seemed as though Wendy had had a premonition when she said to Linda, "The only time I'm going to be in a hospital is when I die."

It is said that the first forty-eight hours after a murder are crucial for police to try to solve a murder. Even after almost forty years, officers at the Toronto Police Cold Case Unit don't plan to give up on who killed the two girls. Sometimes, time can work to their advantage, especially when witnesses — reluctant to come forward at the time of the crime — approach police years later, when fears of reprisal are gone. Linda Harris has had more than her share of hopes shattered, but at age sixty she refuses to give up on the search for whoever killed her younger sister and her best friend until the day she dies.

"You hear about other cold cases being solved," said Harris. "Why not mine?"

Chapter 5

Chrystal Elizabeth Van Huuksloot (1977)

TEENAGERS IN LOVE SOMETIMES do crazy things to express their feelings. Years ago, demonstrating your undying affection meant writing love letters, cliché-drenched poetry, or getting a heart-shaped tattoo bearing the name of your beloved permanently etched into your flesh. Today, teenage infatuation often takes the form of endless abbreviated text messages sent back and forth from cell phones, or posting your innermost feelings on social networking websites like Facebook, Twitter, or MySpace. In the most extreme cases, teenagers will do whatever it takes to be with the one they love, consequences be damned. Some will lie to their parents or steal from friends. In extreme cases, some become involved with drug dealers and other criminal lowlifes who rob them of their innocence, their money, or worst of all, their lives.

Chrystal Elizabeth Van Huuksloot[1] was just nineteen back in 1976, a teenager so deeply in love that she was willing to do anything for her boyfriend, even if it meant bailing him out of jail. Back home in Edmonton she became involved with an older drug dealer named Stacey Harris. During a trip to Toronto, Harris was apprehended by police. Once Chrystal heard the news, she left as soon as possible to free her man from the city's decrepit Don Jail. The child of an upper middle-class family — her father was a planner with an oil company — Chrystal was appalled by the crowded conditions at the decaying institution and, in the words of her father, Leo, "had never seen misery." In just a few days, the stench and filth of the jail would be the least of her problems.

For most of her young life, Chrystal led a safe, unexciting existence, working part-time at places like the local Dutch butcher shop, or as a hostess at the Edmonton Exhibition. By the age of seventeen, her life changed forever when she began associating with drug dealers and others on the fringe of society. She began dating Harris, against the wishes of her father and mother, Teus, who did not approve of the relationship in the least. When Chrystal found work at a local travel agency she left her mother and father's house and moved into her own apartment in Edmonton. Unknown to her, the Department of Justice began tapping her phone, gathering evidence against her new boyfriend. Following his arrest in Toronto on drug charges, Crystal, the devoted girlfriend, was adamant about bailing him out of jail, no matter the cost.

In October 1976, Chrystal bought a $158 return ticket on Air Canada and flew standby from Edmonton to Toronto. She made up a convincing story for her parents about the trip, telling them she was going to Vancouver for awhile to check out hotels for her job at the travel agency. If Chrystal had told them the real story — that she was flying out east to bail her boyfriend out of jail — they would never have let her go. The pretty young woman with the broad smile and curly brown hair packed light, carrying her luggage on the plane. In her tote bag, Chrystal brought one blue dress, one brown dress, a quilted jacket, hair accessories, and a few pieces of jewellery. She certainly didn't plan on staying long in Toronto, but she wanted to look good for her boyfriend.

As she boarded the plane, airline personnel greeting Chrystal were unaware of an unusual item she secreted under her clothing. Around her waist was a money belt, but not the usual manufactured kind you might find at a luggage shop. It was homemade, put together from a silk stocking. Carefully stitched inside the improvised belt was cash, a lot of it. Back in 1976, $3,000 was enough for a down payment on a modest house, and more money than necessary to rent a decent one-bedroom apartment in downtown Toronto for an entire year. Although it was a lot of cash, it was merely one-fifth of the staggering amount Chrystal needed to raise to bail Stacey out of jail: $15,000.

As soon as her flight landed in Toronto, Chrystal went to stay the night with an acquaintance in her North York apartment. The next morning, she took a cab to Gerrard Street and Broadview Avenue in the city's east end, where the grimy old Don Jail had stood for over 120 years, adjacent to its more recent but no less crowded addition. Once the guard called her name, Chrystal met with Harris, and the pair discussed legitimate means of raising the $12,000 shortfall necessary for his bail. Chrystal was elated and left the jail in a good mood, confident she would soon return with the money and put this nightmare behind them. After all, who wouldn't loan cash to a young couple hoping to start a new life together?

Over the next few days, Chrystal sought out anyone and everyone who she thought could loan her money to cover the $15,000 bail. First it was banks and loan companies; all said no. Friends and people claiming to be friends didn't have the money, or didn't want to lend it to her. There were others, including lawyers and bail bondsmen, who flatly refused to advance such a tremendous amount of dough, fearing they would never see it again. After a few days of hearing "no" over and over, Chrystal felt defeated. Upset and trembling, she returned to the grubby jail to break the bad news to her beloved Stacey. Expecting him to tell her to go back to everyone a second time to get bail money, she was surprised by how calm he was when he heard the bad news. Instead of trying to wriggle money out of the same people, Stacey gave Chrystal a name and a phone number for someone he met in jail, a man who would change her life forever.

Ian Lester Rosenberg was known to Toronto Police for all the wrong reasons. A man with a lengthy criminal record, the thirty-five-year-old had a reputation as a hard drinker and an all around tough guy, someone equally unafraid to pick a fight or back down from one. Rosenberg's chosen criminal profession was a perfect match for his fiery, unpredictable personality. As a loan shark, Rosenberg eagerly advanced money to men and women desperate for cash, charging crippling rates of interest for his bogus generosity. His interest rates were so high that in many cases the actual loan dwindled in comparison to the penalties he charged for late payments. Rosenberg always made sure he collected interest payments from his clients in cash, or some other, less pleasant form. When Harris met Rosenberg in the Don Jail, he was behind bars for brutally beating a cab driver with a tire iron after the man refused to pay Rosenberg's exorbitant interest rates. The amount Rosenberg advanced the cabbie was $1,500, but within a very short time, the interest he demanded was $3,000, *double* the amount of the loan. When some down on his luck individual like the unfortunate taxi driver couldn't afford to repay Rosenberg, their next stop was the emergency department of one of Toronto's many hospitals, where nurses and doctors would tend to their broken arms and shattered legs.

Although he dealt drugs for a living, Harris wasn't in the same criminal class as Rosenberg. He wasn't a hardened, institutionalized type of criminal, and was unable to tolerate jail conditions alongside streetwise male prostitutes, pimps, thieves, and self-medicating transvestites. Desperate to get out of the Don Jail, Stacey became fast friends with Rosenberg, and a financial arrangement was soon struck to raise his bail money. Rosenberg would loan Harris $4,000, and charge him $150 per week just in interest alone, amounting to more than 70 percent. The rates offered by Rosenberg were outrageous, but not unheard of, at least not from a moneylender in the business of granting illegal loans.

Back in the late seventies, loansharking was a well-established, illegal, tax-free business, with an estimated worth of $5 billion a year in Canada alone. It was, and is, a lucrative endeavour, linked to numerous organized criminal enterprises, including prostitution, drug trafficking, robbery, and even murder. When it comes to loan sharks, there is a misconception that only poor or uneducated people — unable to secure money from banks or legitimate credit companies — seek the services of these less than reputable characters. The reality is very different.

Doctors, lawyers, businessmen, and others who appear to be well off sometimes have worse financial problems than the average person, caused by fortunes lost in the stock market, bad investments, drug addictions, or thousands of dollars in unpaid gambling debts. Some will borrow, steal, or prostitute themselves to pay off their debts, while others become trapped in the world of loan sharks, and their sky-high, impossible to repay interest charges. Many successful loan sharks don't really care if they ever get their principal back, as long as the high interest payments keep rolling in. If the flow of money stops, then there's a problem. Depending on the loan shark, reminding someone about a missed payment can take the form of a verbal threat. If the warning is ignored, legs, ribs, noses, or arms can and will be broken. In some twisted fashion, these people are the fortunate ones. Broken bones eventually heal, but there's no cure for a bullet in the head, "accidentally" drowning in a lake, or being burned alive when someone sets your house on fire.

Back in Edmonton, Chrystal's parents, still believing their daughter was in Vancouver inspecting hotels for her travel company, were unaware she was actually in Toronto, arranging a deal with a loan shark to get her boyfriend out of jail. She phoned home a couple of times, telling her family she would be back out west in a few days. What she didn't let them know was how bored she had become with her safe, day-to-day existence in Edmonton, and that she was making plans to have her belongings shipped to Toronto to build a new life with her boyfriend. She couldn't wait to be reunited with Harris, put the $15,000 bail unpleasantness behind them, and move on together as a happy, young couple in love.

Over the next few days, Crystal met with Rosenberg and, police believe, another loan shark, to finalize the bail money. Her dreams of getting Stacey out of jail were shattered when, for unknown reasons, the deal with the loan shark fell through. Crystal was devastated. After having no luck getting money from banks or trust companies, Rosenberg was her last resort in Toronto, and that too had failed. Packing her dresses and other belongings into her tote bag, Chrystal then booked standby seats for her flight back to Edmonton, including an additional four seats for a Mister "Peter Piper" and his family. This was an old trick at the time in the airline industry, a way to better the odds of actually getting a standby seat. Her next stop was a taxi ride to the Don Jail and her beloved Stacey. Once there, the barely composed Chrystal told him the loan fell through with Rosenberg, then burst into tears. Between her sobs, she told him how much she loved him, and kept repeating that she'd soon be back with the money to get him out of that horrible place. Once she left the jail, she called Stacey's mother and told her she was returning to Edmonton, but that she would soon return to Toronto with bail money.

Early on the day of October 9, 1976, Chrystal said she was heading to the Toronto International Airport[2], and would be getting a drive from none other than loan shark Ian Rosenberg. It was the last time Chrystal Elizabeth Van Huuksloot was seen alive.

Missing person posters in Toronto and Edmonton gave detailed descriptions of the young woman: five feet seven inches tall, brown hair, blue eyes, 120 pounds. Chrystal vanished just one month before her twentieth birthday, and the story of her life and mysterious disappearance was far from over. There was no sign of her and absolutely no word to her family or friends. Then, almost seven months after the young woman disappeared, the last person she was seen with was found brutally murdered.

Just hours after he was released from the Don Jail on $35,000 bail, where he had been held on charges of extortion and robbery, loan shark Ian Rosenberg was found naked, dead, and bloodied in his girlfriend's bedroom at around 2 a.m. on April 22, 1977. Discovered face down on the mattress, Rosensberg had been shot gangland-style twice in the back of the head at very close range with a heavy, military-style weapon.[3] His lover, a married twenty-nine-year-old woman named Joan Lipson, had also been shot in the head; somehow, Lipson managed to live for another six hours before she died in hospital from her injuries. Tragically, it was Lipson's older daughter, just eight years old, who was awakened by the sound of gunshots before discovering her bleeding, dying mother and her dead lover in the bedroom of her Toronto home.

About two months after the brutal double homicide, Toronto Police made an arrest. On June 16, 1977, James Edward Bass was charged with first-degree murder in the slaying of Rosenberg, described by police as a former "friendly acquaintance" of the dead man, and someone who despised Lipson with undisguised passion. At first, Toronto Police believed the motive behind Rosenberg's murder was a loansharking disagreement between the two men. Lipson, a potential witness to the murder, was killed to keep her quiet. Toronto papers at the time ran photos of Bass, a newspaper draped over his face, being led by homicide officers to his court appearance. It was not the first time, nor would it be the last, that Bass made headline news in the city of Toronto.

Thirty-five at the time of his arrest for the murders, Bass had a lengthy criminal record going back to his teenage years. In 1967, Bass and his brother were charged with fraud when they filed numerous phony auto insurance claims over a thirteen-month period. The bold scam was relatively simple, but its success depended on driving abilities, precision timing, and above all, skillful acting. Bass and his brother would drive a small, foreign-made car or rented truck in and around the city. When they spotted another vehicle in the rearview mirror they would let the driver come close to their car, then unexpectedly slam on the brakes. Without any chance to slow down, drivers behind them would hit their car, sometimes crashing into the back, usually just touching bumpers. The Bass brothers would leap out of the car, one of them grabbing his neck in pain and faking whiplash, the other shouting, "My God, what have you done to my car?" or "Look at the damage you've caused!" In just over a year, the two collected a staggering $10,000 in fraudulent insurance claims before they were caught.

In 1968, Bass made the news again when he and another prisoner attempted an unbelievable escape — from the window of a moving patrol wagon. Bass and other inmates were being transferred from the Don Jail to court when the patrol wagon slowed down at an intersection in Toronto's west end. A woman pulling alongside the police vehicle watched in disbelief as Bass and another man — who managed to break the supposedly shatterproof glass and kick out a section of strong, spot welded wire mesh — were wriggling their way out of the vehicle. Most astonishing was that Bass, a solidly built man almost six feet tall and 170 pounds, managed to squeeze through a window measuring a mere ten by fourteen-inches while handcuffed to another man slightly smaller than himself. The six other prisoners in the wagon made no attempt to escape, but were concealing the sound of breaking glass by singing and shouting at the top of their lungs. Bass and his partner's breakout attempt was foiled mid-escape when the witness frantically waved her arms to get the attention of the officer driving the wagon.

Deemed a "pubic menace" at his 1969 trial for defrauding insurance companies through his fake auto accidents, Bass was sentenced to the maximum: ten years behind bars. Bass was stunned and Judge Everett

Weaver proceeded to provide the incredulous criminal with his reasoning for the stiff sentence. The offences were against people and property, said the judge, and some innocent individual could have been seriously injured or even killed in one of the staged collisions. Bass did not take the sentence well, shaking his fist at Weaver and screaming "Are you nuts?" and "Drop dead!" Bass went to prison, resurfacing time to time over the next few years in the newspapers as a letter writer. While behind bars as inmate number 5872, Bass sent a number of letters to newspapers complaining about conditions at Collins Bay Penitentiary, where he was incarcerated. The *Globe and Mail* published a number of his letters. One was critical of a Royal Commission investigating guards beating prisoners, while another admonished authorities for not passing out Christmas presents to Jewish prisoners. At one point, Bass's cellmate was the infamous Peter Demeter. A Hungarian-born real estate developer, in 1974 Demeter was convicted of hiring an unidentified person to kill his wife, model Christine Ferrari.

Once they were released from jail in 1976 both Bass and Ian Rosenberg were arrested again after a man claimed he was beaten and had his life threatened for refusing to make any more payments to the loan shark. Bass and Rosenberg were charged with assault causing bodily harm, attempted robbery, and extortion. Just over a year later, Rosenberg's former friendly acquaintance would go on trial for his murder. Rosenberg's lawyer believed his client's murder could have been the result of a long-standing grudge between loan sharks.

Both Rosenberg and his girlfriend, Joan Lipson, were buried on the same day, but in different cemeteries. Separated from her businessman husband at the time of her murder, Lipson's obituary did not read out of the ordinary, describing her as a loving mother to her two girls, and devoted daughter to her parents. There was, understandably, no mention about the circumstances surrounding her death.

The emotionally charged trial of James Bass for the double homicide of Rosenberg and Lipson began in March 1978. Described in the press as a "classic whodunit," the prosecutor, Robert McGee, told the jury of seven women and five men, "I doubt if there will be any days in the next few weeks when you will be bored."[4] McGee's comment was prophetic, as the jurors were exposed to a world of violence many of them had never before seen or even imagined could exist.

The trial would prove to be a complex affair for the prosecution, as McGee faced his biggest challenge: convincing the jurors of the motive behind the Rosenberg and Lipson murders. The prosecution contended that nineteen-year-old Chrystal was last seen driving away from Rosenberg's apartment with Bass, and that Bass later told Rosenberg "he had Chrystal in a room somewhere." Bass was afraid Rosenberg would tell police he had done something to Chrystal, so he killed Rosenberg to silence him before he could talk, and Lipson was also shot because she saw Bass killing her lover.

One of the first witnesses to testify was Lipson's young daughter, who testified she heard "five or six bangs" the night her mother and Rosenberg were murdered. Awakened by the sound, she saw a shadowy figure race past in the reflection of her bedroom mirror and move down the stairs. The terrified little girl entered her mother's room to find Rosenberg naked and dead on the mattress, and her mother on the floor midway between the bed and the doorway to the bathroom. Like Rosenberg, Lipson had also been shot at very close range, two bullets tearing through her skull into the floor, a third blackening her arm with gunpowder. As Lipson lay bleeding and fading into unconsciousness on the floor, the little girl struggled to wipe the blood off her face. "Ian," moaned Lipson, fighting to stay alive, "Ian." A next door neighbour also heard the shots and the sound of footsteps walking away from the gruesome scene of the murders.

Tests revealed that at the time of his death it would have been impossible for Rosenberg for fight off his killer or killers. His system contained about twice the legal limit of alcohol, along with traces of Valium, a drug that was often prescribed to treat anxiety disorders; taking the drug while drinking considerably increases the effects of alcohol, and would have made Rosenberg sleepy and defenceless.

From the beginning of the trial, the prosecution had a tough time convincing the jury that Bass was guilty of murder. Since over $400 in cash was found in Rosenberg's clothing, robbery was not a likely motive. Most of the evidence against Bass was circumstantial, including a dusty imprint of a gun in Bass's apartment and an empty cartridge case on the bedroom floor where the couple were murdered. Both were fascinating pieces of evidence, but the prosecution had a hard time tying them to Jimmy Bass. McGee had full confidence in another crucial piece of evidence, a key found in Bass's pocket that fit perfectly in the side door of the Lipson house. Since there were no signs of forced entry at the murder scene, McGee stated that this was the key that Bass used to gain easy access to Lipson's house, where he gunned down Rosenberg and Lipson in their sleep. This theory was soon discredited when Bass's defence team were able to prove the key not only worked in Lipson's lock, but opened the door to several other locks, including Bass's own residence.

A number of prosecution witnesses, terrified to appear in court and speak out against the alleged killer, did not help the prosecution's case against the accused. One witness, a nineteen-year-old friend of Bass's, admitted in a thin, crackling voice that he was terrified to testify, and make Bass "look bad." The witness was also a friend of Lipson's, and recalled how she helped him by typing his university essays for him. He remembered seeing the murdered woman the evening before she died, at a party Rosenberg held at his apartment on the evening of April 21, 1977. The nervous man also remembered seeing Bass and Rosenberg arguing at the same party, with Bass storming out in anger.

During the trial the jury also heard testimony from Ian Rosenberg's eighteen-year-old daughter. The young woman testified that she overhead her father and Bass talking at a party the night Chrystal was supposed to return to Edmonton. Although she couldn't make out the entire conversation, the girl recalled her father asking questions like, "Where the hell is the girl?" with Bass saying something back about "leaving her in a room," and a blue pickup.

Another prosecution witness, a real estate agent, asked for protection under the Canada Evidence Act while being questioned about trying to help Chrystal find someone to loan her money to bail Harris out of jail. The judge told him to answer the prosecutor's questions or risk going to jail. The man said Chrystal gave him $3,000 in October 1976 to help find someone to put up Harris's bail. When the real estate agent admitted to Chrystal that he couldn't find anyone to put up the bail money, she became upset and demanded her $3,000 back. The witness also testified he received a phone call from Rosenberg about the money, and that Chrystal and Rosenberg came by his office to pick up the cash on the night of October 8, 1976. That was the last time he saw her alive.

At one point during the trial, it was Bass's turn to be intimidated, not by the prosecutor but by a courtroom spectator. Bass was on the stand when an enormous man silently walked into court, taking a seat near the front, close to Bass. Immediately, Bass's tough guy demeanour dissolved, and he grew visibly agitated, gesturing toward the man and banging his pen against the side of the prisoner's box to get the attention of his two lawyers. After about half an hour, the silent stranger rose to his feet and left the courtroom as mysteriously as he had entered.

During the trial, details emerged about Bass's relationship with Rosenberg and Lipson. Although he was described as being on good terms with the murdered man, one witness recalled the depth of Bass's loathing for Lipson. Less than a year before the murders, Bass and another man emulated a crucial scene from the film *The Godfather* when they left a bloody deer head on her property. According to the witness — a co-worker who helped the accused man with his gruesome plan — Bass originally wanted to place the head in Lipson's car, but wasn't able to so he dumped it in her driveway.

The weapon and ammunition used to kill Lipson and Rosenberg were not run of the mill, as experts testified during Bass's trial. Both victims were shot from a distance of no more than two feet, with bullets likely fired from a heavy semi-automatic Colt or a copy. The bullets used in the .45-calibre handgun were even more unusual, since they were made for the United States government back in 1965 and unavailable on the open market. Similar bullets were found around the same time in the apartment of a well-known Toronto gun dealer, a man acquainted with Bass and Rosenberg.

The prosecution believed in the strength of another key piece of information, the gunshot residue tests taken of Bass's hands a few hours after the murders. They revealed elevated levels of lead, antimony, and barium, telltale signs that Bass had recently fired a gun, or handled a gun that had been fired within a few hours. Bass's lawyer, John Rosen, was successfully able to deflate this theory and put serious doubt in the minds of the jurors. Bass, he said, had a business repairing pinball machines, which were enormously popular in Toronto arcades at the time. The lead and other residue on his client's hands could easily be the result of working on pinball machine mechanisms, not from firing a handgun.

The accused man presented himself as a tall, handsome figure in court. Taking the stand wearing a neat, pressed blue suit, his curly black hair and thick moustache trimmed and combed, Bass claimed he was being set-up for the double homicide. "Kill Ian Rosenberg and put Jimmy Bass in jail for it," he told the court, ominously adding that there were "many shades of truth" when it came to the accusations against him. Bass flatly denied killing Rosenberg and Lipson, claiming he didn't know Chrystal Elizabeth Van Huuksloot, which prompted Crown Counsel Robert McGee to show him a photo of the missing young woman.

"I suggest you're a liar," said McGee, holding Chrystal's photo in front of Bass's face.

"I suggest you're full of shit," Bass replied, which elicited a gasp from the courtroom.

What about the credibility of witnesses who were testifying against him? asked McGee. Surely they were not perjuring themselves? They were all liars, said Bass, who seemed to have an answer for everything. When asked about his whereabouts the night of Chrystal's disappearance, Bass claimed he was in Barrie, Ontario, about fifty-five miles north of Toronto, picking up ten pounds of hashish for a drug deal. And where was he in the early morning hours when his alleged friend Ian Rosenberg and his girlfriend Joan Lipson were both shot dead at point-blank range in the head? Fixing a broken-down truck on Highway 401, replied Bass.

Police witness testimony contradicted Bass's claim of being out of town. Officers stated that they saw him driving in the general direction of Lipson's house an hour before the shooting. Another policeman testified that Bass was wearing dark clothes prior to the murders, and light-coloured, tight-fitting clothing and no socks after the killings. Yet another constable said Bass told him, "Some guy got it in the head twice with a forty-five and some woman got it three times." Evidence suggested

Lipson may have also been grazed by a third bullet, information that could only be known to the killer, or a confidante. In total, seven bullets were found at the scene; one may have grazed Lipson's head, but medical examiners couldn't say for certain. Bass's lawyer, John Rosen, called the evidence against his client entirely circumstantial, and stated that it raised more questions than it answered. "Bass is guilty of a wasted life, but he is not guilty of this offence," said Rosen.

Over his many years being in and out of jail, Bass developed a long-standing loathing of police, an anger that came out a number of times during the trial. Toronto Police Sergeant Robert Crompton, who knew the accused man from arresting him in the past, testified that Bass once cited the Bible to him, arguing that the cops wouldn't be able to prove he killed two people. Bass, said the sergeant, was trying to pry information from the officer to see how much evidence they had against him. "We have a lot of bits and pieces of circumstantial evidence and it all fits in just like it was Ian [Rosenberg] pointing at you from the grave,"[5] said Crompton. The comment infuriated Bass, who said, "He's not Lazarus. He can't come back from the dead and point a finger at me." While being questioned by Deputy Crown Counsel McGee, Sergeant Crompton said he noticed Bass wrote on the ceiling of his jail cell, "JB versus the crusher," which was Crompton's nickname. Throughout the trial, Bass was fond of name-calling and citing Biblical and historic references. At one point, he said he couldn't wait to "cross swords" again with Crompton.

By the time the trial against James Bass concluded on March 22, 1978, the prosecution had called seventy-six witnesses. Homicide officer Julian Fantino — who became Toronto's Chief of Police years later, in 2000 — testified that soon after being charged with the murders, Bass smirked at him and said, "You won't win this one." In the end, Bass was right. After deliberating for seventeen hours over two days, the jury felt the Crown failed to prove its case; namely, that Bass shot Rosenberg to prevent him from telling police about Chrystal's disappearance. Acquitted of the of first-degree murder charges, Bass walked out of court a free man on April 3, 1978. Smiling, he thanked the jury, hugged his lawyer, then turned and uttered an obscenity to one of the police officers who investigated the case against him.

The murder trial was over, but Bass was back in court just a few days later facing a host of other charges including assaulting police, possession of a dangerous weapon, and extortion. In September 1979, Bass would be sentenced to nine months in jail for the drug charge stemming from his statement that he was out of town picking up hashish at the same time Chrystal disappeared.

Although Chrystal Elizabeth Van Huuksloot has been missing for over three decades, she is not forgotten. When the *Edmonton Sun* launched its first edition on April 2, 1978, the cover story, "Acquittal Deepens Chrystal's Mystery," was devoted to the young woman's disappearance. In the late 1970s it looked as though the secret was solved when a mushroom picker found the badly decomposed body of a female near Elmvale, Ontario, sixty miles north of Toronto. Police believed the remains were Chrystal's, but they proved to be those of another missing female. To this day, Chrystal's photo and physical description appear on numerous websites, including the Alberta Missing Persons and Unidentified Human Remains site and the Doe Network. At the time of her disappearance in 1977, Chrystal's father Leo said he kept all of Chrystal's correspondence in a cardboard box and continued to fill out her income tax forms, just in case. "I don't want to bring her home," he said with sadness. "I just want to know if she is alive."

Chapter 6

Veronica Kaye (1980)

BACK IN THE FALL OF 1980 Veronica Kaye was another typical Canadian teenager who liked to shop, go to parties, and hang out with her friends. Popular, friendly, and gifted with a sense of humour, the eighteen-year-old was more focused on having fun and going out than making a list of long-term life goals and settling down. The child of divorced parents, life wasn't always easy at home. There were rules to follow and Veronica, like most teens, occasionally showed her stubborn side while trying to gain her independence. There were the usual arguments between parents and their children about staying out too late and spending far too much time with friends instead of studying. At one point, Veronica moved out of her father and stepmother's place and began living with her grandmother in the Highway 427 and Bloor Street area of Etobicoke, in Toronto's west end. The rules were more relaxed with her nana, who would sometimes let her stay out late, providing she called to let her know where she was.

On Friday November 7, 1980, Veronica was planning to buy a few things at the Square One Shopping Centre in Mississauga, a place that had everything a teenager could possibly want. Before going to the mall, Veronica made a quick stop at a photo lab, Cherish Photography, in a small strip plaza at 500 Hensall Circle in Mississauga. It was where

(Ontario Provincial Police)

Just eighteen at the time of her disappearance, Veronica Kaye was going to the Square One Shopping Centre in Mississauga when she disappeared on November 7, 1980. Her body was not found until almost a year later and whoever killed her is still on the loose.

her friend Elaine worked, and Veronica was there to pick up some clothes she was borrowing — a bag with a pair of jeans and two tops — for a party the next night. She left the photo lab around 1:30 p.m., telling Elaine she was getting a ride from someone who was waiting in outside in his car, and that he was going to drive her to Square One to do some shopping. Veronica didn't say who the driver was, but promised to give Elaine a call later that day. Thinking nothing more of it at the time, Elaine went back to work. It would be the last time Elaine saw her friend alive.

Saturday night came and went, and Veronica didn't show up to the much-anticipated party. The next day, there was still no sign of the eighteen-year-old. By Monday, her family was worried. Sure, staying out late, sometimes all night, was something Veronica would do, but never without phoning and letting a family member know her whereabouts. By Monday November 10th, her worried grandmother hadn't seen or heard from Veronica in days, and called Toronto Police to let them know her granddaughter was missing.

Was it possible that Veronica was a runaway? asked police. It was highly unlikely, since there wasn't any good reason for her to leave her grandmother's home. She was fed and taken care of by her nana, who helped her out with a few dollars here and there. Life was good at Nana's. Veronica could come and go as she pleased, as long as she called to let her know where she was staying and who she was chumming around with. She was also going to start a new job the very next day, a part-time position at a local Mississauga pizza parlour, so running away was out of the question.

Although her younger sister disappeared thirty years ago, Veronica's sister Cherilyn Lafferty still has sharp, painful memories of the day she found out Veronica was missing. At twenty-two, Cherilyn was four years older than her sister, one of the many Ontarians who at the time were moving out west to Vancouver to find work. When her father Ron called her apartment, Cherilyn's phone had been damaged the night before and wasn't working properly. The crackling line kept cutting in and out, and she managed to convey a message to her father that she would call him back collect from a phone booth in a few minutes. She knew her younger sister was living with their grandmother, and as soon as she heard her father say "Veronica is missing," Cherilyn immediately knew her baby sister hadn't run away, but that something terrible had happened to her.

"My dad told me, and I remember my knees buckling, feeling nauseated, and squatting down in the phone booth just bawling my eyes out, because I knew right then that there was something tragically wrong, because Veronica would have called my nana to say she wasn't coming home, and she wouldn't have worried my grandmother like that," said Cherilyn. Just a night or two earlier, she remembered experiencing the worst nightmare she ever had in her life. Although she couldn't remember exactly what caused her to wake up, she later found out her grandmother had a similarly upsetting dream, right around the same time. "I don't remember what it was about, but I woke up sobbing, and I often wonder to this day if it was some type of signal or message."

Just seven weeks after her sister's disappearance, a local paper followed up with the family in the days before Christmas 1980. Accompanying the article was a photo of the four girls — Cherilyn, Veronica, Julie, and Melissa — taken during a much happier time, the holidays the year before. At the time, their father wanted to remain optimistic but couldn't help feeling as though his missing daughter was dead. "It would be more of a shock to see Veronica walk in that door Christmas morning than for the police to come and say they'd found her body," said Ron Kaye. "I've taken this whole situation apart and put it together again and I can't come up with any other answer except she's not alive."

In the weeks following her disappearance, numerous tips came in to police, but none materialized into solid evidence and Veronica was not found. After hearing the news that her sister was missing, Cherilyn came back home from Vancouver, and the family became involved in the search, printing posters of Veronica and distributing them across Mississauga in the hope that someone, somewhere, remembered seeing her. When a loved one is missing, families will often go to any lengths for information. At one point, Cherilyn went to a psychic, who told her a white van was involved and that Veronica was in a wooded area in the Orangeville area of Ontario.

Months passed, and there was still no sign of Veronica. Around 9:30 on the morning of October 9, 1981, almost a year after her disappearance, two men were walking a dog in a wood lot off Duffy's Lane in Caledon, Ontario, when they came across a horrific sight. Lying on the ground was a body. Still dressed, it was nearly skeletonized, and appeared to have been in the woods for some time. Police were called to the scene and the remains were taken in for forensic testing. Information was circulated across Canada and the United States, and in a few days the body of Veronica Kaye was identified through her dental records.

At the time she went missing in 1980, Veronica was about five feet two inches tall, 120 pounds, with shoulder-length brown hair, and a fair complexion. When she was found almost a year later, she was wearing the same clothes she'd had on when she disappeared: a long sleeve maroon shirt, red, down-filled nylon vest, blue jeans, blue socks, and brown running shoes with a white stripe. The bag holding the jeans she borrowed from her friend Elaine was missing and her purse was nowhere to be found. A forensic examination was conducted, and newspaper reports at the time stated Veronica was beaten and suffered numerous blows to the head before she died. There was no mention made if she had been sexually assaulted. Her sister, Cherilyn, remembers hearing that the back of Veronica's skull was fractured, and that one of her baby fingers was broken, as if she was trying to ward off a blow.

For police, the hunt for a killer was on. For Veronica's family, the many months of uncertainty over what happened to their daughter had come to a close, but an unsatisfying one. Her remains were found, but whoever killed her was still out there, free and living life. For families of murder victims, the emotions that come with the discovery of a body are often mixed. They are often grateful the remains of their loved one have been located, but many questions remained unanswered. Who killed Veronica? Was it a stranger, or someone she knew? Was there anything that could have been done to prevent this tragedy? Some questions simply cannot be answered, even after thirty years.

"Your life is never the same," said Cherilyn. "The guilt, the shame and remorse of what you 'could have,' 'should have,' or 'would have' done, even though you know intellectually those are wasted emotions, but you just can't help it." The last time Cherilyn saw her sister alive was when she flew in from Vancouver for a party in Mississauga they were both attending. She remembers Veronica telling her she loved her. Veronica was standing on the road and called out to her sister, "And keep in touch."

Even after her sister's remains were found, Cherilyn hasn't been able to feel a sense of finality about her sister's death. At Veronica's memorial, attended by her many friends and family, she remembers standing in front of the closed casket and her father telling her that Veronica "wasn't there." At first, she believed the comment was made in the spiritual sense, that her soul had departed her body. The comment was actually literal. There had been a delay in returning Veronica's body to the family, and most people at the crowded memorial were unaware her coffin at the time was empty. "We're at the memorial, and Veronica's remains weren't even there," said Cherilyn. "They were there in time for the burial, but not in time for the memorial, so that was weird. I've never had a feeling of closure."

Was Veronica the victim of a serial predator, a man who drove around Ontario picking up young women in the seventies and early eighties who were hitchhiking, and robbing them of their lives? While police are not confirming if such a person of interest exists or existed, the number of other unsolved murders and disappearances of young women in Southern Ontario within a close geographic proximity cannot be ignored.

In November 2009, on the twenty-ninth anniversary of Veronica's disappearance, Ontario Provincial Police announced a $50,000 reward for information leading to the arrest and conviction of the person or

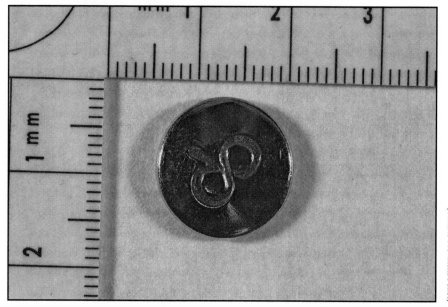

A small, metallic, clip-on button found underneath the remains of Veronica Kaye in 1981. Depending on how the button is viewed, it resembles a numeric number "8" or the symbol for infinity. This piece of evidence was not released to the public at the time of the murder. Police today hope it can be used to track her killer.

persons responsible for Veronica's murder. In cold cases, witnesses sometimes feel more comfortable approaching the authorities years after the fact with information.

"We are confident that someone out there has the missing piece of information that will resolve this case," said Detective-Inspector Andy Karski of the OPP's Criminal Investigations Branch. "The passage of time, for one reason or another, may allow those people with information about the case to finally come forward and provide police with a vital clue or tip that may lead to an arrest."

In 2009, the OPP also revealed another unusual item for the first time in their investigation: a small metallic button just over half an inch (1.5 cm.) in diameter. Police determined the button, found underneath Veronica's remains, did not come from any of her clothing. The button has several unusual characteristics. It is a clip-on, not sewn to a garment, and has a unique, slightly raised design on its face. Depending on how it is viewed, the button looks a great deal like a numeric number "8," or the symbol for infinity. It is hoped that whoever killed Veronica was wearing clothing with the button attached to it, and that this tiny piece of evidence can be used to help identify and catch a killer.

"We have no idea how that button got there," said Karski. "We are desperate for one small break and it may come from forensics or from somebody seeing that button."[1]

Sergeant Nikki Randall from the Caledon OPP said the button was investigated years earlier, when Veronica's remains were found. "There was a lot of investigation done into the button at the time," said Randall who, along with her colleagues, is contacting a number of manufacturers and searching websites and blogs on the Internet for information and photos. Randall said the OPP have received a number of tips since the photo and details about the button were released, and are hopeful for a break in the thirty-year-old cold case.

Although decades have passed since Veronica's murder, it still isn't known how she got from Cherish Photography in Mississauga to the woods in Caledon. Veronica and her friends did hitchhike sometimes. Did she get a ride with someone she knew or a total stranger on the afternoon of November 7, 1980? Her friend Elaine never saw the person who was apparently going to give Veronica a ride to the Square One Shopping Centre. At the time, police believed the young woman was "probably murdered while hitchhiking."[2] Following his daughter's murder, Ron Kaye wrote a number of letters to the mayors of Toronto and Peel asking to have hitchhiking banned, and encouraged parents to talk to their children about the dangers of thumbing a ride.

Cherilyn Lafferty said her sister's remains were found with a bus transfer issued by Mississauga Transit for November 7, the same day she went missing. "She had a bus transfer, so that's what makes me want to think it may have been somebody who drove by and saw her and said, 'I'll give you a ride,' somebody she knew, or the bus was taking too long and she thought, 'If I don't get a ride, I'll jump on the bus.'"

While it is possible that police will garner leads from members of the public who have seen news items in the papers or on television, or official information posted on the Ontario Provincial Police website, the Internet has become a place where armchair sleuths have posted their unsubstantiated theories about who murdered Veronica on various websites and blogs. One individual went so far as to actually name a suspect, who is now deceased. Much of the information and specific details that these self-styled "detectives" post online may seem convincing, but it's not gained through first-hand knowledge. They're just going on old newspaper and magazine articles written about the crime. Such theories would be beneficial, if they were true. When police are sent to investigate they often turn out to be fabrications or outright lies, perpetrated by individuals who are often mentally unstable, addicted to drugs or alcohol, or who have unresolved issues with their parents or a close relative and invent false allegations to "get back" at them.

For police and the families of murder victims, these hoaxes are not only disruptive, they can be emotionally devastating. Unfounded online "theories" not only waste time for the police who investigate them to see if they have any validity, but resurrect painful feelings for family members who are forced to relive the death of their loved ones through the eyes of a stranger. In Veronica's case, at least one individual — who went so far as to create and post videos online of the "search" for evidence and bodies years after the murder — contacted the family directly, giving them false hope about bringing Veronica's killer or killers to justice.

After thirty years, police believe there may be someone out there able to solve the mystery of who killed Veronica Kaye. Even after all these years, it is possible that a tiny piece of evidence the size of a button will finally bring a killer to justice.

Chapter 7

Susan Tice and Erin Gilmour (1983)

BETTER KNOWN TO THE WORLD simply as DNA, Deoxyribonucleic Acid is a truly splendid thing. Present in all living organisms, save for a few viruses, DNA is nature's genetic fingerprint, revealing not only information about us but our mothers and fathers. Initially used as an identification technique in the mid-eighties to detect the presence of genetic diseases, DNA has become a valuable scientific tool — perhaps the most valuable discovery — to modern-day criminology. First used to convict a criminal in the United States in 1988, DNA is derived from evidence collected at crime scenes, such as semen, blood, skin, saliva, and hair with the root attached. Countries around the world, including England and the United States, have created national DNA databanks. In the U.S., the Federal Bureau of Investigation's National DNA Index System contains DNA from not only evidence taken at crime scene evidence, but from convicted criminals as well.

In Canada, the National DNA Data Bank can be traced back to 2000,[1] and has produced matches for police forces across the country. Two of the matches involve women murdered in Toronto in the same year, in unrelated crimes, months apart. In life, it is unlikely Susan Tice and Erin Gilmour would have known one another, since they were different in almost every way, from age to life experience and social standing to career. Yet when a match was made in 2000 positively linking the women through DNA from their killer, whatever differences they may have had became far less important than the evidence that they were both raped and murdered by the same man, who remains at large to this day.

"Back then, they didn't know that these two cases were connected," said Toronto Police Detective Sergeant Reg Pitts, head of Toronto's Cold Case Squad. "Both women were murdered in 1983, four months apart, four kilometers apart, and killed by the same guy. They were very similar geographically, the timeline was obviously close, they were killed in much the same manner — stabbed and strangled and sexually assaulted — but you don't really know for sure until you have some DNA, and that wasn't done until 2000. It's the definitive link, this DNA matches that DNA."

Back in the summer of 1983, the life of forty-five-year-old Susan O'Hara Tice was at a personal and professional crossroads. A loving mother to four children and a devoted wife, for many years Tice had followed her husband Fred as he worked his way up in the business world, moving her entire family from one city to the next. A professional investor, Fred's most recent position was a post as vice president and director at Wood Gundy Investments Limited in Calgary. As she had done a number of times before, Susan dutifully packed the family's belongings and moved the household out west. The family had been living in Calgary for about three years when they separated. Their friends and family were surprised at the unexpectedness of the split. Susan and Fred had known one another for many years, having met at Hamilton's McMaster University where Susan graduated as a nurse in 1960. An extremely bright, energetic, and caring woman, Susan later graduated with her master's degree in social work from the University of Toronto in 1980, and spent a great deal of her time trying to help others realize their full potential by working with disadvantaged youth.

Their marriage over, Fred and Susan moved back to Toronto, but lived in separate residences. He moved into a townhouse on Ontario Street, while Susan bought a house for herself at 341 Grace Street, near Harbord Street. The popular area, widely known as Little Italy, re-

A forty-five-year-old who was recently divorced, Susan Tice had only been living in her new home in Toronto for a short time when she was found murdered in August 1983. DNA testing conducted in 2000 revealed that Susan Tice and Erin Gilmour were killed by the same man.

(Toronto Police Service)

mains home to countless stores, restaurants and cafes, and tiny storefronts serving Sicilian ice cream. Susan moved into the house in June 1983, and was getting settled in over the next few months while looking for a job.

On Friday August 12, Susan left Toronto with a canoe strapped to the roof of her car, and headed to her hometown of Leith, Ontario, a tiny village near Owen Sound, and the final resting place of acclaimed Canadian artist Tom Thomson. Tice was there to visit her family and catch up with old friends. She returned to her Grace Street home just two days later, and was last seen on the evening of Sunday August 14. No one saw her again for a couple of days. By Wednesday, relatives were getting concerned. Susan missed a family reunion. Her brother-in-law went to her house to check on her. Mail was piling up. Susan was discovered in a second-floor bedroom, dead. She had been stabbed a number of times in the chest and lungs. According to Toronto Police, a door had been left open and the house had been ransacked. When they interviewed Susan's neighbours, one thought she heard screaming late after Tice returned home, but thought she might have been having a nightmare, and didn't investigate to see if the screams were real or not.

By late September, after weeks of investigation, police believed that Tice, a social worker who devoted herself to her children and helping others in need, was brutally murdered by an intruder for less than $75 in cash. To this day, the rape and murder of Susan Tice is still unsolved. The case would remain an isolated one for the next seventeen years, unconnected to any other murders in the City of Toronto, until DNA recovered from semen in 2000 connected Tice to the murder of beautiful, young socialite Erin Gilmour.

As head of Toronto's Cold Case Squad, Reg Pitts may have moved up the ranks in the police service over the years, but the unsolved Gilmour murder case has never left his thoughts. He was on duty as a young police constable working out of 52 Division the night of December 20, 1983. It was bitterly cold, with an average temperature of -12°F, and the police received a call about a "possible suicide" in an apartment above a shop. The location was Hazelton Avenue, a street in the heart of Toronto's trendy Yorkville area, known for its many upscale fashion boutiques, jewellery stores, and world-class beauty salons.

Police soon arrived at the scene, an apartment above a clothing boutique named Robin's Knits, a white stucco building at 37B Hazelton Avenue. Since there was no access to the apartment from the store, police went down a laneway to get inside the two-bedroom apartment. Upstairs, in one of the bedrooms, was the body of Erin Gilmour. Officers tried resuscitation, but it was too late. Just twenty-two years old at the time of her murder, the attractive blonde girl with the shoulder-length hair had been sexually assaulted and stabbed repeatedly, with one wound piercing her heart. Detectives were soon able to create a timeline of the last hours of the young woman's life with the help of her boyfriend, who found Erin on her bed.

The discovery of Erin Gilmour's body took place literally minutes after she was killed. A pretty girl with the face and figure of a model, Gilmour had been working on and off at Robin's Knits while attending school. Living in the apartment upstairs from the store was ideal, and Erin was only a few doors away from Shelagh's, a furniture store owned by her aunt. She hadn't lived in the apartment for very long, only two months, and moved into the area because she was near family and felt protected.

On the bitterly cold Tuesday evening that she died, Erin was planning on going out for a quiet dinner with her boyfriend, twenty-four-year-

Just twenty-two years old at the time of her murder, Erin Gilmour was killed in her Yorkville apartment on the bitterly cold evening of December 20, 1983. Police were able to link her killer to the murder of Susan Tice, which had occurred a few months earlier. He remains at large.

old Anthony Munk. He said he would be by her apartment at nine o'clock. She finished work at about 8:45 p.m., locked the store for the night, went outside, and walked down the laneway about fifty feet to her apartment at 37B Hazelton Avenue.

By the time Anthony arrived at Erin's apartment, it was closer to 9:20. He had stopped at a bank machine to get some cash and arrived a bit later than expected for their dinner date. The street level door didn't have a peephole. It had been left ajar — not all that unusual, since she could have left it open anticipating his arrival — and he went inside, calling out her name. There was no reply. He called out again, and there was still no answer. He went upstairs, calling her name a few more times. Erin wasn't in the kitchen or the living room. Maybe she had stepped outside for a moment to go check on something, or see why her boyfriend was running late? Anthony went downstairs, almost expecting to meet Erin on the stairs. Not seeing her downstairs, Anthony went back upstairs; this time, he checked the bedrooms. Inside the master bedroom was Erin. She was on the bed, raped and dead from multiple stab wounds.

Erin Gilmour was sexually assaulted and killed within a very short time after getting off work, no more than thirty-five minutes. Since there was no direct access to her upstairs apartment from Robin's Knits, police believed that the young woman was followed the fifty feet from the store to her apartment, or that the killer let himself in and waited for her. The only entrance to the apartment at 37B Hazelton Avenue was through the main door. The door was slightly open when Anthony arrived, but it did not appear to have been tampered with. Was it possible that Erin, expecting her boyfriend to arrive shortly, inadvertently opened the door to her killer?

In the days and weeks following her murder, the media explored the many aspects of Erin Gilmour's life. Born on February 3, 1961, Erin immediately entered the world of the Canadian elite. Erin's mother, Anna McCowan, is the granddaughter of Ontario Lieutenant-Governor Colonel Henry Cockshutt. Erin's father, financier David Harrison Gilmour, was the only child of the decorated First World War soldier and financier, Major Adam Harrison Gilmour. Although Erin was born into wealth and the only child of Anna and David, she was far from a spoiled child, and those who knew her thought of her as very kind and understanding. Eventually, her parents divorced. Erin lived with her mother and two half-brothers before moving into her Hazelton Avenue apartment above Robin's Knits. She attended some of the finest institutions, such as Bishop Strachan and the Toronto French School, but wanted to make a name for herself in the world of fashion and design.

Soon after her death, ten detectives from 52 Division were actively looking into her murder, while a dozen uniformed officers went door-to-door in the area, asking if anyone had seen or heard anything out of the ordinary. Although her phone number was not listed, Erin had recently been receiving a number of threatening and obscene phone calls. Police investigated, tracking down the man who was calling her, but didn't believe he was involved. The number of potential suspects was not that great. Erin associated with upstanding people, not criminals or lowlifes. Her boyfriend, Anthony, was the son of Peter Munk, the founder of Barrick Gold Corporation, the world's largest gold miner. The fathers of both Anthony and Erin — Peter Munk and David Gilmour — were long-time friends and business partners.

The rape and murder of one of Toronto's wealthy young socialites shook the city. In 1983, there had been forty-seven murders in the city before Erin was killed, but her death took place in Yorkville, one of the safer areas of Toronto. A year after her murder, police had performed countless background checks and questioned over seven hundred people. DNA evidence was still years away, and would eventually link Erin's murder to whoever stabbed Susan Tice to death four months earlier and just two and a half miles distant. To Reg Pitts, the murders of Tice and Gilmour highlight the fact that although Canada's DNA base is growing, it still has its limitations when it comes to catching a killer.

"The guy could be dead, or he could still be out there," said Pitts. To date, the DNA recovered from semen found at both crime scenes has not yet been linked to other rapes or murders. Has the suspect assaulted other women, or started using a condom? There could be many reasons why the killer hasn't been caught. It's possible that he raped other women but let them live, and the rapes went unreported, or semen samples were not kept for any number of reasons. The crime is also not one that men — in or out of prison — generally boast about committing.

"Rape-murderers usually don't go around telling a lot of other people, so we generally don't get a lot of tips about that," said veteran Toronto Police Detective Robert Wilkinson who, like Pitts, knows many details about the crimes, having reviewed the files countless times over the years. "We get the odd 'hint' if you will — 'Have you thought about this?' or 'Have you thought about that?' — but it's not a tip." The police still receive calls about the crimes, but many of them are more of a suggestion, like checking out the postman who worked the route the days of the murders, than specific.

Like many unsolved crimes, there is still a good chance the man who raped and murdered Susan Tice and Erin Gilmour can be caught and convicted. Police believe the suspect was about eighteen to thirty-five years old at the time he killed both women, and he would now be in his mid-forties to early sixties.

In the twenty-seven years since both women were killed, police have looked at as many as 4,500 people in connection to the murders of Tice and Gilmour. And though the two women couldn't be more different in age, background, appearance, and life experience, they were raped and murdered by the same person. There is a reward of up to $50,000 for information leading to arrest and conviction of the man who killed them, who very well may have gone on to commit other rapes. With his DNA on file, there is a good chance that whoever killed Susan O'Hara Tice and Erin Harrison Gilmour back in 1983 will not spend the rest of his life a free man.

Chapter 8

Sharin' Morningstar Keenan (1983)

OF ALL THE CRIMES MAN CAN COMMIT, none is more cowardly, more unforgivable, than the abduction, rape, and murder of a child. Whenever a little girl or boy is kidnapped at the hands of a stranger, we are soon reminded by the media of other similar crimes, as a flurry of tragic stories from the past reappear and names of victims are resurrected. We see photos of children taken at the peak of their young lives, usually school portraits that look pleasant enough, until the reality sinks in: the happy little kid you're looking at is dead and buried.

All stories of murdered children are tragic, yet some keep coming back to haunt us, like Victoria "Tori" Stafford, Emanuel Jaques, Alison Parrott, Cecilia Zhang, and Holly Jones, to name just a few of the innocent lives lost over the years. In all of these cases, there was some measure of comfort, however slight, that guilty parties were apprehended and brought to justice for their horrific crimes. For almost thirty years, family and friends of Sharin' Morningstar Keenan are still wondering why this beautiful girl was murdered, and how — after all these years — the only suspect in her death has managed to elude capture not only in Canada, but around the world.

To this day, the name Dennis Melvyn Howe[1] sparks a visceral reaction, especially among police who are all too familiar with details of the crime. The sole suspect in the Keenan murder, the manhunt for Howe remains one of the largest in Canadian history, and despite countless "sightings" of Howe in far-off places like the Yukon and Hawaii, not one has proven to be true. To this day, Howe's mug shot, detailed physical description, and aliases are on most wanted posters around the globe. Using computer technology, Howe's face has aged many times, altered to reflect the passage of time. Fatter, thinner, greyer, balder, with facial hair and without, he has transitioned into the Internet Age, and appears on websites for the Metropolitan Toronto Police, the Royal Canadian Mounted Police, Jamaica's Most Wanted, and Interpol, the world's largest international police agency with 187 member countries. Although decades have passed since the murder of Sharin' Morningstar Keenan, the man police consider her killer is still deemed violent and extremely dangerous, not to be approached except by the proper authorities. Assuming he is still alive, Howe will soon celebrate his seventieth birthday. Sharin' will never be older than the nine, the age she was the day she was murdered. This is her story.

The Disappearance

As anyone who lives there knows, Toronto in the middle of January is rarely a winter wonderland. Sparkling Christmas decorations, long gone from stores, have given way to Valentine's Day displays. Even the weather feels like it's trapped between holidays. Skies are grey and bruised, and when temperatures rise for a few days piles of pristine white snow melt, covering streets, sidewalks, parks, and playgrounds with a thick, slushy soup. Sunday January 23, 1983, was one of those typical Toronto days, made even less hospitable by an unending drizzle.

A couple of years earlier, Brendan Caron and Lynda Keenan moved their family from Toronto's east end to the Annex area, in the centre of the city. Close to the prestigious University of Toronto, in 1983 the Annex was an area in transition. Old homes, converted decades before from huge three-storey estates to low-rent, multi-unit apartments, were slowly being bought by single families, gentrified, and resurrected to their former grandeur. A number of homes on Brunswick Avenue remained among the unrestored variety, the kind of places where you could rent a cheap furnished room with a cramped kitchen and bathroom shared by other tenants.

Just steps away from Brunswick Avenue is Jean Sibelius Park, a flat, nondescript piece of land surrounded by old homes on all sides, named after the nationalistic Finnish composer following his death. The streets surrounding the park — Kendal Avenue, Walmer Road, Bernard Avenue, and Wells Street — were familiar to the Keenan/Caron family, who lived on Dupont, a street just six blocks from the park. When Sharin' asked her mother if she could go play, Lynda said yes. It was not an unusual request. Nine-year-old, Sharin' cold be headstrong but was very responsible. She promised to be home from the park by five o'clock that evening. Sharin' set off, and her mother remained at home to look after the two younger children, six-year-old Celeste, and Summer Sky, just four years old.

When Sharin' didn't return by 5:00 p.m., the little girl's parents grew concerned. Her father went to the park looking for her. At the time, Brendan Caron thought she might still be mad at him for a recent tiff she had with little Summer Sky. Her younger brother was slightly hurt during play, and Caron scolded Sharin' in front of her friends. She was upset and embarrassed. At the time, Caron thought she was teaching him a lesson for humiliating her, and hoped walking home with her from the park would make them both feel better. When he reached the park, Sharin' wasn't there. Had she taken another route home by herself? Was she somewhere with a friend? Sharin' had always been mature for her age, a responsible child who always phoned if she was running even a few minutes late. When Caron returned home, he soon learned from his wife that Sharin' wasn't there either, and fear settled over the couple.

Outside, the skies darkened as daylight quickly disappeared and the air grew cold. Six o'clock came and went. At quarter past the hour, Lynda Keenan called police at 14 Division, responsible for serving the Annex area. Lots of kids "go missing" every day, usually turning up at a friend's place, or even in their own home, hiding under their bed, in a closet, or somewhere in the basement. Back then, the police station received about two dozens similar calls every day. Officers were dispatched to the parents' home, arriving around seven that evening. They asked the standard questions: where was Sharin' last seen? What was she wearing? How tall is she? How much does she weigh? What colour eyes and hair does she have? Do you have recent photos of Sharin'? Is it possible she could have gone on her own to the house of a friend or a relative? The parents were told to call around, to ask if anyone had been visited by the little girl. Sharin's description was soon broadcast to police in the area, and they were told to be on the lookout for the missing child. As the hours passed, thoughts of the girl running away evaporated, replaced by a deepening fear. "I'll probably be more relieved than angry when she shows up," said Caron at the time. "We are trying our best not to think the worst."[2]

That evening of her disappearance, police drove up and down the streets in sound trucks, with loudspeakers blasting out Sharin's description, and asking neighbours to check for the little girl. Has anyone seen her? Check anywhere she could be hiding — under your porch or deck, in your backyard, garage, or the bushes on your property. Some neighbours paid attention to the trucks while others — immigrants living in the area unfamiliar with English — didn't know what they were saying. As the evening drew to a close, the sickening thought that someone took Sharin' became a reality.

"I heard on the news that this girl was missing, and searches was one of the things that the police used the auxiliaries for a lot," said Jim Bunting. A former Metro Ambulance[3] employee, Bunting also helped out as an auxiliary police officer. He remembers volunteering to aid in the search for the little girl. During his time with Metro Ambulance, Bunting and his partner were present at many awful places, including the recovery of a number of "floaters" — corpses found in the water — usually in the city's west end, often around Marie Curtis Park or the Humber River. Over the next few days, creeks and rivers would be only a few of the places police searched for Sharin'.

The last place Sharin' was seen before she vanished, Jean Sibelius Park, soon became ground zero for police. Their search centered on the park, and radiated outwards. A small trailer was set-up to serve as a command post. Inside the cramped trailer were a few desks and telephones, where officers fielded calls. On the wall was a large board displaying streets in the neighbourhood. Some of the locals came in with information, and Bunting took down their name and contact information on a card. If the tip seemed especially pertinent, they were sent to talk to a detective in the trailer.

The days following Sharin's disappearance were long for Bunting, starting early in the morning and lasting until seven in the evening. He remembers the police searching the area over and over again, revisiting the same houses when owners or tenants weren't home the first time, and asking for permission to go inside locked sheds and garages. "At the beginning, everybody was tossing up in the air whether this was a missing kid, or an abduction," said Bunting. "The second time around, they were getting desperate. It was obvious by that time, five or six or seven days down the stretch, that this wasn't a kid that had run off. The longer she was missing, the less there was a possibility of her being a runaway."

Bunting remembers a teenager of about fourteen or fifteen coming forward. "She had seen the missing girl, who we now know as Sharin', sometime on the day she disappeared," Bunting recalled. "She saw the girl in the park being spoken to by a man, and later on it developed that this was Dennis Melvyn Howe."

Within days, everyone in Toronto knew the name and the pretty young face of Sharin' Morningstar Keenan. Her name was both memorable and strikingly beautiful. The apostrophe, explained her parents, was deliberate, coming from her sharing nature. Her middle name, Morningstar, was the first thing her parents saw the morning of her birth, July 3, 1973. Sharin's father, thirty-five-year-old Brendan Caron, was a laid-back kind of guy, his long black hair tied in a ponytail. He was a printer who had recently lost his job and picked up a side business selling food dehydrators from his home. The little girl's mother, Lynda Keenan, passed her good looks onto her children. With her brown hair and dark complexion, Sharin' was pretty, confident, and outspoken. The family was spiritual, and soon Lynda lit a small white candle on the mantle. Its purpose, she pointed out, was not to signify hope, but to maintain a light so mother and daughter could get through the ordeal.

Two days after Sharin's disappearance, two senior Homicide officers — Staff Sergeant David Boothby and Sergeant Wayne Oldham — were brought in as observers to aid in the search, which soon expanded to include a nine-mile stretch between the Humber and Don Rivers. Still hoping for the little girl to be found safe and sound, it remained crucial for Homicide officers to be present from the beginning.

"When we were called in, the first thing I wanted done was to go back to square one, right back to the approximation of where she went missing," said Boothby, who later became Toronto's Chief of Police. He asked officers to knock on all doors in the area and request permission to search houses. "There have been many cases where kids have gone missing, and the search goes on and on, and they're trapped in some place right close to the house, and still alive in many cases — they've just got themselves trapped in some situation by misadventure."

In Toronto's north end, a church group combed ravines, while police continued to search abandoned houses, ravines, parks, alleyways, garages, warehouses, railway cars, Sharin's public school, even laundromats. Overhead, police used a helicopter to check rooftops for anything unusual. The word went out to the city's trash collectors to be on the lookout for garbage bags that seemed unusually large or heavy, and to cut them open to see what was inside if necessary.

As the agonizing days of uncertainty wore on, it seemed more and more likely to police that Sharin' did not run away, but was taken, grabbed by someone in the park. Most missing children turn up within a few hours, and Sharin' vanished in the chilly gloom of January a few days earlier. The story that began as a small item in the newspapers soon became front page news, as almost one hundred police and auxiliaries searched for miles around the Jean Sibelius Park, rifling through bins of industrial scrap metal, automobile wrecking yards, and along the waterfront at the edge of frigid Lake Ontario. Ten thousand photos of the missing girl were distributed across Toronto, with many businesses posting them in their front windows. The public was provided with a description of Sharin' at the time she went missing: four feet nine inches tall, eighty pounds, dark brown hair, dark complexion. When she disappeared, the little girl was wearing a brown quilted knee-length coat, a blue and green kilt, white blouse, and brown shoes.

A round-the-clock telephone hotline was set-up, with twenty-five police officers investigating every lead. Some calls sounded legitimate, while others were from crank callers who thought they were being clever, not caring if they wasted valuable police search time or not. The little girl's father saw over a dozen psychics in the days following her disappearance, many of them saying his little girl was near a bridge, a railway, and water.

The elementary school photo of Sharin', showing her with her hair combed back, wearing a red sweater and white shirt, soon became familiar around the city. A few days after the disappearance, the *Globe and Mail* published a new series of photographs that had never been seen before, provided to the newspaper by Sharin's father. The strip of four images were ones that Sharin' took of herself in a downtown photo booth. They revealed a confident nine-year-old girl perfectly at ease with the camera, hamming it up in a series of modelling poses. Caron said the photos provided a better likeliness of his daughter, who usually wore her dark brown hair hanging down over her eyes, instead of pulled back, as in the school photo widely used in local papers.

Eight days after she disappeared, a Canada-wide alert was issued, and police were following up on tips from as far away as North Bay. Sharin's father made an impassioned public appeal for his daughter's return. "Bring Sharin' home. No one will hurt you if you do. If you need help, come forward with Sharin' and I'm sure people will help."[4]

The Discovery

As one day flowed into the next, the search for little Sharin' continued. Toronto Police visited and revisited houses in the immediate area of the Jean Sibelius Park, especially those where they were unable to talk to every resident. Some were out at work, others at school, and some just didn't bother answering the door. One of those houses was 482

Brunswick Avenue, across the street from the park. Two of the officers going door-to-door on Tuesday February 1, 1983, were Sergeant Peter Pickford[5], formerly a police officer in Britain with Essex Constabulary, and his partner, Constable Brian Lawrie, who had joined the force almost a decade before. The two had been partners for about two years.

The system of searching for a lost child is largely the same in both the U.K. and Canada. "It's a well-rehearsed and a well practiced and a well proven technique that we have, with respect to the machinery or the system that kicks in whenever a child is reported missing," explained Lawrie, who was involved in dozens of missing child cases over the years. "Basically it's the same. You start off with last known location, and of course you speak to relatives, and you speak to other people, and you start to work out an ever-increasing circle. Plus, you make use of the publicity aspect of it as well. It is very important that the public knows that this child is missing, because the public are really your eyes and ears whenever it comes to situations like that."

Lawrie, like many officers on the force, is a father, as was his partner. Although both men maintained their police professionalism, it was impossible not to feel deep emotions for the family and friends of the missing girl. "If you're chasing an escaped prisoner, that's another thing. But when it comes to the child, and the helplessness of a child, and the *vulnerability* of a child, then it takes on that importance," said Lawrie, who was detailed from 13 Division to 14 Division to take part in the search. "It was important that we did a more detailed investigation of the vicinity." This included not only speaking to everyone who lived in the immediate area of the park, but anyone who would have a reason to be in the neighbourhood the day Sharin' went missing, including postmen and couriers.

To refresh residents' memories, Lawrie and Pickford carried a basic Identi-Kit composite of the man suspected of abducting the little girl. Based on a description of the person seen talking to Sharin', the image was made up of overlays of parts of the face, such as the forehead, eyes, nose, mouth, and chin. "They looked pretty ineffective, because people weren't used to seeing photographs like that," said Lawrie, "but that's all we had, and of course, our job was to go and interview everybody, and show them this photograph, and see if they could recognize, or had any good idea who that might be. We had done quite a number of houses, and some of them were rented by the room. If someone wasn't home, we made a note, and it went into the report, and at the end of the shift there were staff there who would identify where there were people who hadn't been spoken to, and follow that later. It's quite meticulous, the way those investigations are done."

By the time the sun was setting that early February evening, Lawrie and Pickford had been going door-to-door for hours, concentrating on homes on the west side of Brunswick Avenue. Both officers were cold, sore, and tired. Lawrie suggested they take a break and get something to eat. Pickford said, "Let's do this house here," and the two advanced up the porch stairs of number 482, a rooming house that was up for sale. They knocked on the door, which was opened by an Asian man who was mopping the floor — the superintendent. Lawrie remembers standing on the mats so as not to leave footprints on the wet, freshly cleaned surface. By that point, it was late and getting dark. The man, recalled Lawrie, seemed preoccupied with his work, and wanted to go upstairs. The officers accompanied him to the third floor with him, and spoke to one of the tenants on the floor.

"Who else lives here?" asked Pickford.

"Well, there's a guy on the second floor," replied the tenant.

"Is he home?"

"No, he's not."

"When is he going to be home?"

"I don't know."

"When did you last see him?"

"Eight days ago," stated the tenant.

Lawrie and Pickford were taken aback by the man's exacting comment. Not a week, not two weeks, but *eight days ago*, the exact number of days Sharin' was missing. The two officers looked at one another and asked the superintendent if he had a key to the missing tenant's room. He did, and the three went back downstairs to the locked second-floor room. Once the door was opened, Lawrie was surprised by the condition of the room: it was absolutely spotless.

"Most of these places, we'd expect to find dishevelled, to say the least," said Lawrie, who had spent two years in the military, and found the room extremely tidy, even by military standards. The bed was neatly made, and everything seemed in order. There weren't a lot of places to search — a closet here, shelves there. Lawrie found nothing out of the ordinary in the cupboards, or in the closet, which was devoid of clothes. As Lawrie kept looking around the apartment, Pickford stood in the hallway outside the room, talking to the superintendent, asking questions about the man who rented the room, when did he pay his rent and most important, "When did you last see him?"

That was when Lawrie noticed the refrigerator, and thought, "If he's coming back, there's got to be stuff in the fridge." As he grabbed the handle, the fridge door stuck on the carpet, only allowing it to open a few inches. The fridge was working, but the door didn't open far enough for the light to come on, so Lawrie used his flashlight to peer inside the darkened refrigerator, and saw a green garbage bag with a shirt poking out.

Who keeps laundry in the fridge? thought Lawrie, pulling open the door a little further. At that moment, the bag tipped forward, and a body began falling out, dark hair tumbling over its face. It was Sharin'. Despite all his years of police and military training, Lawrie was stunned by the horrific discovery.

"Shock wasn't the word for it," said Lawrie. "It was a realization." He stood there for a few seconds before turning to his partner and saying, "She's in the fridge." The moment didn't register with Pickford, who continued talking to the superintendent. Lawrie repeated himself more forcefully, "*She's in the fridge.*" After an extensive search of the city for over a week, combing through every vacant lot, every ravine, under porches, and inside garages, the nine-year-old — who Lawrie still affectionately refers to as "Morningstar" — was found stuffed in a fridge just a two-min-ute walk from where she was last seen alive. The two officers immediately called for backup. The sickening realization that the little girl had been murdered was replaced by the need to protect the scene and maintain continuity. Lawrie left the room and stood midway up the stairs, placing himself in a position where he could see the room and keep an eye out

Sharin' Morningstar Keenan was found dead in a rooming house refrigerator ten days after she disappeared in 1983. Her murder sparked one of Canada's largest manhunts for her accused killer, Dennis Melvyn Howe.

to make sure no one entered or left the house. Uniformed officers arrived almost immediately, followed by Homicide detectives.

"As soon as that is discovered, our job is to secure the scene, and secure anybody around the scene," said Lawrie, "whether they are suspects or not, they are certainly potential witnesses if they live in the same house as the body was discovered. So it was important that we secured as much of that scene as we possibly could, including the people at the scene. That was the initial challenge. So then, it was left to the detectives in charge, Boothby and Oldham."

For years afterward, Lawrie and Pickford remained haunted by the pointless waste of the little girl's life. "It was the significance of the garbage bag," said Lawrie. "It bothered me for a long time. I didn't know what the purpose of the garbage bag was, because she was murdered in the room — that's what I understand took place — what would the purpose of the garbage bag be, just to put her in the fridge?"

The event affected the lives of Lawrie and Pickford forever. Both men had seen many lives ruined and discarded over the years, but this one was simply too much to tolerate. The next day, once word got out about the discovery, friends and family called Lawrie's wife to see how he was coping. After being an officer for a total of seventeen years, Lawrie realized it wasn't something he wanted to do any longer and resigned a few weeks after he found Sharin' in the fridge.

"I guess if you spend so much time in other people's garbage, the danger comes when you don't notice the smell anymore," said Lawrie. "And that's what it was with me." After leaving the Toronto Police at age thirty-four, Lawrie took a sabbatical. Soon after, the former police officer received a call from a cousin who had been charged with a traffic violation. He successfully got his relative out of his traffic dilemma, and was inspired to start the Provincial Offences Information and Traffic Ticket Service in May 1984. As Canada's original and most successful traffic court agent, Lawrie and POINTTS continue to represent motorists in court.

Lawrie remembers that awful moment of discovery, but has come a long way since that cold day in February. The same cannot be said of his former partner, Peter Pickford.

Over the years, Lawrie kept in touch with his former partner, who continued working as a police officer. He had been, said Lawrie, a happy-go-lucky sort of guy prior to the discovery of Sharin's body, which took a day to thaw before it could be examined by forensic scientists. The autopsy conducted by Dr. John Hillsdon-Smith revealed the little girl had been raped, manually strangled, and probably murdered within hours of her abduction. This knowledge, and finding her icy corpse in the fridge, left an indelible mark on both men. In mid-May 1987, Lawrie met with his former partner, who seemed much quieter than usual. Two days later, Pickford got up as he normally would, took his dog out for a morning walk, and did some banking. On the way to work he got off at the Rosedale subway station, laid across the tracks, and waited for death. Pickford was just forty years old.

"He was never the same after finding that body. He had a daughter a little younger than the Keenan girl and it really shook him up. It left a big mark," said Lawrie.

Sharin's Funeral

It was a bitterly cold day in the city's Mount Pleasant Cemetery where Sharin' was buried, wind sweeping through a large tent that covered her grave. Lawrie was there, along with other officers, friends, schoolmates and their parents, teachers, and politicians. The funeral procession had just come from the Toronto Buddhist Church, which wasn't large enough to accommodate the hundreds of mourners attending the service. The entire city of Toronto mourned the devastating loss that day, February 4, 1983. At the request of her father, a fund had been established in Sharin's memory. Created for the purpose of promoting creative arts activity for kids, the fund had already raised thousands of dollars, including an undisclosed amount from comedienne and actress Carol Burnett.

While many of the city's residents were mourning Sharin', Toronto Police were busy checking their files for known sex offenders, and tracking down leads. Whoever killed the beautiful little girl had a ten-day head start, and cops were faced with their biggest challenge: who was he, and where was he? The discovery of Sharin's body sparked the beginning of one of the largest manhunts in Canadian history, a criminal odyssey that would span decades.

The Search for Sharin's Killer

Who was the man renting the cheap, $45 a month apartment where Sharin' was found? Was he someone who knew the little girl and was able to lure her to his room? The room where the man lived had a balcony; outside, there was a view of the Jean Sibelius Park, and the melting ice skating rink that a witness remembered seeing Sharin' "splashing about" on before she left with an unknown man.

The rental house at 482 Brunswick had a number of tenants. A couple from Argentina were renting the basement flat, two rooms on the second floor were rented to single men, and students lived in the attic. When the Argentinean husband and wife were interviewed by a reporter from the *Toronto Star*, the man suddenly had the sickening realization that he may have heard Sharin' being murdered. Unable to speak English, Alberto Suarez feared police wouldn't be able to understand him in his native Spanish, and didn't speak to them. The night of Sharin's disappearance,

Suarez heard "horrible banging noises," feet running on stairs, and someone saying "Shush" over and over. The noises were loud and lasted almost three hours, prompting Suarez to rap on the ceiling with a pool cue.

At first, police believed name of the man they were looking for was Michael Robert Burns or Byrne, a thin, weathered-looking drifter who rented the apartment two months before the murder. The man had an aged appearance, was about five feet nine inches tall, with dark brown hair greying at the temples. Witnesses remembered his teeth, which were yellowed and rotting. By mid-February, Toronto Police Inspector Jim Majury created a composite sketch of the wanted man. Police purposely held off releasing the sketch because they wanted it to reflect the most accurate information possible.

Soon after Sharin's father saw the composite drawing, he thought something seemed eerily familiar about the man's face. Then Caron remembered he had met the stranger before — with Sharin. Father and daughter were in the Jean Sibelius Park in the fall of 1982, when they were approached by a man who asked if they'd like to buy some pantyhose. Caron said no, and the man left, but not before he felt that it was "pretty inappropriate" of the guy to try to sell him women's undergarments with his young daughter standing beside him.

Police were able to track the man's employment to Samet Hosiery on Spadina Avenue, in the city's garment district. While searching his apartment, officers found a handwritten list, with odd, paired words on it like "malted milk," "oriental rose," and "gypsy jade." These turned out to be pantyhose colours, which officers were able to trace to the hosiery factory. The owner of the company said the man calling himself Michael Burns was a good worker but not too personable, someone who kept to himself. He hadn't been around for a few weeks, not since the day after Sharin's disappearance, when he asked his boss for an advance to see the dentist. The man got the money, but never saw the dentist.

A day after the sketch of the wanted man was published in the newspapers, Toronto Police received over two dozen tips, including one from a young waitress in a rundown coffee shop in Regina, Saskatchewan. Witnesses described the man in detail, from his weather-beaten skin to his crumbling teeth. More information soon emerged about the man's personality and habits. He was a drinker, favouring Molson Export over other beers. He loved country and western music, and was a relentless chain-smoker — his brand of choice was Player's unfiltered. One witness remembered him effortlessly smoking seven cigarettes in less than half an hour. The man had a boisterous, loud laugh and a very peculiar way of speaking. Instead of calling things by their proper name, everything, even inanimate objects, was referred to as "turkeys." Instead of saying, "Hand me that screwdriver," he would say, "Hand me that turkey."

To be eligible to work in Toronto, the man used a social insurance card from the real Michael Robert Burns from Regina, who lost his card three or four years before the murder. Suspecting the killer had a military background, police made the controversial decision to approach the National Defence Identification Bureau of the Canadian Armed Forces, which kept fingerprints on file of past and present members of the forces. The prints were kept for the sole purpose of identifying "bodies of military personnel and victims of amnesia." The issue raised the question of why the records should be kept at all, and should they be used for police investigations.

In the weeks following Sharin's murder, local papers were full of stories about fearful parents and their equally terrified children, as they tried to cope with a real life monster on the loose, not an imaginary ghost or troll but a flesh and blood sex killer. Many mothers and fathers in the Annex refused to let their youngsters walk to school by themselves, or go playing outside or skating alone. Meanwhile, parents at Jesse Ketchum Public School — Sharin's elementary school — held meetings to try to answer questions from schoolmates like, what happened to Sharin', and when would she be back? One piece in the paper lambasted parents who continued to let their kids go out unaccompanied by an adult, selling Girl Guide cookies or chocolate-covered almonds for school charities. "Children should not be out canvassing door-to-door late at night; they should not be out on their own unless it is to solicit from neighbours they know,"[6] chastised a writer from the *Toronto Star*.

By Sunday March 6, 1983, police had gathered enough information to release the real name of the man believed to be Sharin's killer: Dennis Melvyn Howe. Fingerprints taken at the crime scene matched those of

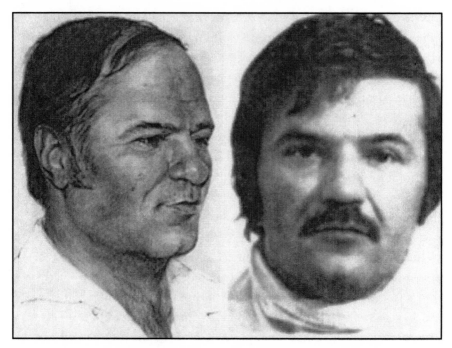

The many faces of a wanted man: Dennis Melvyn Howe, the prime suspect in the rape and murder of nine-year-old Sharin' Morningstar Keenan in 1983. Born in Regina, Saskatchewan, on September 26, 1940, Howe is a chameleon, able to change his appearance quickly through weight gain and loss, and growing a mustache. A man of unusual habits, Howe is a chain-smoking, beer-drinking man who has a habit of calling inanimate objects "turkeys." Assuming he is alive, Howe is likely working at a menial job, or in a remote mining or logging camp.

Howe, whose records were microfilmed by police in Regina and sent to Toronto. The previous witness descriptions were accurate, and detectives were able to add considerable details. Born in Regina, Saskatchewan, on September 26, 1940, Howe had a lengthy criminal record going back to the mid-1950s. He was white, five feet nine inches tall, with brown hair, greying at the sides. His weathered complexion, forehead wrinkles, and a scar under his chin made him look older than his forty-two years. Other distinguishing features of his face included brown eyes, a bulbous nose, and a small gap between his front teeth. His body was hairy, especially his arms and chest. Left-handed, the baby fingers on both hands were crooked and bent inwards. He was known to wear a moustache, and gain or lose up to forty pounds from his 165-pound frame quickly.

Other characteristics emerged that Toronto Police hoped would help identify and apprehend Howe. When he sat, Howe was always erect, with his thumbs tucked under his chin. His walk was fast and flat-footed, which was what led police to believe he served time in the military. He had a habit of lining up his cigarettes on a table, and would hold them between ring and middle finger, close to the webbing. When he held a pen in his hand he would twirl it in his fingers, as if it were a miniature baton. Staff Sergeant David Boothby went to western Canada to learn more about Howe from the people who knew him. He met Howe's half-brother, and immediately recognized some of the facial features of the wanted man. Dennis, said Boothby, had been on the wrong side of the law his entire life.

"When they were growing up in Regina, sometimes there would be a knock at their door, and if they could see it was a police officer, they would say, 'Dennis, it's for you' just by seeing the police officer through the door," recalled Boothby. "He was forever getting into trouble. The other thing was, he was a survivor. This kid, when he was 13 or 14 and the police were looking for him, would survive in a garage or laneway in Regina in the middle of winter, when it was very cold. That's the kind of person he was."

Howe was also a master at conning others into doing as he desired. While in Regina, he lured a nurse into his apartment, telling her he had a little puppy, and that it was very sick and needed help. The woman's heart went out to him. Another time, Howe put up an ad on a store bulletin board looking for a babysitter. He interviewed potential candidates, and even created a fictitious family — including a wife who, he claimed, was very ill — and said he needed someone to look after his young daughter. Using this tactic, he conned a girl and took her on a drive, tied her up, and put the hood of his car up to make it look like he had engine trouble. Fortunately for the girl, a passing driver became suspicious, went over to investigate, and the girl was saved.

Howe has used a number of aliases in the past, including Wayne Edward King, Ralph Ferguson, Jim Myers, and Michael Robert Burns. His job at Samet Hosiery, where Howe worked as a shipper, was obtained under a false name. While at the pantyhose factory, he demonstrated a remarkable ability to learn and retain inventory and stock numbers and was known for being a very good worker, though not the most approachable.

The search for Howe was massive. By late April 1983, a $50,000 reward was posted for information leading to Howe's arrest. Toronto's Homicide Squad soon received dozens of calls from across the city and the western provinces. Truck drivers agreed to have posters with Howe's image plastered on their vehicles, and hostels in Canada and the United States were sent Howe's picture, in case he showed up. Mediacom Inc., a large outdoor advertising company, agreed to put up enormous posters of the wanted man on billboards and bus shelters. The poster campaign — and an increased reward of $100,000 for information leading to Howe's capture — were unprecedented.

"The big thing in these cases is to create so much publicity that everyone is on the lookout for this guy," said Boothby. "On the other hand, from the police perspective, you have to be prepared to deal with hundreds and hundreds of calls and hundreds and hundreds of dead ends after you follow-up the leads." Despite countless tips, a year passed without any solid leads on Howe's whereabouts. In June 1984, sixteen months after the murder, police issued a worldwide alert for Howe, who was also placed on Canada's most wanted lists and with Interpol.

All across Toronto, thousands of people saw the posters of Sharin's alleged killer on bus shelters, with the words, "Warrant for Murder in Toronto Dennis Melvyn Howe," underneath. One of them was Irwin Patterson, a volunteer with a travelogue show on Graham Cable TV called *Have Fun Will Travel*. In addition to his travel program, Patterson had done a number of shows on crime prevention, and thought creating a two-minute short to be used as a station break between shows would help police in their pursuit of Howe. The Toronto Police were enthusiastic, and Patterson interviewed Boothby and Oldham for the segment. This was years before television shows like *America's Most Wanted* and *GTA's Most Wanted* hit the airwaves.

The videotaped interview about an open homicide was unique for its time, and had numerous advantages over static images of Howe. Flanked by large posters of the wanted man in the studio background,

Boothby emulated Howe's many idiosyncrasies, such as the odd, twirling way Howe handled his pen. To demonstrate Howe's quick, flat-footed, almost military walk, police taped Oldham copying Howe's walk in Jean Sibelius Park during a downpour. The final tape, six minutes and thirty-three seconds long, included a detailed description of Howe, his known aliases, and an in-depth account of the case, including the type of jobs Howe held, like roofing, shipping and receiving, and short order cook.

Once the tape was completed and delivered to the police, Patterson was told they couldn't do anything with it, because they didn't have a budget for blank video tapes. Patterson, a cable TV volunteer for a dozen years, quickly came up with a solution. He told police that when movie studios sent commercials to television stations, the promos were only thirty to sixty seconds long, and the rest of the tape was blank, "and when the movie has been through the system, they throw the tapes out," said Patterson. While police contacted movie studios for used tapes, another station, CityTV saw the segment, and made a public appeal for tapes. Pathé News came forward, and offered to make two hundred duplicates for the police free of charge.

Ultimately, nine hundred copies of the tape — considered the world's first "video wanted poster" — were made, earning Patterson a crime prevention award for his volunteer effort. Canada Post offered to send copies of the tapes free of charge, and Patterson remembers seeing a roomful of officers on the floor, stuffing and labelling almost one thousand envelopes. Eventually, the tapes were sent to all cable television operators, broadcast TV stations, and police stations in Canada. Believing Howe might have gone to the United States, additional copies were sent to police agencies in Texas and Southern California, and a French-language copy was made. The sign-off at the end is eerily ironic, since at the time no one suspected that Howe would remain at large for so many years. "It is our hope that you continue to air this piece until Dennis Melvyn Howe is caught. Thank you."[7]

One of the many challenges facing police was the photo of Howe, a mug shot taken a number of years before Sharin's murder. In the picture, Howe was younger and considerably heavier, less scruffy-looking, his cheeks rounder and fuller. According to people who knew and worked with Howe, his face changed considerably as he aged, the creases on his forehead and around his eyes deepening, hair greying, and his face somewhat thinner.

Toronto artist Alexa Phillips[8] was sick at home with the flu when she saw Sharin's father, Brendan Caron, on TV, upset with the police for circulating an older photo of Howe instead of a newer image. She found Caron's plight heartbreaking and wondered why the police hadn't put out a composite sketch to show what he looked like then. She called the police to volunteer her services as an artist, and was quickly accepted. Phillips still remembers going to the homicide department, which reminded her of an old movie; a dingy room filled with cold, grey metal desks. Working from a file of photos and eyewitness testimony, Phillips took a photo of Howe when he was thinner, and aged it, weathering his skin and greying his hair and stubble. As a portrait painter and illustrator, Phillips was aware that certain facial features change as we age but others remain the same, such as the distance between the eyes and the midline of the mouth. Paying close attention to all the details of the wanted man's face — such as his bulbous nose and distinctive crease lines — she created a realistic three-quarter view of Howe in coloured ink. "His co-workers were shocked at how good it was," said Phillips. "They said, 'Oh, that's exactly what he looks like.'"

Creating the illustration over a week had an effect on Phillips, who admits that looking at the portrait still "gives her the creeps" to this very day. At one point soon after she did the drawing, Phillips thought she recognized Howe in downtown Toronto. Sixteen months after the horrific rape and murder, Dennis Melvyn Howe — who remains the only suspect to this day — was still out there, somewhere. Police by that point had chased down an estimated ten thousand clues. The two lead investigators, Boothby and Oldham, refused to be defeated, but did admit their frustration. Oldham described the feeling as "thirsty and being able to get within two inches of a glass of water, but no further. The person is out there. With his lifestyle and past we would have expected to apprehend him a long time before now. Where is he? What aren't we doing? How have we missed him?"[9]

Over the months since Sharin's murder, the police had done a great deal to try to catch her killer. The poster campaign featuring Howe's face on billboards and bus shelters all over the city was unprecedented. The video wanted poster was unique, as was allowing a member of the public to create an age-enhanced sketch. The previous October the police decided to grant the story of Sharin's murder to *Reader's Digest*, because it was a magazine that remained in doctor's offices and waiting rooms for months, and hopefully someone would recognize Howe. Although the article resulted in over three hundred telephone calls, none led to Howe's capture. So why, after so much time, were there no tangible leads in the case?

In 1988, a full five years after Sharin's rape and murder, *Saturday Night* magazine devoted a cover story to the case. "Stranger in the Park" retraced the events surrounding Sharin's death, and the aftermath, including the dissolution of her parent's marriage. Numerous "sightings" of Howe — everywhere from Barrie, Ontario, to Mexico — came in, but as before, none turned up the wanted man. Since Sharin' was killed, her mother Lynda Keenan turned to art to help her with her grief, painting a portrait of her late daughter and holding an exhibition of her work. Caron spoke of his frustration with the investigation over the years, and his belief that if police used tracking dogs earlier to hunt for his daughter, Sharin' might have been found alive. The problem with dogs is that their sense of smell is less precise in colder weather, and in heavily-travelled areas, such as the Annex.

In July 1990, the popular television program *America's Most Wanted* aired a special Canadian edition of the show, featuring two wanted men. One of them was Dennis Melvyn Howe. It was the first time Canadian crimes had been featured on the then two-year-old series. Featuring re-enactments of the hunt for Howe, the show received hundreds of tips in the hours following its broadcast. Wayne Oldham, who had been investigating the crime for seven years by that time, was in Washington to field calls from viewers who believed they had information on Howe's whereabouts. One caller swore he'd once gone fishing with the wanted man, while another said Howe was living in her friend's basement apartment in New Jersey. Both calls proved to be dead ends.[10] At the time, police believed that Howe, a chameleon who lied effortlessly and easily changed appearance, might have been working in the American west. The episode on Howe was broadcast again in April 1991, and generated three hundred possible leads.

In the years since Sharin's murder, police have received hundreds of tips from people who are convinced they've spotted Howe. In 1994, one individual said he recognized the wanted man from a photo in the *Regina Leader-Post* and claimed Howe stayed at his rural Saskatchewan hotel three times between 1987 and 1990. A few years later, following a third profile on *America's Most Wanted*, police received about one hundred tips regarding Howe. At the same time, it was believed Howe could have worked as a dishwasher in one of Canada's remote mining camps in the Northwest Territories. With his ability to change his appearance, an isolated mining camp would be the perfect place for Howe to hide.

Although tips continued to trickle in for years after Sharin's murder, there were no significant discoveries until a macabre revelation in the late 1990s: was Dennis Melvyn Howe dead and buried in a Sudbury, Ontario, cemetery? It was almost inconceivable to think the wanted man's whereabouts could finally be known after so many years. Believing he could be dead was bittersweet, but it would give police and the public some consolation to know that even though justice wasn't served, Howe would never again torment and kill another child.

Investigators followed a lead from a Sudbury Police officer who read an information package about Howe. There were many similarities between the man buried in an unmarked grave in Lasalle Cemetery and Howe, especially the quiet, hermit-like existence both men were known to have lived. Piece by piece, police gathered enough evidence to get an order to have the body exhumed. When Sharin' was murdered in 1983, DNA evidence was not yet widely used, but genetic material — such as blood, saliva, and semen — are often found on clothing, sheets, and bodies of victims. Was it possible these samples, or DNA from Howe's relatives, could confirm the identity of the man in the Sudbury cemetery? Burial records listed the man's name as "Peter Steven Sanderson" — was it Howe's last laugh, using yet another alias for his final resting place?

Although the deceased man was a recluse, police were able to piece together information about his habits and personality. Many of his traits bore more than a passing resemblance to Howe. The man was a drifter — a miserable, perpetually down on his luck kind of guy, full of bitterness and loathing toward others. People who met the man remember it being a thoroughly unpleasant experience, and wanted as little to do with him as possible. He was scruffy, dirty, and often reeked of stale cigarettes, alcohol, and body odour.

A Sudbury area contractor and property owner named Laurent Diotte remembered the man coming in to his office and asking for a job back in 1987. The guy calling himself Peter Sanderson had all the right identification, including a social insurance number and a driver's licence. He came to Sudbury from western Canada, or so he said, and had heard "good things" about the nickel and copper-mining city. Although the man stank and had an attitude, Diotte felt sorry for him, and gave "Sanderson" a job as a labourer and truck driver. He also rented him a cheap apartment. Something about the elusive man — described as "a miserable old goat" by Diotte's wife — made people extremely uncomfortable. The stranger was decidedly a man with a past, but few wanted to know more about the drinker with the tobacco-stained mustache.

By early 1988, Sanderson's work habits changed for the worse, and he was constantly complaining about being in excruciating pain. Some days he came in late, other days he didn't bother showing up at all. By late May, his health declined rapidly, and at one point he lifted his shirt to show his boss a lump on his back. That was the last time Diotte saw Sanderson, who died just a few days later on May 28, from cancer. As inconceivable as it seems, the man fought against being examined by a doctor all that time, and somehow managed to walk, barely, with untreated terminal cancer.

Even though he was dead, the mysterious "Peter Sanderson" was far from finished, and kept surprising the authorities. An X-ray of his head was taken after he passed. Like Howe, the man had wretched teeth and clear evidence of an abscess — a painful, sometimes fatal, infection in his jaw. Doctors did a double take when the head X-ray was placed on the light box. Clearly visible was the triangular, metal tip from an old-

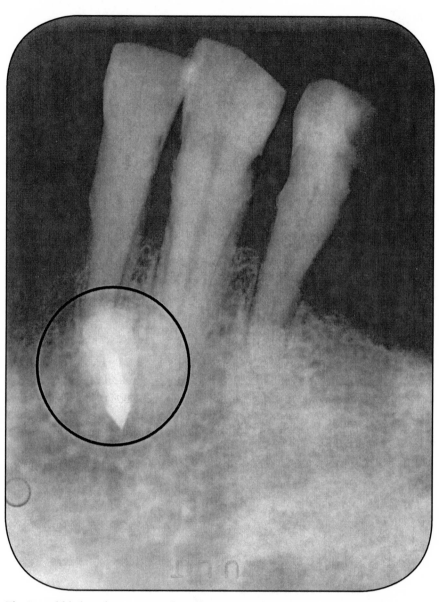

The incredible lengths some people will go to in order to avoid doctors and police: the dental X-ray obtained by police of the man calling "Peter Sanderson." Suffering from a painful abscess in his jaw, he chose to treat the excruciating pain himself — by snapping off the metal tip from an old-fashioned ballpoint pen deep in his jaw. "He just rammed it in, and broke off the tip of the pen to break the abscess," says Toronto Police Detective Robert Wilkinson. "That is how much he didn't want to come to the attention of the authorities."

fashioned ballpoint pen, embedded deep into his jaw. "He just rammed it in, and broke off the tip of the pen to break the abscess," said Toronto Police Detective Robert Wilkinson. "That is how much he didn't want to come to the attention of the authorities."

The man calling himself Peter Sanderson was so unbelievably elusive that Diotte only learned of his death from reading about it in the local paper. The man worked for him briefly, and since Diotte barely knew him he didn't attend the funeral. Now that Sanderson was dead and buried, it was up to Diotte and his family to clear out the apartment they rented to him. They weren't prepared for what they found. It was full of garbage, old rags, and ground-in filth. The rotting body of a dog lay on the floor, dead from starvation after unsuccessfully trying to chew its way through a door. Most curious of all was a plastic bag in one corner of the room; inside were panties and an undershirt that would fit a little girl. Were they the property of Sanderson, or somebody else? In the end, Diotte's daughter threw the items into the trash. That was the end of Peter Sanderson — or so Diotte thought.

Years later, police tracked down Peter Sanderson, alive and well. The *real* Peter Sanderson, a Winnipeg-based father of three in his fifties. His wallet was stolen around 1986, and he immediately reported it to the police. Once his cards were replaced, he didn't give the stolen wallet much thought until he applied for health benefits following heart surgery about a decade later, in 1995. His application was delayed, and he was eventually told he wasn't eligible to receive benefits. *Why?* asked Sanderson. *Because you are dead*, he was told. Government officials thought he was an imposter, until he was able to prove he was who he claimed to be through Government of Canada documents, and matching fingerprints taken when he was in the Canadian Armed Forces. Winnipeg resident Peter Sanderson wasn't the imposter: the man lying in the Sudbury cemetery was the fake, buried in an unmarked grave under his name. The phony Sanderson's rest would not be eternal, however, as police produced a warrant from the coroner to exhume the body.

Toronto Police Detective Wilkinson supervised the exhumation, which took months to arrange. He went to Sudbury the evening before to see exactly where the grave was located. The next morning Wilkinson returned with others, including a forensic anthropologist, before the break of dawn. He had heard the stories about the extreme lengths the mystery man had gone to, going back to a doctor several times for stronger and stronger pain medication, but refusing every single time to be examined. The last time he came in, the man calling himself Peter Sanderson was in so much pain that he could barely stand, his body riddled with cancer. "That's how determined he was not to get involved with the authorities," said Wilkinson, "and that's how it first came to our attention: how does this guy not give his name, and not go to the authorities, for any kind of examination?"

There were a few physical discrepancies between the dead man and Dennis Melvyn Howe, but the similarities were far too many to ignore. The last known sighting of the real Howe was in Winnipeg, and the man in the ground used the identity of someone whose wallet was stolen in Winnipeg. Both Howe and the deceased spoke in a similar strange manner, referring to objects as "turkeys" instead of by their proper name. Both were chain-smokers, gruff, unkempt, smelly, rough-looking men around the same age. Perhaps most important of all: Howe and the deceased went to extraordinary lengths to avoid any contact whatsoever with authority figures, choosing to live in squalor, work menial, almost disposable jobs, and maintain what Wilkinson calls "a fairly low-intensity lifestyle. In the absence of finding Melvyn, with circumstances like this, with this mount of evidence, you can't afford not to take the unusual step of disinternment."

Using shovels and a small backhoe, cemetery workers spent three hours unearthing the casket of the imposter buried under Peter Sanderson's name. The date was September 30, 1999, and to add to the misery of their duty, it was raining. Next to Wilkinson was a forensic anthropologist from Laurentian University. As dirt came out it was placed in a pile next to the grave. At one point, the anthropologist yelled "Stop!" Wilkinson was amazed as the anthropologist reached into the clumps of earth, and pulled out one toe bone, then another, until he soon reconstructed the remains of a human foot. "They are that good," said Wilkinson.

The remains, buried for years by that point, were not in the best condition. "The coffin leaked," said Wilkinson, matter of fact. "The way they dug the grave wasn't quite level. His feet were in the wet part, and that disintegrated." Fortunately for police, the upper portion of the body was in considerably better shape; had it been the other way around, identification may have been impossible. Cordoned off by a barrier, police, archaeologists, and forensic experts emerged with paper bags containing evidence, including tissue and bone samples from the corpse, which was photographed and re-interred. There was no post mortem needed, since police knew the man died as a result of cancer. "There is no mystery to how he died," said Wilkinson. "The question was, 'Who is he?'"

Once the body was exhumed and examined, it became apparent that there were significant physical differences between the man in the grave and the real Dennis Melvyn Howe. The corpse was missing a finger; Howe was known to have all his digits intact. Most surprising of all, considering the state of decay, was the clearly visible tattoo of an eagle across the corpse's chest, wings spread wide in triumph, spanning from one nipple to the other. The tattoo had an amateurish, homemade or prison quality to it. A photo of the tattoo embedded into the corpse's desiccated flesh was taken and published to help identify the remains. The chest of the dead man had an eagle on it, but Howe wasn't known to have any markings on his body. During the sixteen years since Sharin's murder, Howe could, of course, have walked into a tattoo parlour, or lost a finger while working. A chameleon his entire life, Howe maintained an ability to change his looks with ease.

Witnesses who got close enough to the man claiming to be Peter Sanderson recalled him having blue eyes; Howe's eyes were brown. Still, it seemed there were more similarities than differences between Howe and the deceased. The man claiming to be Sanderson left behind samples of his handwriting on weekly work timesheets, and experts were brought in to see if the handwriting matched that of Howe. The final determination of whether or not Howe's body was in the cemetery would be left to DNA testing, which was expected to take several months.

By that time David Boothby — who became Toronto's Chief of Police — had an intimate knowledge of the case, going back to the discovery of Sharin's body in February 1983. He had heard of the many false sightings of Howe over the years, and was cautious not to jump to any conclusions. "I would certainly hope that it would bring some closure to the families — that's the most important part. But I just want to put this thing in perspective. We've probably tracked down 10,000 leads in this [case], and this is one of those things that is troubling because we don't know exactly who this person is. I certainly don't want to get anybody's hopes up."[11]

In a newspaper interview published at the time of the exhumation, Sharin's father expressed his bitterness towards the media and the police. He was angry that no one from the coroner's office told him they were digging up the man who could be his eldest daughter's killer; he only learned of it from reporters who came knocking on his door. He remained upset with police for years after Sharin's death, still believing that had tracking dogs been brought in earlier in the search they would have found his daughter alive.

In January 2000, the DNA test results were in: the decomposing body in the Sudbury graveyard was not that of Dennis Melvyn Howe. The news was disappointing. Could Howe still be alive somewhere after all those years? If Howe wasn't buried in the cemetery, who was? And why would anyone go to such incredible lengths to maintain their anonymity?

The photo taken of the dead man's tattoo was published in the papers, and Toronto Police were surprised when an identification was made. A retired Ontario Provincial Police Inspector recognized the tattoo as one belonging to a person he had wanted from an active investigation. The man was wanted for killing two of his wives years earlier. Both women died under extremely suspicious circumstances. "The way they'd met their deaths is they exited the passenger door of his pickup truck into oncoming traffic, quite a feat," said Wilkinson. "While we didn't get Melvyn, this guy had equally good cause to be hiding."

It has been over a quarter of a century since Sharin' Morningstar Keenan was killed. If she had been allowed to live, the smiling young girl with the dimple in her check would be approaching her forties, and likely a mother herself. Despite one of the largest ongoing manhunts in Canadian history, the only suspect in her murder remains at large.

"It's not as if we're trying to solve a crime," said Toronto Police Detective Sergeant Reg Pitts. "Crime solved. It's finding him. From our point of view, we're not looking for anybody else. We're not looking to verify anything. The evidence is all intact, and we're ready to go to trial the second he is found." Boxes of evidence, reviewed and examined countless times over the years, are ready for a trial that may or may not ever take place. The refrigerator that contained Sharin's body still exists. Many of the retired police officers involved in the case, like Lawrie, Boothby, and Oldham — are still alive, waiting for their day in court to face the monster accused on this monstrous crime.

"There is nothing remarkable about Howe," said Pitts. "He is remarkable in his unremarkableness. You're not dealing with a master criminal. You're dealing with a guy who committed a horrendous crime, and fled the jurisdiction, and somehow has managed to avoid detection. Maybe he died a year after this, maybe that's how he's been so lucky."

Today, the murder of Sharin' Morningstar Keenan may not be as well-known as more recent tragedies, but tips still come in to police on a regular basis. Detective Wilkinson credits the many local police forces in Canada and the United States who have spent a great amount of time investigating leads from other jurisdictions, and passing their findings on to the Toronto Police. He doubts that Sharin's killer is still alive, based on information about Howe. A few weeks before Sharin' was murdered, Howe went to a dentist with serious problems. "Short of having all your teeth out or having major dental surgery, his condition proves fatal," said Wilkinson. "Unless you have major dental surgery, the condition doesn't improve by itself." So distinctive were Howe's teeth that his dental chart was published in a leading Canadian dental journal, in the hopes that any dentist working on a patient would recognize him as the wanted man. To date, not one has. The last known credible sighting of Howe was on a bus en route to Winnipeg. Police believe he had almost no money with him, and the driver remembers him carrying just two garbage bags and nothing else.

While many police believe Dennis Melvyn Howe is indeed dead, others, like David Boothby, think Howe may still be alive, possibly under a stolen name in the United States or working in a remote mining camp in Canada's north, washing dishes or doing other menial, anonymous jobs. "If a 13-year-old kid can spend three or four nights in the alleyways of Regina in the middle of winter, that's a kid who can survive," said Boothby.

The Annex area of Toronto has changed considerably from the way it was back in 1983, the year Sharin' was murdered. The venerable Brunswick House — a popular place for university students to grab a cheap beer or two — is still located at the corner of Bloor and Brunswick. But gone are the many Hungarian restaurants that once served enormous plates of schnitzel and overflowing piles of pork, potatoes, and vegetables called a Transylvanian Platter. There are still a few of the bohemian incense and Peruvian handicraft shops here and there, but these too are giving way to sushi bars and cafes.

The Jean Sibelius Park, where Sharin' was last seen alive, hasn't changed much over the years. It remains flat and somewhat barren, a small city park encircled by houses. It is a great place for parents to let their kids burn off some energy after school. Old wood and metal swing sets and see-saws have been replaced by newer blue, yellow, and red plastic playground slides with safer, rounded corners. There is now a black metal fence surrounding the playground, its purpose uncertain: to keep children in, or keep others out? Just outside of the fenced area is the monument to the man whose name the park honours: Jean Sibelius. Atop the monument is a bust of the famed Finnish composer, his stern countenance glowering down over the playground, watching generations of youngsters grow up like a parent watching over his children.

Near the park stands the house at 482 Brunswick Avenue. It looks much like it did that evening when back when Constable Brian Lawrie opened a fridge door and found Sharin', triggering the hunt for a killer that has gone on for over a quarter of a century. In many ways, the house, like the memories many people have of Sharin', has become frozen in time. It is one of the few structures in the area that hasn't undergone major exterior renovations, like a new brick façade, landscaping, or expensive interlocking stone driveway. Surrounded by trees and overgrown hedges, the house remains perpetually in shadow, even during the day.

Sharin's remains are buried in Toronto's Mount Pleasant Cemetery, the bronze plaque bearing her name without the apostrophe and the words "Shakuni Shosei," a Buddhist translation of her middle name, Morningstar. Beneath the dates of her birth and death are the words, "Walk in balance little sister." Perhaps one day justice will be served, and Sharin' can finally rest in peace.

Chapter 9

Nicole Louise Morin (1985)

ALL ACROSS CANADA, THE SUMMER of 1985 would be remembered as one of the hottest and driest in many years. By the end of July, cities like Vancouver hadn't seen a drop of rain in over a month, leaving locals to slather themselves with coconut-scented suntan lotion, put on sunglasses, and head to the beach alongside hundreds of others to cool off. The unusually hot weather was also felt on the other side of the country, as temperatures in Toronto stayed above the 80°F mark. Backyard and public pools were packed as parents and children struggled to get some relief from the relentless heat. In the borough of Etobicoke, in Toronto's west end, July 30 started out as a hot, sticky, but otherwise normal day for a little girl named Nicole Louise Morin.

Late that Tuesday morning, eight-year-old Nicole put on her orange bathing suit to get ready for a swim. It was a glorious, sunny day. Nicole was on summer break from Wellesworth Public School, where she was in grade three, and wouldn't start again for over a month, leaving lots of time to play with friends. Few things in life looked better to Nicole than dunking her head in the cool water of the pool outside the condominium complex where she lived in the twentieth floor penthouse.

Along with her peach-coloured towel, Nicole carried a plastic bag holding her goggles, a white T-shirt, green and white shorts, a pink

One of Canada's most famous missing persons cases, Nicole Louise Morin was just eight when she disappeared from inside her parents' condominium building at The West Mall in Etobicoke. The search for her has never stopped.

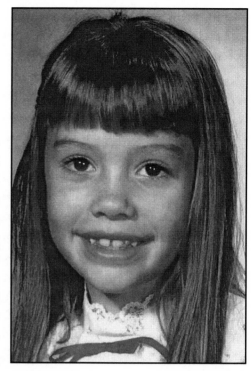

hairbrush, and a bottle of suntan lotion. Just before eleven o'clock that morning, Nicole's friend Jenny buzzed the building's intercom to tell Nicole she was waiting downstairs. Promising she'd meet her right away, Nicole set off from the apartment, down the hall to the bank of three elevators. Back in the mid-eighties, it was normal for parents to feel safe about letting their youngsters play on the building's property, or in the pool by themselves or with friends.

Jenny waited, and waited. After about fifteen minutes she was beginning to wonder where Nicole was, and buzzed the Morin apartment again. Jeannette, the little girl's mother, wasn't overly concerned, thinking her daughter was probably fooling around someplace, riding up and down one of the building's elevators. Jenny continued to wait in the lobby. After about half an hour, Nicole still wasn't there, so Jenny decided to go swimming by herself. Nicole's mother believed her daughter was in the pool with her friend the entire time, and when she checked for Nicole later that day she panicked when she realized her daughter was nowhere to be found. Police were called around three o'clock that afternoon. What had begun as a hot, unremarkable summer day in July would be the beginning of one of the greatest and most baffling missing persons cases in Canadian history.

In recent years, the expression "without a trace" has become overused and something of a cliché. It is rare, practically impossible, for two people or objects to meet *without* leaving a trace. Whenever someone enters or exits a room, he or she leaves and takes microscopic particles from their clothing, hair or dander from their body or head, and dirt or debris from their shoes. "Every contact leaves a trace" remains the cornerstone of all police crime scene examination, a term developed by pioneering forensic scientist Edmond Locard.

Known as Locard's Exchange Principle or Locard's Theory, the "Sherlock Holmes of France" is credited with the study of trace evidence: tiny, often microscopic bits and pieces of material that are used as silent witnesses to aid investigators in their pursuit of wrongdoers and missing persons. "Physical evidence cannot be wrong," said Locard. "It cannot perjure itself, it cannot be wholly absent.... Only human failure to find it, study and understand it, can diminish its value." This cross-transfer of physical evidence occurs whenever there is contact between two items, such as when two people meet. In case of a crime, materials are often left or removed from the scene, including soil, clothing fibres, footprints, paper, paint, dust, or glass. Long before the advent of DNA, Locard realized the importance of so-called genetic fingerprints, such as blood, semen, and saliva. When physical items are combined with DNA, it makes for a mute but powerful witness in court, a witness unaffected by factors that influence human beings like fear, excitement, anger, or forgetfulness that comes with the passage of time. "This is evidence that does not forget."

While evidence never quite "forgets," it must exist in the first place for it to be of any value to police. In the quarter-century since her disappearance, it is astonishing to consider not one tangible piece of evidence — no clothing, and none of the items she took with her to the pool — have materialized in the disappearance of Nicole Morin, a case that remains active in police files, the media, and on the Internet to this very day.

A charming, wide-eyed little girl with dark brown hair and a welcoming smile, Nicole loved McDonald's, and going to the circus and fairs. She was the only child born to Art and Jeannette Morin, married for a dozen years before their daughter's birth on April 1, 1977, and separated at the time of her disappearance. Nicole lived in the condominium with her mother. The area surrounding her building at 627 The West Mall was stark, made up of ranch-style bungalows, nondescript high-rise condos, and apartments surrounded by large, empty stretches of lawn. For police, searching the building where Nicole was last seen was a formidable task. The 429-unit structure had, like many other buildings in the area, multiple underground garages and countless utility, storage, and pump rooms, making the challenge of finding the missing girl even more difficult.

It soon became apparent that Nicole, who was taught by her parents not to talk to strangers, did not wander off on her own. Within hours of her disappearance, Crime Stoppers posted a $1,000 reward for information leading to her discovery. Jeannette was convinced her daughter had been kidnapped, since Nicole had never gone missing before. Described by police as "a well-organized, clever girl," Nicole knew how to make long-distance telephone calls if she ever got into trouble. Police were able to determine the little girl made it to the elevator and downstairs to the lobby, when a woman in the building recognized Nicole from a photo. Many questions remained unanswered. How could a little girl disappear so quickly from a condominium building? Was Nicole abducted? And if she was, did it take place inside or outside the structure? If she was abducted, why didn't anyone hear anything, and why wasn't a single one of her personal belongings — such as her towel, clothing, or pink hairbrush — found anywhere in or near the building or outdoor pool? The seventh-floor female tenant who recognized the little girl from her picture officially remains the last person to see Nicole Morin alive. "That's the last she was seen, but it leaves the dilemma of what happened to her," said Toronto Police Staff Sergeant John Luby, who headed the probe into Nicole's disappearance. "No one saw her after that."[1]

A week after Nicole's disappearance, after conducting numerous searches of her building using tracking dogs, police roadblocks around the building were removed. She was not the type of child to go wandering off on her own, and photos of the missing girl had been distributed in the area, along with her detailed description. Nicole was eight years old at the time of her disappearance, four feet tall, and weighed about fifty-one pounds. She had a birthmark on the right side of her forehead, and pierced, slightly protruding ears. There was a small gap between her front teeth. Local media helped in the search for the little girl; the *Toronto Star* printed six thousand posters showing a photograph of missing eight-year-old, with the caption, "Have you seen Nicole?" and a phone number for Metro police.

To create a more accurate impression of Nicole, Toronto Police approached artist Alexa Phillips[2] to create a piece to show more accurately how Nicole looked the day she went missing. It was the second time the artist worked with the police. A few years earlier, Phillips did an extremely accurate illustration of Dennis Melvyn Howe, the man wanted for the 1983 rape and murder of Sharin' Morningstar Keenan. Instead of using coloured ink, as she had done with the drawing of Howe — a rough, weathered-looking man in his forties — she chose watercolour, a better medium to capture the soft and delicate facial features of a young girl.

"The police said, 'If you could draw her the way she looked the day she disappeared, it might help for people to see her in that outfit,' said Phillips. "They had a good picture of her face, and I had another little girl model for me for the body, and I put the face and the body together." The model was a neighbour's daughter, depicted in the same type of bathing suit that Nicole was last seen wearing, a towel in her right arm and plastic bag in her left hand. The watercolour accurately depicted Nicole, since the girl posing for the painting was the same age, size, and physical build as the missing child.

Soon, the watercolour of Nicole was printed on three thousand reward posters distributed to Ontario police forces, post offices, and business. Two weeks after her disappearance, twenty investigators were working on the case and a $50,000 reward was posted. Toronto Police tracked down numerous leads; unfortunately, several of them were time-wasting hoaxes. One sixty-five-year-old man said Nicole was buried in a field, and police squandered hours searching the area with tracking dogs before arresting the man for conveying false messages and harassment. A few days later, an eighteen-year-old prankster claimed he kidnapped the girl and was holding her for ransom. This, too, turned out to be false, taking precious time away from the investigation. Several searches of parks, creeks, and a ravine near the airport revealed no trace of the missing girl.

Leads continued to pour in. Within a few weeks police had received 1,500 phone calls, and amassed file pages numbering in the thousands. In late August, a month after the disappearance, authorities were looking for a mysterious woman who was last seen on the twentieth floor, where the Morin condo was located. The police desperately wanted to speak to the woman, not as a suspect but a potential witness to Nicole's disappearance. Officers were able to create a composite sketch based on recollections from a tenant who lived on the same floor and remembered seeing the woman in the building. Something about her presence seemed strange at the time, said the tenant, and much stranger in retrospect. She was about thirty-five years old, white, pretty, thin, and had her dark brown hair parted on the left. She wore a white skirt with a black pattern, and a white or cream-coloured blouse and shoes. It seemed peculiar that she was standing at the opposite end of the hallway from the Morin's penthouse apartment, holding a notepad, just forty-five minutes before Nicole's disappearance. It is not known if police were able to track the woman down. She remains someone who possibly saw Nicole and the person or persons who abducted her.

By early November it seemed as though police finally had a significant break in the case. A search turned up a plastic garbage bag containing a black jacket, pants, and a newspaper dated July 31, 1985, with a front page story and photo of Nicole. By that point, police were three months into the investigation. A team of investigators had been working full-time on the missing girl's case. Seventy-five uniformed Toronto Police and auxiliary officers, along with members of the Royal Canadian Mounted Police and Peel Police, performed a shoulder-to-shoulder search of an overgrown area along the banks of the Etobicoke Creek near the airport. Nicole's parents, Art and Jeannette, were present in case they needed to identify any of their little girl's property. Forensic tests later confirmed the clothing uncovered by police turned out to belong to someone else, not Nicole. By this point, officers had interviewed about six thousand people. The search for the missing child expanded into the United States, as posters were sent to police agencies across North America.

For the public there was the eerie feeling that something tragic happened to Nicole. At the time she disappeared, Nicole was one of a number of young girls in the Toronto area who were abducted. The others, Christine Jessup, Sharin' Morningstar Keenan, and, later, Alison Parrott, were all found dead. No physical trace of Nicole has ever been found.

To this day, Nicole's disappearance remains one of the oldest active cases in the files of missing children agencies around the globe, including Child Find, a not-for-profit charitable organization with branches in almost every province in Canada. Back in 1983, when Child Find began, no central registry of missing children even existed. Every year across Canada, approximately sixty thousand children go missing. Some are parental abductions, or youngsters who decide to run away from home. Others are kidnapped by strangers. Many are reunited with their families, while some, like Nicole Morin, remain missing for decades.

"Some days, I find completely heartbreaking. Even talking about Nicole's case will sadden me, because she's been gone for so long, and you just wish you could have had some kind of news for her mom and dad," said Trish Derby, executive director of Child Find Ontario from 2003 to 2009. Since it was incorporated in 1984, Child Find Ontario has been active with police and other agencies to help locate missing and abducted children. Along with local authorities, they assist other groups, such as the Royal Canadian Mounted Police National Missing Children Services, Canada's Department of Foreign Affairs, and the National Center for Missing and Exploited Children in the United States.

In some cases, Child Find Ontario gets a call from parents whose child is missing even before police are notified. Before they take on a case, Child Find stipulates there must be a report filed with the police, and parents have to fill out a detailed assessment form. If the authorities believe the child is missing because of a suspected parental abduction, Child Find will work with the custodial parent. The group also assists in the search for missing children and youth primarily to age sixteen, educates the public on ways to prevent abduction, and advocates the rights of children.

One of Child Find's missions, said Derby, is keeping the missing child's photo in the press, as they have done with Nicole all these years. Her description — along with images of her taken shortly before her disappearance and computer-generated age-enhanced photos — are displayed on electronic screens in Esso gas stations, billing envelopes from Rogers Cable and the Canadian Imperial Bank of Commerce, Toronto Transit Commission display screens, and on the back of transport trucks. "Our role is to help parents any way we can and get those pictures out, because we know pictures find kids," said Derby. "It's really tough watching the families endure this, so I'm hoping that by working on the cold cases, we can keep them alive in the media." When tips come in to Child Find Ontario, they are directed to the proper police authorities and sometimes forwarded to other governmental departments, such as foreign affairs.

Decades have passed since she was last seen, yet the bizarre disappearance of Nicole Louise Morin remains active to this day. There have been various re-enactments on television over the years, the most recent being *GTA's Most Wanted* in 2007.[3] The program marked Nicole's thirtieth birthday, and revisited the place where she was last seen: the building at 627 The West Mall. The video appears on a number of websites, including YouTube, and is linked to many other unsolved and missing persons sites on the Internet.

A tremendous tool for informing the public, the Internet has tragically also become a haven for sexual predators, a place where men and women pose as youngsters to build trust, luring kids into dangerous, sometimes deadly situations. The problem has grown so large that police will talk to school kids about the perils that come with making "friends" over the Internet, and the risks that come with divulging personal information, like where they go to school, and their interests. The old saying "Don't talk to strangers" has gained a whole new meaning in today's digital age of text messaging, cell phones, and meeting total strangers online who could be thousands of miles away, or as close as the next street. In the United States, even the Federal Bureau of Investigation has become involved, creating a parents' guide to Internet safety. In Canada, *Cybertip.ca* — the country's national tip line for reporting the online sexual exploitation of children — has experienced over 12 million hits since 2005. In Canada many youngsters think surfing the net is safe, yet court records are bulging with horror stories of middle-age men hooking up with young boys and girls through online chat rooms, establishing a "relationship," and meeting them in rundown motels and out of the way places for sex. Worldwide, few nightmares remain as unimaginable as those perpetrated by Marc Dutroux, a Belgian man convicted of horrific crimes against children.

One of the most despised men in modern-day Europe, Marc Dutroux, remains relatively unknown in North America. Dutroux was first convicted of committing a series of violent crimes back in 1979, while in his early twenties. Within a few years his sexual perversions grew and Dutroux was arrested in 1986 along with his then-wife for abducting and raping several girls. Although he was sentenced in 1989 to thirteen years behind bars, Dutroux, an electrician, was released on parole just three years later, despite warnings to prison officials from his mother and being described in a medical report as "a perverse psychopath, an explosive mix." Paroling Dutroux proved to be a disastrous mistake on the part of the Belgian Government; he went on to kidnap six girls between 1995 and 1996. Only two of the girls survived the "Belgian Beast's" concrete, soundproof torture chambers, housed in the half dozen homes he owned. That Dutroux's light sentence had allowed him to rape, torture, and murder children prompted a revolt among the outraged citizens of Belgium; 350,000 of them took to streets in October 1996 to protest a system that protected abusers and killers of innocent boys and girls. The case also created a greater awareness among the European populate that these monstrous crimes can, and do, take place.

Dutroux was not only part of a large-scale Internet pornography and prostitution ring, some believe he was the leader. One of the worst instances of child porn was uncovered in the Dutch town of Zandvoort in 1998, when investigators exposed a large-scale pedophile ring operating out of an apartment. Inside, police found thousands upon thousands of explicit images of children, along with client lists from across Europe and the United States. Since that time, authorities have uncovered pedophile rings in Britain, Australia, Austria, France, Finland, Italy, and other countries, seizing countless photos and videos of children as young as a few months old being drugged, raped, tortured, and killed. As inconceivable as it may seem, perverted customers will pay handsomely for "home movies" of their twisted sexual fantasies involving little boys and girls, often $5,000 U.S. or more for extremely "limited edition" videos limited to ten copies.[4]

In Europe, one group helping to expose the dangers of child pornography and children being bought and sold as sex slaves around the world is the *Fondation Princess de Croÿ et Massimo Lancellotti*, known to North American authorities as Foundation Princess of Croÿ. Based in Brussels, Belgium, the group was founded in 2003 by Jacqueline de Croÿ, with her cousin, Princess Maria Massimo Lancellotti, later joining her as a supporter. The foundation collects vast amounts of data, news releases, articles, and photos of missing and exploited children. The number of girls and boys they believe are the victims of pedophiles in Europe is staggering. In 1998 it was ninety thousand; by 2008 the figure mushroomed to an estimated two million. Like many organizations dedicated to missing children in North America, researchers for the foundation are unpaid, donating their time to try to make a difference in the lives of abused boys and girls.

Back in 2004, two of the foundation's researchers believed they uncovered photos of Nicole Morin, who disappeared almost twenty years earlier. Images of Nicole from a Canadian police website appeared similar to those of the Zandvoort children found on a Dutch website named Buro Zoeklicht. A group fighting for the rights of sexually abused children, Buro Zoeklicht offers support to parents, caregivers, and victims, and follows strict procedures when reporting their findings to police. They are also involved in tracing child predators, collecting information, and presenting their findings to the authorities. Their website features photos of dozens of missing children. Some are clear, while others are grainy images captured from video cameras. Photos are identified by number, not by name, and anyone recognizing a child is encouraged to submit a report over the Internet.

Groups like Buro Zoeklicht and the Foundation Princess of Croÿ — whose aim is to protect children from being victimized by Internet predators — must be vigilant when dealing with questions from strangers. "Internet contacts are complicated, and we never know who is behind the screen," said Jacqueline de Croÿ. "That guy could even be the murderer. It's not the safest job in the world, so we must be careful."

Technology has rapidly become a many-headed monster. On the one side, police, child safety agencies, and missing persons websites use the Internet to help track pedophiles and recover abducted children. On the other side, sexual predators pretending to be someone they're not visit online chat rooms and social networking sites to meet youngsters and gain their trust. Many abusers take images or videos of the kids they molest, and researchers examine those pictures and try to match faces of stolen children from around the world.

One technique used to match pictures of faces is biometrical analysis. Using sophisticated computer technology photos are analyzed. Common areas of the face are minutely calculated, compared, and tested thousands of times. Jacqueline de Croÿ believes that the comparison to Nicole on images they obtained are so close that they cannot be ignored. The technology analyses features of the face that do not change with age, such as the distance between the pupils or the nostrils, and identifications of less than 300.000 points are considered a match by the Foundation.

"The metrical difference between the pictures of Nicole and that of Zandvoort is of 285.429 points, much lower than 300.000, in such a way that it is undeniably the same child," said de Croÿ. The photos used in the Foundation's comparison, however, are not ideal. The full-face school portrait taken of Nicole in Canada is crystal clear and well-lit, while the image seized in Holland is a three-quarter view, grainy, slightly blurry, and dark. The Foundation does not believe Nicole was necessarily taken out of Canada to Europe, but that she was likely attacked by someone in her building. Canadian police have not commented on the photos.

In North America, another group keeping Nicole's name active in the media is the Doe Network. A volunteer association formed in

2001, the Doe Network assists law enforcement agencies in solving cold cases, unexplained disappearances, and identifying victims from North America, Australia, and Europe. Their mission is to "give the nameless back their names and return the missing to their families." Through the Internet, volunteers search for clues and possible matches between missing and unidentified persons, and approach the media for exposure on these cases. To date, the group has made forty-seven matches of missing and unidentified persons, and unidentified remains.

"We constantly have others that are awaiting DNA testing, or dental comparisons, so there are always more possibilities waiting," said media representative Angela Ellis. The group is comprised of over two hundred volunteers across North America, and works mainly with cases that are ten years or more old. The demand for a website featuring more recent cases prompted Ellis to start a sister site in 2005, the North American Missing Persons Network.

Like many Canadians, Ellis remembered hearing about Nicole when she was younger, along with the stories of other young girls murdered around the same time, like Sharin' Morningstar Keenan in 1983, Christine Jessop in 1984, and Alison Parrott in 1986.

"Those girls were really on my mind, and they were the main reason why I became interested in cold cases," said Ellis, who spends forty to fifty hours per week working on profiles and updating information. To help keep these stories alive, Ellis frequently contacts the media during May, which is Missing Children's Month, and on major anniversaries of a child's disappearance.

When a child goes missing our memories of them become frozen, recalling them as they were when they were young. In cases where children have been missing for many years, as with Nicole, police, parents, private investigators, and missing persons organizations often call upon the services of forensic artists. Drawings, clay facial reconstructions, and computer-enhanced images are valuable investigative tools that serve a number of purposes. Police use them to help apprehend criminals. They can be used to help identify the remains of the deceased. One of the most unique applications for forensic art is age enhancement, taking images of a child and "aging" them to what they would look like in the present day. The results are often nothing less than astonishing, considering the challenges facing the forensic artist.

As we grow older, our appearance can change considerably. Some people may "age" better than others, but there is no stopping the advance of time. Parts of the face, such as the nose, begin to droop. Ears start to sag, wrinkles deepen, and the hairline begins to recede to varying degrees. Age progression illustrations attempt to capture the aging process of a missing person and bring them up-to-date where no recent photographs exist. Several factors determine how we will appear over time, including genetics, physiology, chemistry, behaviour, and lifestyle. If a missing individual is known to abuse drugs, drink excessive amounts of alcohol, or smoke, they can appear very different from a person who has a healthy lifestyle. An otherwise attractive man, woman, or child can rapidly appear to be ill, thin, or years older than they really are because of substance abuse.

When it comes to trying to locate missing children, age progressions are an effective tool. In Nicole Morin's case, the little girl who went missing in 1985 at age eight would now be a grown woman. To mark Nicole's thirtieth birthday in 2007, forensic artist Diana Trepkov created an age-enhanced drawing of Nicole for the television program *GTA's Most Wanted*. The process, she said, is 75 percent science, and 25 percent art.

"I'm infatuated with faces," said Trepkov, who began drawing at age twelve. Over the years, she has worked on almost one hundred cases for families, private investigators, missing persons groups, and police departments in Canada and the United States. Many of her clients are referrals from others who ask her to create drawings of missing family members.

Before she puts pencil to paper, Trepkov researches the case through photos, takes notes, and, if possible, studies photos of the parents and other family members. The best images to use as a reference are clear photographs taken head-on, like school portraits. By looking at the shape of someone's skull, Trepkov can determine proportions, and how an individual's face is laid out. When she created her illustration of Nicole, Trepkov knew it would be a challenge. Like her other age-progression

(Diana P. Trepkov)

Forensic artist Diana P. Trepkov working on an age-progression drawing of Nicole Louise Morin. Here the artist, working in pencil, blends the hair.

drawings, she worked entirely in pencil, because of the medium's ability to capture the many fine details of the face. Trepkov may draw two different hairstyles in a portrait, parted in the middle, since it is impossible to determine how a missing person's hair will look in the future.

The detailed, age-enhanced drawing of Nicole at age thirty took Trepkov somewhere between eighteen and twenty hours to complete. Whenever she does a drawing of a missing child she remains optimistic, believing the little girl or boy is still alive out there, somewhere in the world.

When a child is abducted, the family left behind is never the same. As months turn into years, every missed holiday, every birthday, every

Mother's Day and Father's Day serves as a painful reminder of a life left incomplete. Over time, searches are scaled back, as police move onto newer cases. In March 1986, nine months after she literally vanished, a special task force set-up to investigate Nicole's case was disbanded. Up to that time, the probe into Nicole's disappearance was the most extensive in Toronto Police history. An estimated 25,000 man hours were spent tracking down leads. In less than a year five thousand people were questioned, including several hundred sex offenders, and police followed up on countless leads from phone calls, anonymous letters, even the occasional psychic. None turned out to offer any solid information leading to Nicole's whereabouts.

With police efforts to find Nicole slowing down, volunteers sold carnations in downtown Toronto in the hopes of raising $15,000 for the Nicole Morin Trust Fund. The money was earmarked for covering printing costs of new colour posters with Nicole's photo and information, and paying for private investigators specializing in missing kids. Generally, police are not in favour of private investigators working on certain cases, and went on the record stating they did not support Nicole's father, Art's, efforts to raise money to pay for a P.I.

In late 1986, the Etobicoke building where Nicole was last seen was canvassed again by police, who handed out flyers hoping to trigger residents' memories of the little girl. Soon after, Art placed ads in the personal sections of Toronto's three major daily newspapers, asking anyone with information to mail it to a special box number. At one point, he quit his job, set-up a small office, and dedicated himself to searching for his missing daughter, sending out fifty thousand posters to police agencies across North America, along with posters of Nicole to dozens of Canadian embassies worldwide. Attempts by Nicole's parents to salvage their marriage failed, and they finally separated in 1987. Finding his daughter became an obsession. "You want to find answers but there are no answers,"[5] said Art, who also travelled throughout Canada and the United States to search for his missing child. His belief at the time was that his little girl could have been taken out of the country, and that it was necessary to search for her, no matter where she might be.

Three years after her bizarre disappearance, Nicole's room remained the same. Her pink and white canopied bed was in the same place, along with her Porky Pig lamp, white dresser, and embroidered prayer. Art Morin was selling his condominium and Nicole's parents were not on speaking terms. Jeannette had been living in the condo with Nicole, while Art paid maintenance fees, taxes, and $50 a week in support. He was a driver for a dry cleaner at the time of his daughter's disappearance, and moved back into the condo with his wife for a period after Nicole disappeared. The two were unable to reconcile.

In the years since Nicole vanished, her unexplained disappearance has been the subject of countless theories. Some believe she is alive and well, but doesn't actually realize who she is, having forgotten her real identity decades ago.

Older missing persons cases like Nicole's tend to attract a great deal of attention, and over time facts can become so blurred that they obscure the truth. A number of women have contacted police and other agencies claiming not only to know where to find the missing girl, but that they in fact *are* Nicole. Others are desperate attention seekers who, for reasons known only to themselves, waste valuable time and resources. It is also not uncommon for police to receive calls from adults who have long-standing grudges against their parents, claiming their mother or father abducted or killed someone. More often than not, the ridiculous stories these people concoct are transferred from one unsolved cold case to another, and once police investigate the stories fall to pieces.

In the years since her disappearance, Nicole Morin has been the subject of countless theories. Some believe she was abducted and fell victim to a pedophile, while others suspect she is alive somewhere in the world, no longer remembering her true identity. Another theory surrounding Nicole's disappearance is that she was abducted by members of her father's fundamentalist church group. Aware of problems in the marriage, there has been much speculation over the years about a pencilled note Nicole wrote a few months before she vanished, which simply said, "I'm going to disappear." Police believed the note was fantasy, but others considered someone from the church, aware of the impending divorce, took it upon themselves to kidnap Nicole.

(Diana P. Trepkov)

Age-progressed drawing of Nicole Louise Morin, who went missing at age eight in 1985. The illustration depicts Morin as she would appear considerably older, at age thirty.

Since her disappearance, police have had a number of leads that appeared promising. In September 1988, Toronto Police investigated a forty-one-year-old American drifter named Lovie Riddle. Claiming to be "The Interstate Man," Riddle bragged about killing thirty people, and said he kidnapped Nicole and passed her along to someone else. Riddle's assertions sounded convincing enough for police travelled to the United States to investigate, but they found no credibility to his claims. Years later, Toronto Police also investigated Francis Carl Roy, a man who raped and killed eleven-year-old Alison Parrott.[6] Again, nothing concrete came out of the investigation.

Along with missing persons organizations and police, Nicole's father, Art, has been extremely involved in trying to find his only daughter over the decades. Her image is photo-enhanced occasionally, and in 2001 an updated picture of Nicole showing her as a woman in her mid-twenties was sent via the Internet to over one thousand Crime Stoppers programs in seventeen countries worldwide. The likeness was created by a forensic artist at the Virginia-based National Centre for Missing and Exploited Children. In the past, her image and description would have to be stuffed into envelopes and sent to police agencies and the media through the post office, a long, tedious, and expensive process. With the emergence of the Internet, Nicole became the first missing person in Ontario in Crime Stoppers' history to have her face publicized worldwide.

Of all Toronto missing persons cases, the uncanny disappearance of Nicole Louise Morin has received the most attention. A year after she went missing, the reported cost for the investigation was $1.8 million. She continues to receive media attention around the anniversary of her disappearance, and Nicole's photo and detailed description are displaced on a number of websites in Canada and the United States, including the Doe Network, the Texas Department of Public Safety, and the Royal Canadian Mounted Police. Notably, her potential abductor has been the subject of a profile by renowned FBI agent John Douglas.

At the time she disappeared, Toronto Police spoke to many residents in the area and investigated known pedophiles living nearby. Although police have done follow-up interviews over the years, it becomes impractical to talk to someone about where they were and what they were doing on a specific date. People often have a hard enough time remembering what they did the week before, and Nicole has been missing for over twenty-five years.

"This one case has people saying, 'Look at so and so,' because there really are so few clues in it," said Toronto Police Detective Robert Wilkinson. "She really just vanished off the face of the earth. She went in the elevator and poof, she was gone. There's no physical evidence to say, 'We can connect you to a crime scene.' It could have been somebody dropping somebody off, somebody passing through, or somebody visiting from out of state."

Police have pursued a number of unusual leads over the years. At one point they travelled to Quebec to interview Art Morin's brother-in-law, who was convicted of murdering Morin's sister, Gertrude, in 1961. The man was originally sentenced to the death penalty, but the sentence was commuted, though he has since died. He was not in Toronto at the time Nicole vanished. The man held a grudge against the Morin family. About two years after Nicole disappeared a thirty-year-old woman was strangled to death in the same West Mall apartment complex. Police investigated but were unable to find a link between the missing girl and the murdered woman.

Recently, police followed-up with a young woman who appeared to look like Nicole would today, based on age-enhanced photos. The woman was adopted as a little girl, and remembers very little about her childhood. "It is very difficult to investigate somebody, and try and recall, 'Who were your parents?' said Wilkinson. "We're looking into the possibility that Nicole isn't dead — she may very well be alive in some strange circumstance, so we've not discounted that possibility."

Today, Art is in his early seventies. His only daughter would be a woman of thirty-three, likely married with kids of her own. In the event Nicole is found one day, her DNA is on file with the Toronto Police and a positive match can be made. Police have not ruled out the possibility that the pretty little girl who went missing and left no trace is out there somewhere, alive. In the meantime, we wait for news that she has been found, and her father holds onto the few physical reminders he has of his missing girl, a box of her schoolwork assignments and old Father's Day cards.

Chapter 10

Frank Roberts (1999)

ALL GREAT INVENTIONS BEGIN with an idea. The idea might come from the mind of an ordinary person, an industrial engineer, or a brilliant recluse silently toiling away at a laboratory. Some inventions are entirely original, while others are created in an attempt to improve products that already exist. In time, the stories behind the origin of countless gadgets, gizmos, thingamajigs, and whatchamacallits become the stuff of legend. Like everyone else in the world, inventors eventually die, but their inventions — and the tales behind them — live on.

The stories surrounding how all great inventions came into being are often a carefully blended cocktail of fact, fiction, technology, and mythology. Even everyday items have a story behind them, and many products have become so embedded into our everyday lives that we refer to them solely by their brand name. "Please pass me a Kleenex," or "Hand me that roll of Scotch Tape" are phrases heard every day around the world. Generic products may have flooded the market, but we rarely find ourselves asking for a facial tissue or cellophane tape.

Many inventions are the result of years, even decades, of hard work and innovation. Some are put on the market quickly, while others sit and wait until someone else comes along, and finds a new use for an unused product. Post-it Notes were born from an idea during a church sermon. A chemist at 3M came up with a low-tack adhesive that was strong enough to attach to paper and other flat surfaces, but come off and reattach without damaging the surface. Higher-ups at the company weren't impressed, and it wasn't until years later that another employee at the company realized that the adhesive could be used to hold bookmarks in place in church hymn books. Today, these distinctive yellow squares of sticky paper are found in virtually every office on the planet.

"Genius is one percent inspiration and 99 percent perspiration," is a quote from legendary American inventor, Thomas Alva Edison. Another quote attributed to Edison, not quite as well-known, is: "Anything that won't sell, I don't want to invent. Its sale is proof of utility, and utility is success." A genius who took out over one thousand patents during his lengthy career, Edison was the rarest of breeds, an inventor who realized the importance of marrying new products with commercial success.

Many inventions credited to "The Wizard of Menlo Park" — named after the place in New Jersey where he established his lab — were not entirely the result of his own mind. Generations of school children have been taught Edison invented the incandescent light bulb, omitting the fact that British chemist and inventor Sir Joseph Wilson Swan actually came up with the first modern light bulb in 1878, while Edison, who also came up with the idea independently, registered his patent in 1879. Folks were litigious even back then, and Edison tried to Sue Swan for patent infringement, but the matter resolved itself amicably when the two men merged their production forces in 1883, as the Edison and Swan United Electric Light Company. Even back in Edison's day, the stories behind many inventions were muddied.

One hundred years after Edison invented the light bulb — at least, *his* version of the light bulb — another invention was being formed over 300 miles north of New Jersey in Toronto, Ontario. Like many products, especially ones claiming to benefit health, this one was born of necessity.

The story of how the Obus Forme came into existence is no less mesmerizing or full of contradictions than the stories surrounding the man laying claim to its invention. Equal parts an outspoken salesman and an individual who carefully guarded his private life, Frank Roberts was fast approaching age fifty back in the late seventies. He had spent much of his working life in various sales roles, as an importer of Danish furniture and housewares, and, briefly, operator of his own gift shop in a strip plaza. None of his ventures were especially remarkable and it's unlikely that Roberts would be remembered as a business legend, were it not for two things: a tennis accident that led to a revolutionary new invention, and being gunned down gangland style outside the company he created in the early morning of Thursday August 13, 1998.

According to company literature and countless interviews with newspapers and magazines over the years, the OBUS Forme — short for Orthopedic Brace Upright Support — came into existence following a back injury Roberts sustained while playing tennis with his daughter, Joy, in 1979. The accident left him in a body cast for a month. Fearing the likelihood of surgery if he reinjured himself, Roberts created his own back support. He kept the body cast, cut it in half, and added foam padding for comfort. Soon, he had a flash of insight: why not make and sell these back supports to the general public? Working in his garage, Roberts created a fiberglass prototype and, as the story goes, consulted a rheumatologist, orthopedic surgeons, and chiropractors before settling on the final design. Allegedly, Roberts had been working on a support for several years *before* injuring his back, but this piece of information, like others surrounding the Obus Forme, are contradictory.

No matter what the truth is behind the evolution of the Obus Forme, the marketing behind it was nothing sort of brilliant. When Roberts's back support went on the market in 1980, it generated volumes of free business for its creator, largely through word of mouth. Not all of Frank Roberts's early business ventures were resounding successes, but no one could ever deny that he was a natural salesman.

The son of second generation Jewish-Americans, Frank Rabinovitch was born in Boston on April 23, 1931. By the tender age of thirteen, entrepreneurial Frank was importing cheesecake from New

York and selling it in his neighborhood. It was a charming, benign anecdote about a man who would in time become loved and loathed, respected and reviled in equal parts. Following his murder, the public soon discovered the multi-faceted life of the Obus Forme inventor as police searched for clues. Who would want Frank Roberts dead? That is the question Toronto Police have been trying to solve for the past dozen years. As with any murder investigation, police dug into the background of the victim, looking for known associates who may have wanted him killed. Officers soon discovered that trying to piece together his professional and personal life was akin to repairing a shattered crystal vase. You can find some of the fragments and put them back together, but many of the tiny, glittering shards remain elusive, and will never be recovered.

"There is that one case that just bugs the crap out of you, that you want to solve. There's not a day that doesn't go by that you don't think about it," said Ray Zarb. Every homicide detective will have an unsolved case in his or her career that frustrates them for years after the crime took place. Some officers retire with that one case still open, still unsolved, and ruminate about it years later. For Zarb, the murder of Frank Roberts is one of those cases. A Detective Sergeant with the Metro Toronto Police Homicide Unit, Zarb has been the officer in charge since Roberts was shot and killed in the parking lot outside his factory in broad daylight on that beautiful, sunny August morning in 1998. In the years since the murder, Zarb has learned more, and knows more, about the late Mr. Roberts than most of the victim's friends or family ever will.

When Zarb calls the investigation "multi-directional," it is a monumental understatement. Whether working for others or for himself over the decades, Roberts was a lifelong businessman and few, if any, successful entrepreneurs avoid picking up an enemy or two along the way. Married three times, Roberts was divorced at the time of his death, and dating a much younger and much-married woman in Florida. There were also the lawsuits for copyright infringement that Roberts threatened over the years to protect his bestselling product, the Obus Forme.

"This case has been led by the police's push to unfold and find the directions, and of course, Frank had a lot of directions," said Zarb.

"You've got family, business associates, anybody who may not have liked his business practices. Every business has its competition and its rivals, and Mister Roberts had them, in other businesses in the medical back support business."

Trying to make sense of the enigma that was Frank Roberts is like trying to understand other rags to riches stories. There is something innate that comes from people who have suffered and grew up to make something of themselves. It is hard for the so-called "younger generation" to follow, but anyone who lived during times of extreme hardship — the Great Depression or the Second World War — know what it's like, especially those children born of Jewish, Ukrainian, Polish, Italian, or other heritages with last names that differ from the norm. These circumstances create a hunger that never dies, and a determination to constantly do better than the long-deceased relatives preceding them. For Roberts, the creation of the Obus Forme was the pinnacle of his many years of hard work.

In order to try to understand who Frank Roberts was, it is essential to know where he came from. Like much of his history, the inventor's background is filled with numerous discrepancies. His biography in the *Canadian Who's Who* states Roberts went overseas to fight in the Korean War after graduating from high school, and was a Prisoner of War. Other sources say he was in the Coast Guard. There is contradictory information regarding Roberts's education. His official biography claims he studied Industrial Design at Yale, the prestigious Ivy League university in New Haven, Connecticut. There are, however, no records of Roberts graduating from the three-century-old institution. Older editions of the *Who's Who* also state he attended the University of Connecticut. Like Yale, there are no documents indicating he was a student there. He was also listed as a member of the Ontario Association of Certified Engineers. Although there are several organizations with similar-sounding names, the one listed by Roberts does not exist.

Certain details of Roberts's personal life can be verified. Back in May 1954, Roberts married nineteen-year-old Annette Goldman, who was to become the first of his three wives, and the mother of his three children, David, Joy, and Brian. At the time, Frank was practically a kid himself, just twenty-three, and managing a restaurant in Newton, Massachusetts. In 1959, he moved his young family to Toronto to join his older brother, Walter, who had married a Canadian. Soon, the Roberts family celebrated the arrival of their son, Brian.

Roberts was working at his new career, building upscale new homes in the growing suburbs of Toronto. Leaving the actual construction to professional contractors, Roberts stuck to selling the homes under his company name, Diamondhead Ltd. By 1967 Diamondhead was no more, and the restless Roberts soon moved on to other business ventures. He became a salesman for Danesco Inc., a Montreal-based importer of Danish furniture and housewares. The job, which required a great deal of travel, eventually took a toll on his marriage and he and Annette divorced. The split was far from amicable, ostensibly leading Roberts to write an exposé entitled *I've Got The Children*. Like many areas of Roberts's life, it is not known if his book was ever published, or if it even exists.

By 1976, Roberts's import brokerage business led to the opening of his own gift shop in the west end of Toronto. Within a year his store, Widdicombe Gifts and Linens Inc., was out of business. In his mid-forties, divorced, and needing a way to make money, Frank Roberts would soon come up with a product that revolutionized back care. Following his 1979 tennis injury and the creation of the back support, Roberts needed a name for his product. He came up with Obus Forme, from the French word for shell. The name, easy to remember and slightly exotic sounding, worked.

A natural-born salesman, Roberts capitalized on the best and least expensive form of advertising there is: word of mouth. Rags to riches stories always make good copy, and newspaper and magazine reporters — many of them suffering from back pain as a result of sitting in front of their typewriters for hours on end — were especially receptive to Roberts's stories about the development of his revolutionary new back support. Writers at the *Toronto Star*, the *Globe and Mail*, and a host at radio station CFRB all tried his back rest, loved the comfort it provided, and praised the Obus Forme in print and on the air.

"Metro inventor is the toast of those with aching backs" was one of the earliest of a number of stories touting Roberts and his new in-

A natural born salesman at work: one of the earliest-known photos of Obus Forme inventor Frank Roberts, published in the Toronto Star on June 26, 1980. Described as the "toast of those with aching backs," Roberts is demonstrating his new back support to seventy-five-year-old Ivy Budarick. Less than twenty years later, Roberts would be found shot to death in the parking lot of the company he created.

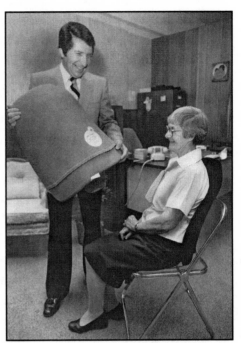

(Jeff Goode/GetStock)

vention. Penned by *Toronto Star* columnist Lotta Dempsey for her Inside Story section, the piece is definitely more advertorial than editorial in its content. Featuring a large photo of a smiling Roberts demonstrating his new backrest to seventy-five-year-old Ivy Budarick, the Obus Forme "is winning raves from suffers of arthritis, low back pain and rheumatism," read the caption. The article refers to Roberts as a one-time china and gift sales agency owner, and mentions local Toronto notables raving about his newfangled back support, including figures like CFRB Radio personality Wally Crouter, "Who not only talks about Frank Roberts' Obus Forme on the air every month or so (gratis), but has spread the news to hundreds of grateful users."[1]

To further promote his new product, Roberts loaned Dempsey her very own Obus Forme. She was so convinced of the benefits that she bought one of the back supports, describing in exacting detail the materials used in its construction — polycarbonate foam, non-allergenic zip-off covers — and the cost, a "one-time capital expenditure" of $59.96. The medical aspects of the product, however, are discussed in general, even cryptic, terms, stating that the well-known Toronto orthopedic surgeon who designed the prototype wished to remain anonymous. Highly unusual, since many doctors who invent new technologies are glad to not only take credit for their work, but even have the device named after them. The location of Roberts's sole showroom in a downtown medical building made it sound as though he had his own lab in the Mayo Clinic. "His tenancy in the prestigious Medical Arts Building in itself is an endorsement, since scrutiny is meticulous."

Other glowing pieces about Roberts's invention soon followed in the *Globe and Mail*, which carried numerous ads for his products throughout the 1980s. In 1982 the *Globe*'s society columnist, Zena Cherry, wrote a laudatory piece about the many converts to the Obus Forme. A wealth of well-known locals were using the Obus Forme, she wrote, including then-mayor of Toronto, Art Eggleton, Lieutenant-Governor John Black Aird, six-foot-five, 260-pound wrestler Lord Athol Layton, and, of course, Cherry herself. Later that year, consumer advocate Ellen Roseman wrote a more objective article about the Obus Forme, and other back pain relieving devices made by competitors that had sprung up since Roberts put his support on the market. Some seemed absurdly impractical, like a carry-along, brown plastic foot stool, meant to elevate one foot while standing in place to maintain a proper pelvic tilt, much like brass foot rails found in old-fashioned taverns. Others were back support devices resembling the Obus Forme, which was much too close for Roberts's comfort.

"Mr. Roberts's former bookkeeper recently started making Ortho Rest, a product so similar to Obus Forme that he's being sued for design infringement,"[2] stated the article, which also mentioned a product called SitRite, "A metal frame with coil springs wrapped in plastic," selling for $45. The product sounded similar to the Obus Forme, and Roberts had good reason to be upset. It was estimated he sold twenty thousand Obus Formes in 1981 alone, and threatened suing competitors with copyright infringement numerous times over the years.

One businessman who remembers Roberts is David Johnson. A former medical products salesman, Johnson is now the president of Innotech Rehabilitation Products Inc. He met Roberts for the first time in the late 1980s, at a party. In time, he presented a friend's unique cold pack technology to Roberts, who was going to market it as Soft Ice, used to treat muscle inflammation. He hadn't heard anything negative about Roberts, other than perhaps that he was an aggressive businessman, "And very litigious about things, as I was soon to find out," said Johnson.

"We were marketing this cold pack product in the United States and we were marketing in Canada, and along comes this cease and desist order from lawyers saying this is a Frank Roberts product. I mean, it was quite ridiculous," said Johnson. "He couldn't tell you how to build the thing. Somehow — and this wasn't the only time this happened in my life — he got his name on the patent for the cold pack in the U.S. We knew it was fraudulently obtained, and we responded to the cease and desist order as, 'No, we won't be ceasing and desisting, and we reserve the right to sue you at a later date.' And that was the end of that issue. He was attempting to shut us down, but he never sued us. I guess when you finally get into the light of day in a court of law, and the judge looks at him and says, 'Well, how do you build this product, since you invented it?' and if he couldn't answer those questions, what's he going to tell you?"

Johnson's company sells a line of back support products under the EmbraceAIR name, along with other items such as pillows and treatment cream used to relieve and prevent muscle spasms and joint pain. He questions stories about how the Obus Forme came into being and the overall effectiveness of the product. Back in the seventies, it wasn't uncommon for anyone suffering a back injury to have spinal surgery, and require a body cast. Johnson said the prototype Roberts made from his original cast would have worked for Frank Roberts, but no one else, since it was molded to the specific contours of his body. Also, there was nothing to support the five lumbar vertebrae in the lower back. This prompted Roberts to add a small removable pad that attaches to the front of the backrest with strips of Velcro. Too much curving of part of the lower back is called lordosis, and Johnson said the Obus Forme's adjustable cushion isn't all that effective compared to his products, which "actually allow you to inflate that area, so you can accommodate the correct curve of your spine." The EmbraceAIR products, said Johnson, are of a more professional level, scientifically proven to work, and recommended by chiropractors.

"I remember Frank saying to me that his mission in life was to have his product sold everywhere, exactly like Campbell's Soup, or Coca-Cola, and that's exactly what he wanted to do," said Johnson. Over the years, Roberts's techniques for marketing the Obus Forme were nothing short of brilliant. In addition to paid advertising, there were many celebrity endorsements, most of them free of charge. There are photos of Roberts giving comedy legends Mel Brooks and Carl Reiner custom monogrammed backrests, and another of Roberts's son, Brian, standing next to martial artist and actor Jackie Chan. On the *Arsenio Hall Show*, *MacGyver* actor Richard Dean Anderson brought one of the famous back supports and used it during his segment. Roberts was so appreciative that he sent Anderson a monogrammed Obus Forme for the free publicity.

There were, of course, the paid advertisements for the Obus Forme, placed in magazines and newspapers, especially in the pages of the *Globe and Mail*. Throughout the mid-1980s, a company called the Back Store heavily promoted Obus Forme in the sports pages of the *Globe*. Roberts and Toronto Blue Jays broadcaster Jerry Howarth were close friends; the two men shared a mutual passion for baseball. The Back Store ads used Howarth's photo and touted him as "Toronto Blue Jays announcer and the voice of OBUS Forme." Some of the ads were combined with a cut-out coupon that readers could send in for the chance to win an Obus Forme and tickets to see the Toronto Blue Jays. The company also ran a rare politically inspired advertisement on the front page of the *Globe's* Report on Business section on Monday October 26, 1992. It was the day Canadians voted on the Charlottetown Accord, and the tongue-in-cheek ad used the names of key political figures: "Mulroney. Parizeau. Manning. We'll support everyone."

Throughout the eighties and early nineties, much of Roberts's personal life remained private. When his first marriage ended, Roberts wed Beverly Ordon Moldaver, a divorcee fourteen years his junior. After seven years of marriage, the couple separated in 1987, and divorced in 1991. By then, Roberts was already living with French-born Dominique Leval, who would become his third wife until they too separated, on Valentine's Day 1995. It would be the year the *Globe and Mail* published another glowing piece on Obus Forme and Frank Roberts. The article was one of the last published during his life, and would remain unremarkable, except for the eerily prophetic final line: "In fact, Mr. Roberts says the design of his Back Rest makes it look at home anywhere — even in a Mercedes."[3]

Thursday August 13, 1998, was a beautiful, warm sunny day in Toronto, and life was good — or so it seemed — for Obus Forme founder Frank Roberts. One year and a day earlier the lifelong baseball fan realized a dream when he threw the opening pitch at the Toronto Blue Jays home game. Although Roberts was sixty-seven years old and his third marriage was over, he was dating a woman less than half his age who lived in Florida. At thirty-one, Etty Sorrentino's age wasn't so much of a problem as the fact that she was a mother of a young child, and she was still married.

Like most successful, self-made men, Roberts was a workaholic, often staying late after the rest of the Obus employees had left for the day, working weekends, or arriving early, long before the rest of the staff showed up. The Thursday morning of his murder was no different. A creature of habit, Roberts pulled his Black Mercedes SL 500 convertible coupe into his reserved parking space around 7:30 a.m. The low-rise Obus Forme factory, at 550 Hopewell Avenue in the west end of Toronto, was located in an area comprised of houses and commercial buildings. Many of the neighbours knew Roberts, if not by name, then certainly by sight. On his way to work that morning, Roberts stopped to buy a bag of bagels for his employees. Turning off the ignition, he got out of his Mercedes, and went to the trunk to fetch the bag. Moments later shots rang out, and Roberts, struck in the head and chest, crumpled to the asphalt. A woman living across the street from the factory ran over when she heard the shots to see Roberts on the parking lot, his face and shoulder covered in blood. Although an ambulance raced him from the scene of the shooting to Sunnybrook Hospital, it was too late. Frank Roberts, businessman and larger than life inventor of multi-million selling Obus Forme, was dead before he reached the hospital's emergency department.

(Toronto Police Service)

Scene of a murder: moments after he arrived at the Obus Forme factory in his black Mercedes SL 500 convertible coupe (centre) on the morning of August 13, 1998, Frank Roberts was shot to death; one bullet in his head, and a second in his chest.

That morning, Toronto Police Detective Sergeant Ray Zarb was advised by his staff sergeant that he was on call for the next homicide in the city. He had never heard of Frank Roberts before that time, and immediately raced to the scene of the shooting. A two-block radius was quickly cordoned off, and police began a large-scale canvass of houses and businesses in the area — like the nearby auto repair shop — in an attempt to find potential witnesses to the murder. Zarb directed the uniformed officers as they went from house to house, and business to business, looking for witnesses to the shooting. "I would say if you look at all the family, all of the employees that worked at Obus, then the surrounding neighbourhood, than the factories in the area that may have had some information, you're looking at a few hundred people," said Zarb. "People heard shots, but nobody saw the assailant run or drive away."

Along with other detectives, Zarb soon began the process of piecing together the life of the late Frank Roberts. According to published reports, Roberts had a brief conversation with a man just moments before he was shot twice. The gunman was described as white, medium

Protecting the crime scene: soon after the shooting occurred police arrived, closed off the area, and immediately began interviewing neighbours and people working in the area.

build, about five feet eight inches tall, with dark hair, wearing a long-sleeved, dark shirt. The weapon used to kill Roberts was a handgun. Police can't discuss specifics about the weapon or its calibre, other than to say the bullets recovered from Roberts's body were not a match to those from any other crimes.

All areas that could potentially hold clues were searched by police. More than a dozen officers scoured vacant lots and land around nearby railway tracks. Vehicles were dusted for fingerprints, and police sawed a chunk of bloodstained asphalt about the size of a large cardboard pizza box from the parking lot and sent it out for testing in the hopes of yielding further information. When they arrived for work that cloudless morning, Obus employees, many of them immigrants, were greeted by the sight of yellow and black police tape, and dozens of officers. As soon as they were told that Roberts was dead, many of them broke into tears. Obus employed an estimated 150 people, and many credited Roberts as giving them their start in Canada and in business. In time, police interviewed hundreds of people, including Obus employees, neighbours, people working in the area, delivery men, anyone who had a reason to be in the area.

Others rushed to the scene as soon as they heard news of the shooting. One of them was Dominique Leval, Roberts's third and most recent ex-wife. After hearing about the murder from a friend she sped to the Obus factory, where she saw police collecting evidence. Sobbing, Leval said the murder was beyond her comprehension. "Everybody loved him so much because he was such a good man," she told the *Toronto Star* in her thick Parisian accent. "When people are successful, they sometimes have enemies or someone is jealous (of them). I just don't know why they would do this."[4]

Relatives, friends, and the many Obus Forme employees who said Roberts treated them like family were left to deal with the shock of his death. For police, the lengthy investigation into his murder was just beginning. "This case has been led by the police push to unfold and find the directions, and of course, Frank had a lot of directions," said Zarb. "You've got family, business associates, anybody who may not have liked his business practices. Every business has its competition and its rivals. The victimology can take you everywhere. You try to peel the onion of that person, and find out what really happened, and is there evidence? We're lucky when there is forensic evidence that can tie you back to a potential suspect — DNA, fingerprints, hair and fibre — all those nitty-gritty things in this case did not exist." During the course of their investigation, police were faced with the challenge of wading through much of Roberts's early life and business activities in retailing, importing, and real estate development. They did not rule out a disgruntled former employee or acquaintance being behind the murder.

Front page stories appeared in all the major Toronto papers, all asking the same question: who wanted Frank Roberts dead? Over four hundred people attended the funeral service for the father of three and grandfather of thirteen on August 16, 1998. In the weeks following his murder, the details of Roberts's personal life — which he kept carefully guarded for years — were about to become public, such as his relationship with the married Etty Sorrentino. The two had been dating for about three years, and Roberts was supposed to go to Miami the day after he was killed. During the time they dated, he allegedly bought her expensive gifts, including jewellery, clothes, and a black Mercedes, and hired a lawyer to handle her divorce. Detective Zarb flew to Florida to talk to Sorrentino and her husband. It turned out that the Sorrentinos were in Italy on a holiday at the time of the murder, and that Etty had actually been away for most of the summer and not seen Frank in quite some time.

Once the press heard about the older man–younger woman angle, they tried to get any information they could as quickly as possible. A reporter and photographer from the *Toronto Sun* flew to Florida to speak with Sorrentino, and she proceeded to slam the door in their faces — but not before they snapped a photo of the young woman holding a cordless phone — and a handgun. Sorrentino lived on the ninth floor of Mystique Point Drive, a luxury condominium complex in an exclusive Miami suburb. Roberts, who vacationed regularly in Florida over the years, bought a condo on the twenty-fourth floor of the same building back in 1992. Just a few years later, by 1995, Roberts was apparently planning on retiring in Florida, and was spending considerable time, sometimes months at a stretch, in the Sunshine State.

Sources at the time said Roberts's generous nature — buying pricey gifts for Etty — also extended to paying her credit card bills, which were reported as being in the range of $20,000 a month. There were many other expenses in Roberts's life. Sorrentino was pressuring him to renovate an expensive American property he bought in 1997. In January 1998, he took out an $830,000 mortgage on his home in Willowdale, Ontario, at a high rate of interest: prime plus 5 percent. The reasons why he needed such a large sum of money were unclear. In July 1998, Roberts sold the Florida condo he'd had since 1991. It was near the Turnberry Isle Resort and Club, a world-class club where Roberts was a member — but he didn't renew his membership for 1998. Strangest of all was his recent purchase of a $5 million life insurance policy, making one wonder if Frank Roberts had a premonition about his own death.

At the time of Roberts's murder, it appeared Obus Forme was doing well. Over two million of his famous back supports had been sold in Canada, the United States, and twenty-six other countries. The company was recently listed in the *Financial Post* as being one of the best-managed companies in Canada (1995–96), and Roberts had been selected as one of the Top 100 Entrepreneurs by the *Ontario Business Journal.* Annual sales of the Obus Forme were said to be in the $20 Million range. Like any business, Obus had its detractors. There were the ongoing legal battles over copyright infringement and the fourteen-year patent for Roberts's famous back support was coming to an end. Before he died, Roberts was debating if Obus should go public.

In the weeks following the entrepreneur's murder, newspapers and magazines published a rash of articles about the need for businessmen and women to bolster their personal safety in the cutthroat world of business. The murder of a well-known Canadian executive was the prefect news hook onto which companies in the security business could hang their story. For several months terms like "criminal stalking" and "soft targets" were used to describe executives like the late Frank Roberts. These men and women were seen as vulnerable, largely because of their work ethic. Many of them were creatures of habit. By arriving at work at the same time every day, and in the same vehicle, they made themselves easy targets. "Like sexual assault, stalking and harassment are very personal, perhaps embarrassing and taboo subjects. More often than not, until their lives are directly threatened, victims naively choose to resolve the situation alone,"[5] wrote *Canadian Business* shortly following Roberts's murder. One company, Mississauga-based security company Genesis Security Consultants, issued a gruesome press release about Canadian businessmen, stating, "It's a wonder more executives are not lying in pool's [*sic*] of blood."

A year after his death, police were still following leads in what remains one of the city's most complex murder investigations. A few days after the shooting, Toronto Police received a call from a person who provided "vital information" about the case. Police couldn't reveal exactly what was said, and made numerous pleas through the media for the individual to call them again. To this day, they are still waiting. A Crime Stoppers re-enactment was shown on TV, but generated no concrete leads that could help solve the murder. Described by police as "one of the purest whodunit cases you'll ever see," detectives were led in countless directions during their investigation. Did someone from Roberts's past want him dead? Was his killer someone holding a more recent grudge? Within a year, police interviewed more than 1,500 people, amassing an enormous database of transcripts, and over thirty file boxes full of information.

Frank Roberts was gone, but the company he founded was far from finished. About a year after his murder, his son Brian broke the silence and was interviewed about his vision for the future of Obus Forme. It was time to move on, said the younger Roberts, who had been in his father's office perhaps five times since the murder. Brian was a fifty-fifty partner along with his father, but he didn't always share the same point of view when it came to running the business. After the murder, Brian bought Frank's shares from his estate. "Frank had often stood in the way of Brian's aggressive plans for Obus Forme, people close to the company say. When he was no longer there to put his foot down, things began to change dramatically."[6]

A number of changes were indeed in the works. Since the company was established in 1980, new products had been introduced here and there, such as an $89 portable travel version of the popular Obus Forme called the Everywhere. Under Brian's leadership, the push to introduce and distribute new products — including an alarm clock that made nature sounds, massaging foot baths, backpacks, sound therapy machines, and a backrest with heating and massage options — became much more aggressive. All along, father and son had different ideas when it came to marketing. Frank's plans were modest, selling the Obus Forme in kiosks in malls across Canada; Brian's vision was larger, and included distribution to large retailers like Shoppers Drug Mart and Canadian Tire. There were plans to market many new products, nine in total, by the end of 1999. For the first time in the company's history some of them would be sourced offshore, in countries like China, Thailand, Vietnam, and South Korea, where turnaround times were fast, and labour costs considerably less than in Canada.

Brian, who left university to work with his father when Obus Forme began in 1980, was eager to change the corporate mentality that had existed at the company. The suit and tie dress code was considerably relaxed, and employees were given more freedom to be part of the decision-making process. The company's long-time tagline was also updated from "the backcare experts" to "the bodycare experts," in an attempt to appeal to a younger marketplace focusing on lifestyle and health. At age thirty-eight, the younger Roberts epitomized the youthful, health-conscious target market, with personal physical pursuits ranging from karate to boxing and running marathons. "He possesses so much energy that he sleeps just two hours a night," stated one article, which said his work ethic also included showing up at the office early, often before 5:00 a.m.

Drastic expansion, cheaper offshore production, a new line of products, and an updated image could not save the company from its financial woes. By 2005, the business was running into monetary troubles following their expansion into the American market; Integral Orthopedics, Inc. acquired Obus Forme in April of that year. In 2008, ten years after the founder Frank Roberts was shot and killed in the parking lot of the company he built, Obus Forme was forced into receivership, crippled by an accumulated debt of nearly $11 million. A court-appointed receiver put the business up for sale, and an Ontario judge approved a bid from HoMedics, Inc., an American-based company that manufactures and markets health, wellness, and relaxation products.

Although the company founded by Frank Roberts is no longer in Canadian hands, products are still sold under the Obus Forme name, especially their innovative backrest, which has come a long way since it was invented by a struggling salesman back in 1979. Twelve years have passed since Roberts was murdered and many leads have dried up, but as long as Roberts's murderer remains at large, the case is far from over. Detective Sergeant Ray Zarb believes there is someone out there who knows the truth.

"I feel that it will be solved," said Zarb. "I have to keep that hope, at least for myself and the family, who have been patient with me. Every victim's family wants closure. They want to know who's responsible, and to move on with their lives. It's never going to be the same, but at least there's that sense that a chapter has ended." Sometimes, witnesses come forward years after a murder, and are more open to discussing what they saw or know. It is rare, but not unheard of for someone to approach police decades later with information. "I've had cases where people have called that are 40 years old, and thought they were solved, and 'I wish I had told the police that information many years prior,'" said Zarb.

The strange demise of Frank Roberts exposed the professional and personal life of one of Canada's most successful businessmen, and in the process raised more questions than answers. The murder has the earmarks of a professional hit, committed in the early morning hours of August 13, 1998, outside the place Roberts felt most at home: the business he founded in his garage, based on an idea for helping fellow back pain sufferers. There are many chapters in his life, but the last one — who killed him, and why — has yet to be written.

Chapter 11

Domenic and Nancy Ianiero (2006)

IN THE AREA OF MEXICO KNOWN as the Mayan Riviera, luxury four and five-star resorts glisten like a string of precious jewels for miles along the highway, all the way down from the Cancun International Airport. Once passengers get off their respective flights and make it through customs, they must weave their way through swarms of men and women dressed in neon orange, yellow, or bright blue T-shirts, all of them promising free jungle excursions in exchange for a minute of your time, sixty seconds that quickly turn into a two-hour sales pitch for time-shares. Unseasoned travellers who make eye contact are quickly surrounded, as brochures, free maps, and coupon books are shoved into their hands. Experienced tourists, many of them already dressed in sandals and shorts, tighten their grasp on their carry-on bags, look straight through the high-pressure salespeople, and make a dash for the automatic doors and freedom.

Once outside the air-conditioned airport, weary travellers are greeted by a blast of hot air and the distant rustling sound of palm trees and traffic. Immediately past the airport doors they are welcomed by grinning locals selling light beers like Corona, Modelo, and Bohemia, served with a twist of lime and salt for five American dollars per can. After a four-hour plane ride, *nothing* tastes better than an ice-encrusted can of beer.

Just a few feet away from the beer booths the nauseating stench of diesel exhaust is overwhelming. Dozens of buses, vans, and taxis sit idling, waiting to take tourists to their resort destination. Drivers make the trip along the 307 Highway from Cancun to Tulum countless times every day, stopping briefly at one resort to let people off before moving on to the next, like worker bees endlessly pollinating flowers. On many of the buses fast-talking tour guides grab the driver's microphone and ask, "Is everybody happy?" Everyone roars "Yeah!" in unison, and white plastic cups filled with more beer are passed around. Welcome, *turistas*! Kindly leave your inhibitions at the airport.

In Mexico, driver warning signs and speed limits posted along the highway are more of a suggestion than a rule. Near the side of the road, crews of small, powerfully built Mexican workers are engaged in a multitude of physical tasks. Some are sweeping discarded soda cans and fast food wrappers, robotically stepping out of the way at the last possible moment as buses full of tourists whip past close enough to make their torn T-shirts flutter in the wind. Others are busy operating massive bulldozers, ripping up trees, soil, and shrubbery for what will become the foundation of another massive luxury vacation property. Just a few years ago, much of the area was jungle, home to howler monkeys, pumas, lizards, and tropical birds. Today the animals are being squeezed out to make way for elegant resorts with imperial-sounding names like Grand Riviera Princess and the Riu Palace; compact, all-inclusive cities, constructed entirely of marble, granite, and glass.

Originally known as the Cancun-Tulum Corridor, the area was rechristened Riviera Maya — or Mayan Riviera, depending on who you're talking to — back in 1999. The name comes from the long road running south from Cancun to the magnificent ancient archaeological ruins at Tulum, along the Caribbean coastline. All things considered, the new name is decidedly sexier than its predecessor, conjuring images of the French Riviera, on the Côte d'Azur. Much like its French counterpart, the Mayan Riviera is home to brilliant blue skies, turquoise waters, pristine white beaches, and beautiful, tanned women and men. The most notable difference between the two Rivieras is that in Mexico it's possible to spend a week feasting and drinking for about $2,000. Off-peak season, or during hurricane weather from June to November, the rates can be even lower. In France, where the Euro is king, one must actually be rich in order to live it up on the Riviera. In Mexico, travellers can exchange one Canadian dollar for at least ten pesos and pretend to be someone they're not for a couple of days.

On the way to the Mayan Riviera's many resorts there are still signs of old Mexico — a boarded-up gas station, a rickety fruit and vegetable stand — but these are rapidly giving way to iconoclastic American mega corporations like 7-Eleven, McDonald's, and Home Depot, which acquired Home Mart, Mexico's second largest home improvement retailer, back in 2004. With its economy on the rise, Mexico is a country of contrasts. On the median across from one luxury resort under construction, a thin woman who looks like she's about to topple over is pushing an old man in a creaky wooden wheelchair. A moth-eaten, striped blanket covers his lap and pale stumps poke out where his legs are supposed to be. When cars and trucks come to a stop at *topes*, the highways unmarked speed bumps, they move from one stopped vehicle to the next, silently pleading for change, his hand rattling an ancient McDonald's coffee cup containing a few coins. This is the Mexico that their tourism board doesn't want you to see; the Mexico that few vacationers want to acknowledge.

For many Canadians, the Mayan Riviera provides exceptional value for the tourist dollar and offers a great deal more to see than other inexpensive southern destinations, like Cuba, where side trips to Havana are about as exciting as it gets. Mexico is rich in archaeological ruins, like Chitzen Itza (one of the most important sites of the Mayan culture), Tulum, Coba, and many others. At ecological parks like XelHa and Xcaret, tourists are welcomed to swim alongside nurse sharks and parrot fish, or take a leisurely stroll through a jungle paradise.

Repeat travellers to "winter getaway" destinations like Mexico, Cuba, and the Dominican Republic often refer to the resorts as all-inclusives. Canadians with time on their hands and a few dollars set aside make the flight south several times a year. For them, the resort itself often doesn't matter, as long as it meets several criteria: *Warm weather?* Check. *Rating of four stars or higher?* Check. *All the booze and food you can eat?* Double check. *Book the trip, before I change my mind.*

Mexico is seen by many as the place to escape Canada's brutal winters. But the country has recently become known for more than its warm waters, blue skies, and glistening white beaches; it's also known for attacks on unsuspecting tourists, unbridled police corruption, and, in some cases, murder. Compounding the problem, local police will rarely investigate crimes, choosing instead to totally dismiss the allegations as the product of a tequila-fuelled imagination, ignore them entirely, or even laugh them off as "pranks." In some instances, local police do take an interest — when they feel they can benefit financially. Often they'll ask for a few hundred American dollars in exchange for rounding up the perpetrators and "correcting" their behaviour, which usually means beating them to within an inch of their lives.

Not all that far away from the highway security checkpoints of Mexico's resorts, the country's drug trade is rampant, merciless, and deadly. Border cities like Tijuana experience three or four murders *per day*, and no one is exempt from the brutality of drug lords and their bloodthirsty minions. Innocent bystanders, including young mothers and their infant children, have been gunned down on the streets and in their cars, caught in gang crossfire. Honest Mexican police officers fighting the war on drugs have been decapitated, their heads discovered with their police ID cards and credentials crammed into their mouths. The corpses of journalists who dare to write about Mexico's drug trade and name suspects have been found on village and city streets first thing in the morning, their remains riddled with dozens of bullets.

Perhaps the harshest punishment inflicted by drug lords is reserved for squealers, those brave or foolish enough to turn against their fellow dealers and jeopardize their illicit livelihood. Some have been found dissolving in vats of corrosive substances like lye, their flesh, blood, and bone turned into a thick chemical stew. Others are dumped like sacks of trash by the curb outside their homes, their mothers and fathers discovering their bodies, bearing the marks of torture. To ensure they've made their point, drug lords will often pin notes to the bodies, written warnings informing whoever finds them that this is the fate of anyone who rats on a drug dealer, or steps on his turf.

On rare occasions the good guys come out ahead. Recently, police posed for photos beside one of their recent biggest hauls: a mountain of red, plastic-wrapped bales of marijuana totalling more than 563 kilograms, over 1,200 pounds. There is plenty more where that came from. What North American police and United States Drug Enforcement Administration agents fear is that the organized crime and brutal violence that comes with the drug trade will also travel north.

Those fears are not unfounded, nor are they exaggerated. In 2008, the U.S. Justice Department said Mexican gangs are the "biggest organized crime threat to the United States." In an attempt to bring the violence under control, Mexican President Felipe Calderon sent armed troops across the country, but soldiers and police are outnumbered, outgunned, and unable to deal with drug lords who think nothing of taking a human life. In 2007, over 5,300 people reportedly died in Mexico as a result of drugs and gang violence. In some cases, relatives refused to claim the bodies of the murdered sons, brothers, fathers, sisters, or mothers, fearing reprisals from gangs. Far from improving, the situation is worsening by the day, and innocent people are getting caught in the crossfire.

For Canadian and American tourists looking for a cheap, fun-filled vacation, this is not the Mexico they know and love. That is the *other* Mexico, the country's evil twin, a dark place where murder, police corruption, drug wars, gangs, beatings, rapes, and robberies are everyday tragedies. The battles waged over cocaine remain illusory to them, something best relegated to unread articles in newspapers and magazines. When you're sitting on a partially-submerged stool by a five-star resort's poolside bar, drinking your fifth piña colada of the day and slipping into comfortable numbness, the last thing you want to think about are young mothers being gunned down.

For years, luxury vacation properties along the Mayan Riviera have had their share of controversies, many of them quickly hushed up by resorts smart enough to know that bad news travels faster than ever thanks to the Internet. From January to December 2005, 675,216 Canadians travelled to Mexico. In 2008 that number significantly increased, to 1,144,650. Every year, the numbers keep growing. For many tourists from Canada and the United States — especially places like Texas, where bigger is better but unlimited is the best — the reasons to visit Mexico are simple: it is vastly cheaper than a trip to Europe and closer than many other southern destinations. The weather is consistently warm and, with the exception of the rainy season, precipitation lasts for just a few minutes. The food is tasty and abundant, and the alcohol is free flowing. Why worry about not being able to drink the water when there is plenty of beer to be had?

On websites like *TripAdvisor.com* people post honest reviews of their experience at resorts like the Barcelo Maya. Some are from nitpickers who complain about towels not being fluffy enough, but the majority come from experienced travellers who raise valid points about the resort, including quality of food, amenities, and location. Occasionally, the comments are about darker things, including muggings, hotel safes being broken into, balcony doors that won't lock, and tourists being threatened, beaten, even raped. Other sites, like *www.playa.info*, contain forums about every aspect of Playa del Carmen and the Riviera Maya, the good and the bad.

Much like Cancun, the Mayan Riviera has seen more than a few suspicious deaths of the "did he slip while drunk, or was he pushed off the balcony?" or "was he killed in a hit and run, or was he beaten to death?" variety. For families of tourists who died in Mexico, there is often a lingering doubt about the circumstances surrounding their demise. Were they indeed the victim of an accident, or were they murdered by locals? In the highly controversial unsolved case of Canadian couple Domenic and Nancy Ianiero, one of the few established facts is that they were the victims of murder. Beyond that, the case has been mired in rumour and innuendo, cruel inferences, and outright lies.

On the morning of February 20, 2006, the Ianieros — a couple in their fifties from Woodbridge, Ontario — were found brutally murdered in their hotel room. That was just the beginning of a highly publicized nightmare that continues to this day for their family. Since the double homicide almost every story dealing with crimes against Canadians in Mexico that's published in newspapers, magazines, or on the Internet refers to the Ianieros. It has become a *cause célèbre*, a complex political firestorm involving high-ranking government officials from both Mexico and Canada, allegations of police incompetence, cover ups, misinformation, and endless speculation and finger pointing over suspects and motives.

In the four years since the double homicide, both Canadian and Mexican authorities have been widely criticized for how the case was handled, not just at the time but also in the weeks, months, and even years that followed. Mexican authorities have been accused of making comments so inflammatory, so wildly misleading, that they would make Machiavelli blush with shame. In Canada, the authorities have been lambasted time and again for doing little, if anything, to protect the safety and security of its citizens abroad.

In almost every way imaginable, the murders of Domenic and Nancy Ianiero serve as a tragic example of how *not* to conduct a murder investigation. The Canadians blamed the Mexicans, the Mexicans faulted the Canadians, and almost everyone blamed the hotel — perhaps deservedly. Instead of properly preserving the crime scene, the room in which the Ianieros were found — Number 4134 at the Barcelo Maya Beach Resort — was quickly cleaned. Blood and potential evidence was mopped up almost immediately after the discovery of the bodies, long before police arrived at the crime scene. Was this, as some have claimed, an attempt to cover up the murders and destroy evidence, or a clumsy, misguided attempt by the management to make things appear "normal" for other guests?

To add to the family's grief, lurid crime scene photos showing the couple lying in pools of blood were soon leaked to the media. The images were published in a widely circulated Mexican tabloid and eventually found their way online. If pictures that were crucial to an investigation were slipped to the Canadian press and published, several people would undoubtedly be fired or put in jail.

"What does that tell you? The integrity of the whole investigation was shot," said Mark Mendelson. "If that would have happened here, the investigators would have gone out of their minds." A former long-time officer with the Toronto Police Service, Mendelson spent fourteen years in Homicide, investigating over one hundred murders and countless suspicious deaths, not just in Toronto but around the world, including the U.S., Bangladesh, and Jamaica. Soon after he retired from the force, in 2005, he set up his own company and now works as a licensed investigator. Ironically, he was a guest at the Barcelo Maya for his niece's wedding just over a week before the Ianieros were murdered, and was widely consulted in the media after the homicides for his familiarity with the resort and observations on how the investigation was handled.

Of the investigation itself, some Canadian police officers, lawyers, and private investigators have said, without sarcasm, that viewers of television shows like *CSI* and *Law and Order* would likely be more knowledgeable and have done a better job of locking down the crime scene, gathering evidence, and maintaining the chain of custody than the Mexican Police. Even though maids were cleaning up the blood, it is important to remember that crime scenes are rarely, if ever, uncontaminated.

"They have their own agenda. They don't like guests knowing that someone has been murdered the next block over," said Mendelson. The first step that should have been taken was to seal off the entire area, not just the room where the bodies were found.

"Lockdown," said Mendelson. "Lock it completely down. Lock the whole main building down, and make it a crime scene — it *is* a crime scene. Don't let people in there with buckets of water, and get every security guard coming in there and having a look, and then the police arriving, and forensic guys in and out — lock it down. It's Homicide 101. You only get one shot at the scene: once the scene's contaminated, the scene's contaminated. Once it's gone, it's gone. And every time someone walks into a crime scene, they bring something with them, and they leave something out with them. It may be innocuous, it may not be, because you haven't examined the scene."

Even though hotel maids cleaned much of the blood by the time police arrived, Mendelson said there is still a great deal that could have been done, such as determining the size of the area, the dimensions and layout of buildings and rooms, and the locations of entrances and exits. Many guests at the resort were not questioned at the time of the murders or in the days that followed. Literally dozens of potential witnesses got on a plane and flew home without so much as a statement being taken by Mexican Police. Proper police procedure would see all guests and staff being interviewed, including those who may have seen the Ianieros in the hours before the murders. Interviewing guests, said Mendelson, could have given local authorities a better sense of any suspicious person or persons paying extra attention to the couple.

"Were they [the Ianieros] in discussions with anyone else?" asks Mendelson. "Were they more comfortable with certain staff members at the bar, and had long conversations? Were they hanging around other people who obviously weren't part of their party? Was someone trying to schmooze up to Mr. Ianiero? You want to find out who they socialized with, and what they did. Did anyone see anything untoward? Was he flashing money around? Was he wearing a lot of jewellery, and having people come up and say, 'Oh, let me see that bracelet,' or whatever. Just to give you an idea of what they were doing, and of course, you're doing all this after the fact, and playing catch-up."

Mendelson said that the old adage, "everybody is a suspect," is not all that inaccurate. "With any homicide, you start at home, and you work your way out … You eliminate people as you go. You alibi them, you confirm their alibi or corroborate their alibi, and you remove them, and you move the circle wider and wider and wider. You start with your victim. Who is your victim? What's your victim all about? What does he do? Who are his enemies? Who has he pissed off? Who has he had other issues with in the past, be they legal issues, or personal issues, threats in a club, or whatever. You start there, and you find out. People don't just get stabbed in their hotel rooms for no reason. It's rare, it's the rarest, so that's where you start, and you go out from there. You're chasing after the fact. You're chasing a government that is changing its tune every fifteen minutes with a different tact, a different direction; police that have a reputation for not being very efficient or very good, also being corrupt. So you've got an uphill battle."

Following the murders, a number of hotel guests approached Canadian police of their own volition, stating that no one ever approached them for their statement in Mexico. The problem, said Mendelson, is that these tourists were contacting police several weeks after the double homicide, long after they had returned home from Mexico. "They're saying it from here or other cities, so yeah, it was botched-up," he said. "You always want that first, pure version."

Just days after the killings, Mexico's state Attorney General, Bello Melchor Rodríguez y Carrillo, said the murders were the work of professional killers, going so far as to state on the record that the murderers were, in fact, Canadian. "Based on the tests that we have completed, we are very certain [they are Canadian]," he told the Canadian Press. Although he later changed his story about the killing being a professional hit, the damage had been done. His unfounded theory about the status of the killers and their country of origin was repeated in newspapers and websites around the world, distorting how the case was handled.

As someone who has investigated mob murders, Mendelson said the widespread theory initially put forward by the Attorney General is unlikely. "I've been involved in murders involving organized crime, and this is not the scenario they follow," said Mendelson, who questions not only the reasons for the murders, but the choice of weapon used by the killer. "Traditionally, organized crime doesn't use edged weapons, they use guns. To me, it has all the hallmarks of a robbery, unless you can find some sinister plot that would require him [Domenic Ianiero] to be killed, it's a robbery." It is also doubtful that there would have been any reason to kill Mrs. Ianiero if organized crime was behind the murders.

The thought of someone hiring professional contract killers in Canada to travel all the way to Mexico to carry out a hit may sound intriguing, but the odds of successfully plotting and committing a double homicide in another country are very low. There are too many risks involved. Even before leaving Canada they could be seen and photographed. There are airplane tickets to deal with, manifests listing the names and seats of passengers, passports, countless airport security cameras, checkpoint after checkpoint, metal detectors, security guards, X-ray machines, and customs agents, to name a few of the potential roadblocks. To Mendelson, a professional hit man flying all the way to Mexico just doesn't fit. "In one day, they could have been killed in Woodbridge," said Mendelson. "It just seems like a lot of work, and a lot of risk."

By all accounts, fifty-nine-year-old Domenic and his wife Nancy, fifty-five, were not just kind and generous parents and grandparents, but thoughtful and loving to everyone they knew, making them about as unlikely a target for murder as you would ever find. Domenic was semi-retired and worked as a real estate agent, selling mainly residential properties. The people he worked with considered him friendly and easygoing. Both Domenico and Annunziata were born in Italy, but met in Canada in 1964, and married in 1968. The parents of three daughters and a son, the couple devoted much of their time to looking after their children and, eventually, their grandchildren. One of their daughters, Lily, was getting married, and instead of having the wedding in Woodbridge, Ontario, they decided to fly down with family members to Mexico. It was going to be a pleasant, much-needed break, especially for Nancy, a devoted grandmother who hadn't taken a vacation in about ten years.

The wedding party of eighteen flew to Mexico and checked into the Barcelo Maya Beach Resort on Saturday February 18, 2006. A party was held the next night and lasted until about two in the morning. Domenic and Nancy left for their room before the party ended, around 11:10 p.m. They were still tired from the flight, and Domenic's foot was bothering him, apparently the result of a cyst he had recently developed.

The next morning, the parents of the groom knocked on their door shortly before 8:30, as they had made plans to go for breakfast together. There was no answer. They tried knocking again. No one came to the door. Others were called, including the bride, groom, and several guests. They tried knocking on the door yet again; still there was no reply. An employee from the resort was called and the door to the Ianiero's room was opened with a master key. No one could have been prepared for what they found.

Inside, both Mr. and Mrs. Ianiero were on the floor, dead. Nancy was discovered in the bedroom, face down, and Domenic, shirtless, was in the ensuite bathroom on his back. Both were lying in unimaginable amounts of blood, the result of their throats being slashed. The scene erupted into chaos. Guests in other rooms remember hearing people crying, swearing, and the sound of glass breaking. Two female guests staying in a room across from the Ianieros opened their door, and remembered seeing a number of people in the hallway, sobbing and visibly upset. The two thirty-something women — long-time friends who lived in Thunder Bay, Ontario — had been at the Barcelo for about a week by then, celebrating a friend's wedding that was unconnected to the Ianieros. The pair had gone to bed shortly after midnight, and didn't hear anything unusual until the commotion in the hall the next morning.

As unbelievable as it may seem, several guests remained unaware that the murders had taken place. When a Chevrolet Suburban hearse pulled up later that day, to take the bodies to the Funerales Del Caribe in Playa Del Carmen, some guests believed an elderly person had passed away from natural causes — these things happen, even on vacation.

The two women from Thunder Bay soon checked out and got a ride back to the Cancun International Airport. On the way out of the resort they were not approached by hotel staff, stopped by anyone in authority, or questioned by the police. The pair returned to Canada, totally unaware that within hours they would become the prime suspects in the brutal murders of Domenic and Nancy Ianiero; an accusation that would hang over their heads for years to come.

The day of the murders, Mexican State Attorney General Bello Melchor Rodríguez y Carrillo said the prime suspects were two other Canadians who had already left Mexico. The lurid story was immediately picked up by Spanish-language newspapers that published front page stories about the crime the next day. Early reports stated that the Ianieros were found wearing jewellery and that both were stabbed to death with a kitchen knife, when, in fact, their throats were slashed and the murder weapon was never recovered. Initial news reports in Canada spoke about a Canadian couple being brutally killed at a "posh Mexican resort" where they were attending their daughter's wedding. Foreign Affairs Canada was able to confirm that a homicide had taken place, but did not immediately release the couple's names or details about how they died. One of the

Mexican newspapers in Playa Del Carmen used no such discretion when they published the names of the victims, along with speculation about the motive for their murders.

On the surface, there appeared to be no valid reason to kill Domenic and Nancy Ianiero. The statements made by the Attorney General of Quintana Roo — that the murders were a professional hit — not only tainted the investigation from the onset, but made it seem as though the Ianieros were somehow involved in mob activities. Bad news travels fast. The family had to endure the misfortune of being stigmatized because of their mother and father's Italian heritage.

The murder of two Canadians at a five-star resort in Mexico was the first of its kind to take place in the Internet age. The result was crime scene photos and misinformation — in Spanish and English — being disseminated across the globe at lightening speed. Until recently, news of the Ianiero homicides would have been transmitted to newspapers through wire services, dot matrix printers, and grainy photos sent via fax. Today, anybody with an Internet connection can read or circulate their views on anything, even someone's perceived guilt or innocence, without checking facts, verifying sources, or separating truth from fiction. The unchecked spread of the photos touched off a war of words between the governments of Canada and Mexico that rapidly threatened to explode into an international incident, with accusations flying between politicians and lawyers.

Before the Ianieros there had been other cases of tourists being murdered in Mexico, but this one was different. The homicides did not take place in a dangerous town or village, or during a wild, alcohol-fuelled party in Cancun, a city that attracts approximately 2.7 million visitors every year. The murders took place on the Mayan Riviera, behind the walls of a secured resort, a serene spot many people believed was almost as safe as being in Canada.

In order to appreciate how difficult it would be for a cloak-and-dagger type killing to take place in one of these resorts, one must first understand how they are designed, constructed, and operated. Many of the four and five-star vacation properties on the Mayan Riviera are unlike hotels in North American cities, where someone off the street can walk into the lobby and ask questions about rates and amenities before deciding if they're going to stay there for the night. These are expansive, multi-million dollar properties, comprised of a series of big and small buildings interconnected by walkways and roads, often one road for guests and an out of the way back road for deliverymen and resort staff. Restaurants, pools, athletic facilities, bars, reception areas, and guestrooms are often set far apart. Some of the larger resorts use multi-passenger, modified golf carts, and even electric trains to shuttle guests and their luggage back and forth.

In many ways, these resorts more closely resemble updated versions of walled medieval cities, encircled by secure, high stone barriers illuminated by multiple spotlights. Almost all of the bigger properties, like the Barcelo Maya, are accessible by a single road leading off the highway to the gate. Closed-circuit monitors, electronic barriers, intercom systems, and manned security booths keep track of guests arriving and leaving the resort. Guests must give their room number and sometimes ID, such as a birth certificate or passport, to guards at the gate every time they enter or exit. There are security cameras and guards patrolling the grounds twenty-four hours a day, making it virtually impossible for a killer to sneak onto the property, track down the Ianieros, kill them, and leave undetected.

In the media the story was dubbed "Murder in Mexico." While barbs were being traded back and forth about who should have done what and how the investigation should be handled, the Ianiero children were left to deal with the brutal and unexplained deaths of their mother and father.

Two days after the killings, Mexican Police reiterated the earlier stories about the murders being carried out by Canadians. As "proof," they offered bloody footprints found leading from the Ianiero's room to where the two women from Thunder Bay had stayed. For anyone possessing a modicum of common sense — and who had seen the grisly photos and cell phone video of maids hurriedly mopping the blood from the room and the hallway — the most obvious conclusion would be that the cleaning staff tracked some of the blood from the crime scene to another room, or rooms, while doing their rounds. The authorities, eager to release the names of the killers, are unable to do so right away, since sloppy record taking by staff at the Barcelo doesn't reveal if the spelling of the names is correct, or even if they are the names of men or women.

Within a few days, Mexican Police stated they had the names and photos of the two Canadian suspects. Stories in a local newspaper suggested that a third person was involved. Police won't say where the photos were from, although it was later revealed by guests at the hotel that security appeared tight, with guards toting walkie-talkies and constantly snapping photos of vacationers. Some of the guests didn't consider the photos an invasion of privacy, while others felt that the relentless picture taking wasn't just annoying, it was unnerving.

Less than a week after the murders, the Attorney General for Quintana Roo backpedalled on his earlier assertion that the Ianieros were killed by members of organized crime. Instead, the women who stayed in the room across the hall — two single mothers from Thunder Bay — were now the primary suspects, along with a third person.

A week after they were killed, the bodies of Domenic and Nancy Ianiero were returned to Canada for burial. Before any funeral could take place, the Toronto Regional Coroner, Dr. David Evans, stepped in and invoked Section 15 of the Coroner's Act, giving him the right to examine a deceased person arriving in Ontario if foul play is suspected. Even though the Ianieros were the victims of murder, the international law requiring bodies to be embalmed for transportation still applied, and they arrived already autopsied and embalmed, raising concerns that yet more evidence had been lost. However, some of the most important evidence was still intact, namely the knife wounds on the couples' throats.

"That doesn't horribly hamper an autopsy," said Mark Mendelson. "It makes it a little more difficult at our end to do it, but wounds are wounds, entrance shots, and gunshot wounds."

While the Ianiero family was making funeral arrangements, the two women from Thunder Bay were holding a news conference, stating categorically that they had absolutely nothing to do with the murders in Mexico. There wasn't anything in their backgrounds to suggest they could be capable of committing a violent act like murder, but as outrageous as the accusations were, there was a legitimate threat that they could be extradited to Mexico, a foreign country with a vastly different system of justice than Canada, to face charges of murder. The thought of being shipped off to a country where they had no understanding of the law or the language, where corruption is rampant, to languish in jail for years, was terrifying. To make matters worse, the Canadian government was slow to take any initiative in the investigation, and took a week to go on the record about the murders.

"We have a situation where Mexican authorities almost by the hour, the story changes," said Public Security Minister Stockwell Day. "At one point the Mexican authorities said there were two people, another time they said there were three; then they said it was a professional killing. Now recently they've been saying we know where they [the killers] are in Canada, we've got their addresses. The thing is taking on bizarre proportions."[1] Day added that the motivation behind Mexico trying to "deflect responsibility" and pin the blame for the murders on two young Canadians was that the country is a prime tourist destination — murder is never good for business. For the two young mothers from Thunder Bay, the words of Canadian government officials were of little comfort. The prospect of extradition to Mexico was beginning to look more and more like a reality.

In Canada, newspapers published editorials about the murder allegations, and were quick to tell their readers that they should consider travel destinations other than Mexico. The *National Post* said Mexico's law enforcement and system of justice needed drastic reforms and until that happened, "Canadians planning their next vacation in Mexico might have reason to look elsewhere." Others, like radio talk show host Bill Carroll, encouraged his listeners to forego trips to Mexico entirely. Newspapers were flooded with letters and emails from irate readers denouncing Mexico, saying the country, its police, and its government were corrupt, and unworthy of Canadian tourist dollars. Some called the Mexican judicial system "ludicrously and deliberately incompetent," and dismissed the outrageous allegations against the two Thunder Bay women, calling it "preposterous."

About two weeks after the murders, the Ianiero's friends and family gathered at a Woodbridge funeral home to pay their respects to the slain couple. By that time, the York Region Police were involved in the homicide investigation. Officers were placed outside the funeral home, taking notes of cars and visitors. Two days later, March 6, 2006, Domenic and Nancy were taken to a Woodbridge church before their burial, while dozens of news cameramen stood outside on stools to get images of mourners entering and leaving the church. At one point during the hour-long service a member of the family told everyone gathered there, "You shouldn't have to defend your name," addressing cruel inferences that the couple were targets for assassination.

Over the next few weeks more news surfaced in Mexico. A sample of hair found in Nancy Ianiero's hand was tested for DNA. Many believe it belonged to the killer, but the results reveal that it was her own hair. Subjecting the hair to analysis was necessary, but if a well trained forensic team had been at the crime scene, they would likely have suspected that the hair belonged to the victim, not the suspect.

"It's not surprising," said Mark Mendelson. Bodies are sometimes found with strands of their own hair clenched in their hands, such as drowning victims who flail and reach out for anything they can. "People do it when they're dying. It's a natural physical reaction."

The confusion and contradictions that began the moment the bodies were discovered continued throughout the entire month of March, as stories were published about what was said, who said it, and how the investigation was being handled in Mexico. Mexican Attorney General Bello Melchor Rodríguez y Carrillo — widely quoted in the media for singling out the Thunder Bay women as the killers — soon changed his story again. The duo were never suspects, he said, just potential witnesses. Inexplicably, Vicente Fox, then-president of Mexico and known for making outrageous comments, spoke to the media, repeating the Attorney General's earlier assertion: the Ianieros were killed by Canadians, and the murders were not random. For the women from Thunder Bay accused of murder, and the family of the Ianieros, this was madness.

As incredible as it seemed, the Attorney General made even more inflammatory statements, baseless accusations that could have been corrected with a single phone call to Canada. The ex-husband of one of the Ianiero daughters was a member of a Guatemalan hit squad and involved in the Mexican drug trade, according to Rodríguez. The statement would be laughable, were it not for the damage already caused by the Attorney General's previous unsubstantiated comments. The comment would backfire. Not only was the ex-husband not in Mexico at the time of the murders, he was a court officer who worked for the Toronto Police, and a friend of the private investigator — a former detective — sent to Mexico to investigate the murders. Even when this knowledge was presented to him, Rodríguez repeated the erroneous statement a few months later. The knowledge that he was mistaken did not seem to deter the Attorney General from his pursuit of justice, right or wrong.

Nancy and Domenic's only son, Anthony, retained the services of respected Canadian lawyer Edward Greenspan, who immediately criticized the Mexican president for speaking about the case as a head of state and interfering in the investigation. It proved to be the beginning a highly charged war of words between Greenspan and Mexican authorities. A meeting was held in late May with Greenspan, Anthony Ianiero, and Bello Melchor Rodríguez y Carrillo. The results were less than satisfying. Greenspan stated that the Mexican Attorney General — the man who was supposed to be investigating the murders, not making unfounded allegations — was "arrogant, pompous and downright rude." Following Greenspan's request for information Rodríguez replied, "We're not here to answer specific questions."

These remarks did not sit well with Greenspan. "No president of a state should get involved. No president should give marching orders to the police," he told the CBC. "This investigation has turned into some form of political football. It will be impossible to reach a fair conclusion."[2] Ultimately, Greenspan was right. The murders are still unsolved. Even though four years have passed since his meeting with Rodríguez, his opinions of him remain the same.

"The Mexican Attorney General has never changed his spots, whether it was the first time I criticized him, or the second time, or the third time," said Greenspan from his downtown Toronto law firm. "He issues false information. He issues false releases [and] makes statements that are simply not true, like he couldn't care less what the truth is. And I've not seen any change. I've seen him retreat a couple of times, but as far as I'm concerned, he's not retreated from his central lines, which we feel in some cases are made up as he goes along."

For the two women from Thunder Bay, accused by Mexican authorities of the murders, the fight to protect themselves and their reputation was far from over. To compound their fears about possible extradition, a Mexican newspaper, *Novedades de Quintana Roo*, received a strange tip: an anonymous letter postmarked from Hamilton, Ontario. The typewritten letter stated that the Ianiero's killers are Canadian. The letter, which arrived soon after the murders, went on to suggest that authorities should investigate three people who flew from Cuba to Cancun the week of the murders; two Canadians and one Latino, possibly a Mexican. "Will you please ask the police to check out the possibility of Canadians flying from Cuba to Cancun on the week that the murders took place?" the writer asked.

For Greenspan, the Thunder Bay women were never valid suspects. He later said that any misguided notion about the two — later dubbed "soccer moms" on CNN's *Nancy Grace* show — being cold-blooded killers is "a tragic sideshow." One of the reasons that they were considered suspects, according to Mexican authorities, was the presence of blood in their room.

A private investigator on retainer with Greenspan's office was soon sent to Mexico to see the police files, and check out the crime scene at the Barcelo Maya. "I don't think it's a cover-up," said Christopher M. Downer of allegations that blood was mopped from the floors almost immediately after the bodies were discovered to destroy evidence. "I think it's a tourist thing, and they [the Barcelo resort] don't want to interrupt the day-to-day activities, so as a result of that, they got people traipsing up and down the hallway, as opposed to it being cordoned-off."

Today, Downer is a private investigator on retainer for Edward Greenspan; for twenty-four years he was an officer with the Toronto Police Service, before retiring with the rank of detective. In June 2006, Downer flew to Mexico with a Spanish-speaking lawyer from Greenspan's office. As a former officer, Downer is aware of how police protocol is handled in Canada, and soon discovered the differences in how the two countries conduct homicide investigations. One of his main goals was to get access to the Mexican Police file on the case, which was difficult in Toronto without receiving photocopied pages with entire sections blacked out. They applied for, and received, a power of attorney, which enabled him to view the whole file.

"With the power of attorney, we were able to gain access to the entire murder file. So we actually stayed with the lead investigator in the police station — not literally — but we were with him four or five days straight, maybe 12, 13 hours a day, going over everything in the entire police file," said Downer. "And any questions they [Mexican Police] had — they're not familiar with Canada — we were there for that purpose, to actually assist them in solving the murder."

The entire investigation in Mexico was fraught with contradictions and unanswered questions, many of which could only be answered by reviewing the original file. What actually happened to the Ianieros? Were they targeted, or the innocent victims of a robbery gone wrong? How well, or poorly, did local police investigate the homicides? Downer and the lawyer were allowed to look at the file, but not bring it back to Toronto. The first time they reviewed it, remembers Downer, it contained no mention of the two women from Thunder Bay. The second time he looked at the file, there was reference to a television converter found in the women's room that had Ianiero blood on it. Rodríguez, the Mexican Attorney General, stated traces of blood from the Ianiero's had also been found in other areas of the room used by the Thunder Bay women, including the key slot, bathroom taps, and the refrigerator. "The evidence is clear," said Rodríguez. "The Canadian couple was killed by professionals with experience in these kinds of jobs. It was not done by an amateur." He also alleged the killer or killers tried to clean the blood in the hall and the room.

"They wanted no evidence or no suggestion that any harm had come to anybody in that hotel," said Ianiero family lawyer Edward Greenspan. "And so, when they cleaned up the room and took their mops across the hall, the bloody mops left blood on the trail over to the room across the way." It is now widely believed that any blood found in the room of the two women from Thunder Bay was transferred there by maids on the soles of their shoes, their mops, and the rags they used to clean the Ianiero's room.

"As far as the file was concerned, there was nothing in there about the Thunder Bay women being suspects, with the exception of photographs of them being in a wedding party," said Downer, who said the Mexican Police did the right thing when they retained all photographs taken of wedding parties around the time of the murders. As for the crime scene being in disarray, Downer said that was a situation created by the hotel, not the officers. Local police didn't arrive until about ninety minutes after the bodies were found, and the federales — Mexican Federal Police — didn't show up until even later, long after the crime scene had been disturbed by maids. To add to the confusion, an all-clear was issued by someone and the crime scene was taken down before it was fully examined — then it was put up again.

"You're already losing evidence that is already there, because of the cleaning that is happening before you arrive," said Downer. "Given everything that happened, I actually thought the Mexican Police did a better than anticipated job. I was impressed with the work that they did. I also looked at it as a lack of training, and they just had a different way of doing investigations than we did."

In Mexico, police examine and process homicides very differently than in Canada. Instead of detectives doing the legwork and questioning witnesses, the Mexicans assign a lawyer to the file. To complicate matters, authorities in Mexico are extremely process oriented, sending many formal letters and requests. In Canada, police officers use notepads to initially record information. In Mexico, Downer found that officers' notes were typed, not handwritten. When he asked to see the original notes, he was told that that wasn't the way they did things in Mexico, and no notepads were ever found, raising the question: what was used to take notes in the first place? Another challenge facing Downer was language. When an English speaking person in Mexico gives as interview to police, a translator interprets what they are saying; in Canada, interviews are taken down word for word, and can be used weeks or months later. "What they do down there is they have someone paraphrase what you're saying," said Downer, adding these witness statements aren't as accurate when someone is translating them directly.

Downer's experiences with Canadian authorities in Mexico were puzzling. After arriving with the lawyer, he soon made contact with the Canadian Embassy in Mexico City, not for the purpose of asking them for information, but to let them know he and the lawyer were Canadians, and they were in Mexico to look into a murder investigation. Inexplicably, members of the staff refused to come out and talk to him. Downer remembers standing outside the Canadian Embassy while the lawyer accompanying him was on a phone, calling embassy personnel *inside* the building. Considering a Canadian investigator had travelled all the way to Mexico to delve into the murders of two *other* Canadian citizens, being told by his country's embassy that they wouldn't speak to him was bizarre. Over the phone, staff told the lawyer that Downer would have to email officials in Ottawa first, and that Ottawa would then contact embassy staff in Mexico to give them permission to meet with him. Ironically, just a few hours after being told he couldn't speak to Canadians at the embassy, Downer and the lawyer met with a Mexican national ambassador, who not only didn't have any issues speaking with him, but went so far as to arrange a meeting with Attorney General Rodríguez.

"I thought that was fascinating, considering that we were Canadians and were there to assist, and we couldn't get our own government or their representatives to actually come out and meet with us," said Downer. Despite the Attorney General's belief that the two women from Thunder Bay were responsible for the murders, there was another, more viable suspect: a security guard at the Barcelo Maya who had disappeared the day after the murders and has not been seen since.

A former Mexican soldier and bodyguard to a Quintana Roo governor, thirty-six-year-old Blas Delgado Fajardo was working as a security guard at the Barcelo Maya resort for six months before the murders of Domenic and Nancy Ianiero.

Following their arrival in Mexico, the Ianieros ate dinner and went to their room. They were both tired and the cyst on Domenic's foot was causing him some distress. Many of the corridors and rooms at the Barcelo look exactly alike, and the couple got lost. Tired and in pain, Domenic hailed Delgado as he was driving by in a golf cart. The security guard obliged and drove the grateful couple to their room. Delgado claimed to have some medical training and offered to massage Domenic's foot, to ease the pain. He was apparently in the Ianiero's room around 12:30 a.m. for half an hour, attending to Domenic's aching foot, and returned a few hours later, at 2:30 in the morning. The butchered bodies of the couple were discovered about six hours later.

For months, lawyer Edward Greenspan tried to determine if Mexico's Attorney General had issued a warrant for Delgado's arrest, and was repeatedly given the runaround. Rodríguez released a press statement saying an arrest warrant was issued. One of Greenspan's lawyers, Todd B. White, soon confirmed that was a lie.

"They [the Mexican Attorney General's office] claimed that Blas Delgado was located in the United States, and that a request was made through Interpol, and that extradition had been confirmed with the federal government of Mexico — no Interpol request has ever been made, no warrant, no request for extradition, and no Americans have ever been contacted. He just lied through his teeth," said White, a senior lawyer working with Greenspan on the case. "They would say, 'We have found Blas Delgado in the United States of America.' 'Whereabouts?' 'In Florida, or Texas, or California.' Well, that's a big area to find a guy, unless they found him in three parts, which is crazy. And our lawyer would make applications to confirm whether or not any of this was done; all of it was a lie. They've never taken any steps to locate him in the United States or Mexico."

The Ianiero's room at the Barcelo had been ransacked. Initial reports said a lamp was knocked over, drawers opened, and personal belongings strewn about, but nothing valuable was missing. The room safe was found open. Records indicated it had been opened a dozen times the day they were killed. Domenic's wallet was still in his back pocket when he was found, and Nancy's handbag was intact on the top shelf of the closet. A bag on the bed had been rifled through, but it didn't seem as though anything was missing.

Italians often give money as a gift to newly married couples. However, all the wedding gifts were left back in Canada, and no large amounts were taken down south. The Barcelo, like many other resorts in Mexico, was accustomed to hosting wedding parties, and whoever killed the Ianieros may have believed there was cash from the wedding in the room.

Private Investigator Downer methodically recreated a sequence of events leading up to the murders. Since there was no sign of the room being broken into, it is believed the Ianieros let Delgado — the security guard with a military past — inside to attend to Domenic's sore foot. At one point, Domenic went to the ensuite bathroom, to the right near the main door, and sat on the edge of the bathtub, soaking his feet. In many Mexican resorts, room doors are opened and lights are activated by using a plastic, electronic key card reader, located immediately inside the room. Once the card is inserted into the slot the lights turn on; as soon as the card removed the lights go out.

Downer believes Delgado, who was already in the room, yanked the card from the slot, plunging the room into darkness. Coming up behind Domenic, knife in hand, he grabbed the older man, who kicked and flailed his legs and feet, splashing water all over the bathroom. In seconds, Delgado slashed his throat from ear to ear and Domenic fell to the bathroom floor, on his back. Nancy, realizing the room had suddenly gone dark, heard the commotion and grabbed her purse, fumbling to find the second room card. Walking in darkness, she almost reached the front door when Delgado grabbed her from behind. As he slit her throat she fell to her knees and slumped face down to the floor. The Ianieros, happily married for thirty-seven years, were dead.

"The person who did this didn't leave the room right away," said Downer. "They actually took the duvet off the bed, and tried to stuff it under the door to try to avoid the blood going into the hallway." When the bodies were found, police found a Hudson's Bay card underneath Nancy's remains and another card on top of her. Since the balcony door was still locked, the killer, allegedly Delgado, must have left through the front door. Assuming he is the killer, a man with military training like Delgado would be bright enough not to leave fingerprints or the murder weapon behind — no fingerprints were reported found at the scene. Downer soon learned that Mexican Police ran out of Luminol, a chemical used to detect traces of blood, and had a hard time getting any to use at the crime scene.

A knife had been found on the beach near another resort. It was handed over to Thunder Bay Police before being sent to Toronto for forensic testing, but was determined not to be the knife used in the killing.

Even though he disappeared immediately after the murders and was a person of interest, it took several months for a search warrant to be issued for Delgado's premises. The first thing Downer asked was: did the police seize his clothes? "The inference was, he [Delgado] had met Domenic the night before, and massaged his foot, and then the next night, he came back and he killed them. The night of the murder, he was all dressed in black, not in his uniform. I'm not the forensic guy, but there could be bits of transference from Domenic onto this guy's security guard clothing, so why not seize the clothing?" Mexican Police did find a potentially crucial piece of evidence in Delgado's room: a cardboard coaster with telephone numbers written on it. Tragically, the coaster wasn't properly kept in an evidence bag — instead, police glued it into their file. "Maybe protecting evidence isn't exactly their expertise," said Downer, shaking his head.

At the time of the murder, all employees at the Barcelo Maya were required to have their photograph taken. The only image of Delgado that was provided to Greenspan's team was a blurry, black square. To date there has been no trace of the man believed to be the Ianiero murderer, and that remains the only known image of Blas Delgado Fajardo.

———————

For the two women from Thunder Bay, the nightmare of being the prime suspects in the Ianiero murders dragged on for years. Despite meeting with Foreign Affairs Minister Peter MacKay, and being told their case would get the government's "highest priority," there was no follow-up. The women soon created a website[3] for others to share their experiences about Mexico, and to lobby Canada's federal government for a travel advisory.

"As has been widely publicized in the media, on February 23, 2006, we became the prime suspects in the internationally renowned Ianiero murder case that occurred at the Barcelo Maya Beach Resort in the Mayan Riviera, Mexico on February 20, 2006," they wrote. "Despite a complete lack of evidence to link us to this horrific crime, as is demonstrated by Mexico's own official police file, we remain the prime suspects in this case and have even been deemed 'professional assassins.' This was officially reiterated by the lead investigator in the case, Bello Melchor Rodríguez, as recently as April 2007, during an exclusive interview with *W-Five*. Today, as the Ianiero family searches for justice, we continue to fight to clear our names of this horrific allegation, with little or no support from Foreign Affairs Canada."

Deeming Mexico unsafe, the women urged the Canadian government to better protect its citizens abroad. They believed that "political agendas" were at work to protect the country's lucrative tourist industry, an industry that — despite numerous attacks on tourists from Canada and other countries — shows no signs of slowing down. "When the president of Mexico chooses to comment on an open murder investigation stating 'Canadians are responsible,' then one must question the true motives behind the officials involved in the case."

The women from Thunder Bay were discussed on a *W-Five* documentary, and on the U.S.-based *Nancy Grace* program on crime and justice. The two so-called "soccer moms," petite women who regularly attended church and volunteered in their community, lived under the spectre of extradition to Mexico. Not until July 2009 were they no longer considered suspects by Mexican authorities. During a press conference, lawyer Edward Greenspan confirmed the sole suspect was Blas Delgado Fajardo. "There is now an arrest warrant for him and him alone," said Greenspan. "Anything that filtered through the Attorney General became evidence that he wanted to move the crime away from it being a Mexican in the region killing Canadians. That was his primary purpose in life on this case. If that was his job, he performed his job admirably. He lied about everything."

Although the Ianiero children were pleased that an arrest warrant was issued, the key suspect in the murder of their mother and father still has not been caught. Instead of the murders of Domenic and Nancy Ianiero being a case of "Canadians murdering Canadians" — as stated by Bello Melchor Rodríguez y Carrillo, the Mexican Attorney General for Quintana Roo — it was most likely a robbery gone tragically wrong.

In the years since the murders the names Domenic and Nancy Ianiero have become a lynchpin for almost any story about murder and corruption in sunny Mexico. Since their bodies were found on February 20, 2006, other Canadians have died in Mexico, murdered or killed under questionable circumstances. In January 2007, young Woodbridge native Adam De Prisco, just nineteen, was killed outside an Acapulco nightclub. A Mexican doctor attributed the death to a hit and run driver, but the teen's family and friends maintain he was beaten to death. In May 2007, an Alberta man, Jeff Toews, thirty-four, died after allegedly falling from the second-floor balcony of his Cancun resort hotel; his family maintains that due to his head and back injuries, he was beaten to death. Just a year later, in May 2008, a twenty-nine-year-old named Bouabal Bounthavorn was shot in the head three times in his hotel room in the city of Cabo San Lucas. His girlfriend was shot in the foot and survived.

Most recently, in September 2009, a sixty-year-old woman from Quebec was found brutally murdered in her apartment on the Mexican island of Isla Mujeres. After living between Canada and Mexico for years, retired financial consultant, mother and grandmother, Renée Wathelet finally decided to move to the tranquil island just months before her death. She had been stabbed multiple times and her throat was slashed. Wathelet kept a number of personal blogs documenting her life on Isla Mujeres, and had recently been writing about a twenty-four-year-old boatman named José, a "veritable encyclopedia" full of wondrous stories. A man named José Joaquin Palacios was arrested trying to flee the murder scene. The apparent motive was a robbery, which resulted in her murder. Immediately before her death, Wathelet wrote about the beach she loved on one her blogs: "Lost in thought, I arrive at the little cove where every morning, I take time to take time. A moment in which I can attune my breathing to the rhythm of the waves; a moment in which I look to the north, towards Montréal — hello everyone, yes I think of you every morning!" An hour later, the woman her friends called "The Nomad" was dead.

There are numerous other questionable cases, not all of them involving murder. Brenda Martin, a women working in Mexico who invested money in a fraudulent scheme with her former employer, spent more than two years in a Guadalajara-area jail, some of it sedated and on suicide watch. She returned to Canada in May 2008. Some members of Parliament called for a boycott of Mexico to protest her treatment.

Canadians have not been the only victims of Mexican injustice — far from it. In recent years there have been numerous cases of American citizens being kidnapped and held for ransom. In 2007 alone, at least twenty-six San Diego County residents were kidnapped and held for ransom. Some were recovered safely, a number were wounded or died. Recently, two female real estate agents were kidnapped in southern Tijuana after showing a property to a prospective buyer. The kidnappers — inept, desperate, or just plain greedy — demanded $350,000 U.S. for their safe release, which was quickly whittled down by the women's families to $27,000, approximately one-thirteenth the original ransom amount. Before the women could be released, authorities were able to track down the vehicle used by the kidnappers. Thankfully, they were released unharmed, and three men were arrested for the crime.[4]

In August 2007, the Ianiero family launched a lawsuit against the tour operator, claiming breach of contract, negligence, and emotional distress. They also claimed that the tour operator did not warn them that there was a greater risk in travelling to Mexico than other tourist destinations, and that the Barcelo Maya had inadequate security. There were also allegations of improper screening of hotel security guards, that ground level patio door locks were broken, and that some doors were missing deadbolts.

The man believed responsible for the deaths of Woodbridge couple Domenic and Nancy Ianiero remains at large. He has not been seen since the night of the murders. "Personally, I don't think they want to find him," said private investigator Downer. "He used to be a bodyguard for the Governor General, and I would imagine in his travels he's seen a lot of things he obviously shouldn't have seen. Remember, this is all speculation, but it might not be in their best interests to find him, assuming he's alive."

Chapter 12

Seven Feet Under (2007 to Present)

IN WHAT HAS BECOME ONE OF the greatest mysteries to come out of British Columbia since the first documented sighting of mythical lake monster Ogopogo in Lake Okanagan back in 1872, a number of feet have been washing up on the West Coast's idyllic shores. Not just any feet, but human feet, and not merely a foot here or there, but *seven* of them since August 2007. Waterlogged and decaying inside athletic shoes manufactured by Adidas, New Balance, Nike, Campus, and Reebok, the different-sized feet are from both males and females. Except for a few, most have not been linked to any one person.

There is something especially unsettling about discovering parts of a body — especially when they come inside of an article of clothing, like a shoe — that have been washed onto beautiful beaches like some ghoulish gift from the sea. The mystery of the disembodied feet has generated more questions than answers, namely, where did they come from? Are the people the feet were once attached to still living, or dead? If they are dead, did they die from natural causes, suicide, accidents, or were they murdered?

Of the first six feet that were found, four were determined to be from males and two were from females. The most recent foot was discovered on Tuesday October 27, 2009, by two men walking along a beach at

Number Six Road and Triangle Road, in Richmond, British Columbia. Like the other feet, this one was discovered inside of an athletic shoe, a Nike, size eight and a half. Within just a few days, the British Columbia Coroner's Service was able to identify the foot as belonging to a twenty-five-year-old male from the Lower Mainland. The man, whose identity was withheld at the request of his family, had been missing since January 2008, and was identified through DNA analysis. Based on details from his family, police did not believe foul play was involved in his death, and that his foot separated from the rest of his body thorough natural disarticulation, caused by a combination of decomposition, warm water, and marine life activity.

With the discovery of each new foot, media attention exploded, not just in Canada but worldwide. While it is not uncommon for human remains to be found floating in water or washed up on beaches, tangled in seaweed, the number of feet being recovered in a relatively short time did little to quench the public's morbid fascination. International magazines and newspapers around the globe, from Australia's *Melbourne Herald Sun* to the *Guardian* in England, have featured stories about the gruesome discoveries. Along with the news came the inevitable theories and morbid, tasteless puns, like "something's afoot," "toe the line," "I'm stumped," and "one step at a time." Press conferences by police in British Columbia have featured large maps with pinpoint locations of where the feet were discovered, and photos of the shoes in which the rotting remains were found.

Is it possible all of the feet came from men and women who chose to commit suicide, died in accidents, or perished in natural disasters? So far, none of the found appendages reveal telltale marks of having been removed from the rest of the body through mechanical means, such as a knife or saw, yet the sheer number of feet that have been discovered on British Columbia's beaches have inevitably led to countless theories. Were the remains from victims of Asian human trafficking, or the bodies of people killed in the Indian Ocean tsunami in 2004? At least two hundred thousand people perished in the tragedy, and many of the bodies were swept to sea and never recovered.[1] Neither theory holds much credibility. Oceanographers were able to determine that the bodies the feet came from originated along the West Coast, and forensic experts concluded that the feet separated naturally from the leg, not cut or hacked off. Although floating human remains can travel a considerable distance, it is nearly impossible that body parts from Tsunami victims could have travelled all the way from Asia to the shores of British Columbia. They're more likely to have originated off the Straight of Georgia.

Others have speculated the feet are from the bodies of victims of organized crime, drug dealers, or stowaways who were savagely dumped overboard. Some believe they could be the remains of men missing from a 2005 plane crash off Quadra Island, or bodies from a boating accident. Are they the remains of drowning victims, since there is no evidence of foul play, such as cut marks on the bone? Possible, but again, highly unlikely; finding so many feet in such a short period of time without any accompanying arms, legs, torsos, or heads would be a remarkable coincidence.

Some have posed scenarios that are far more nefarious than drowning or accidental death. Are these washed up remains the result of a sick prank by a twisted individual working at a funeral home or mortuary — or someone else who would have access to cadavers? Even more disturbing: do these feet come from the victims of a serial killer? The theory is unsettling, and not as farfetched as some might believe.

In just a few years, over twenty men have disappeared from the Vancouver area, never to be seen again. Were they the victims of a murderer who disposed of the bodies in water and let nature take care of the rest? Why would just the feet be found, and not the remaining parts of the body? There is a morbid explanation for why body parts, even entire sets of remains, can sometimes be preserved and look "fresh" for years after death.

Depending on the weather and climate, the condition of a human body can change considerably in a very sort time. In dry, hot temperatures, such as those found in the desert, it is possible for a body to quickly lose its moisture and literally mummify. Remains found in damp earth or cool water can take on a waxy appearance, and develop adipocere, from the Latin words for fat (*adipo*) and wax (*cera*), especially in areas of the body prone to fatty accumulation, such as the breasts, buttocks, cheeks, or abdomen. Adipocere is the result of a chemical reaction that occurs when fat reacts with water and bacterial enzymes, which break down into fatty acids and create a greyish-white or brown, soap-like substance sometimes called grave wax, mortuary fat, or the thoroughly repugnant expression, "corpse cheese."

Bodies or body parts kept under cool conditions, such as moist earth or cold water, can remain remarkably well-preserved. There have been numerous cases of bodies being exhumed in cemeteries a century after being buried and being easily recognizable, as if they had just been interred a day or two earlier. With the added protection of athletic shoes to guard against marine creatures, disarticulated human feet submerged in cold water can sometimes survive intact for years. Many athletic shoes are made out of leather attached to tough synthetic materials, like woven nylon, plastic, and foam, which can float for hundreds of miles. It is also possible, but very unlikely, the washed up remains are the result of the erosion of a cemetery. It is a possibility, because there have been cases of graveyard remains being washed out to sea, but extremely doubtful, because the remains would likely have been reduced to a skeleton years earlier.

Still, the main question remains: if feet are being found on British Columbia's beaches, where are the rest of the bodies? Even if heavier sections, like the head, naturally came apart in water and sank, surely something — an arm here or a leg there — would eventually be washed ashore?

For a father and his twelve-year-old daughter, finding a human foot in a shoe was the last thing they expected on an otherwise pleasant summer day back in 2007. On August 20th, the father and daughter, who were visiting from Washington State, were cruising British Columbia's Strait of Georgia, along Jedediah Island, when they spotted a men's athletic shoe. It was a right, size twelve, blue and white mesh Campus brand, manufactured and distributed in 2003, primarily in India. Out of curiosity, the little girl looked inside and found a sock. Opening the sock, she made a horrific discovery. At the time, police believed the foot had separated naturally from the rest of the body, and that foul play was not involved.

Just six days after the first foot was found, a couple named Michèle Géris and George Baugh were hiking along a trail above a beach on Gabriola Island when they saw a shoe wedged between a cedar and an arbutus tree. Using his wife's walking stick, George toppled the sneaker onto its side. Clearly visible were the remains of a sock and a weathered-looking section of bone, about the height of the shoe. After calling police, the couple remained at the scene. They were flipping through the local paper and read about the young girl finding a foot in a shoe less than a week earlier. This athletic shoe was a size twelve, like the other foot, and they were convinced this was the corresponding appendage. Not only was that foot not a match to the other, this shoe was primarily white, the manufacturer was Reebok not Campus, and this was also a right foot! The odds against finding two male feet less than a week apart in the same general area, both wearing size twelve athletic shoes but coming from different people, were astronomical.

Almost six months passed with no other feet found. For officers from Delta Police, the Royal Canadian Mounted Police, DNA analysts, and B.C. Coroner's Service, it looked as though the mystery of the floating feet was perhaps nothing more than a bizarre coincidence. Then, shortly before Valentine's Day in 2008, a third foot was found. On February 8 of that year two forestry workers made the macabre discovery on Valdes, a tiny Island community accessible only by float plane or private boat. Detectives from the Vancouver Island Major Crime unit were sent to search the area, but were unable to find any other body parts. To add to the mystery, this third blue and white shoe came from yet another manufacturer, Nike, and was a different size than the previous two shoes, a men's right size eleven. Investigators were able to determine the footwear was produced in 2003, and sold throughout Canada and the United States for a very short time, from February 1 to June 30, 2003.[2] Like the other decaying feet, this one was found in a sneaker and wearing a sock. Sent to the coroner's office for testing, the first, second, and third foot were all found within a close proximity, on islands less than forty miles from each other.

Just three months after the discovery of the third foot a fourth appendage was found, adding to the mystery. Believed to have been washed down the Fraser River, the foot — like the three before it — was still dressed in a sock and sneaker. This time, however, the right foot was a woman's size seven, a blue and white New Balance runner produced in 1999, and sold through many major retailers. The foot was spotted on May 22, 2008, on Kirkland, an island in the Fraser Delta between Richmond and Delta, British Columbia. Kirkland is an uninhabited island, its caretaker discovered the shoe partly submerged in the water while walking along the shoreline. Police determined the area to be a crime scene, and sealed off a section of beach while they searched the island for other human remains. None were found. The discovery reignited concerns from the public and endless questions from the media. How far can ocean currents carry the feet? How long can waterlogged sneakers stay afloat? What was the source of the feet? Did they come from people who died in plane crashes or boating accidents? Could they be the remains of people who committed suicide, or the murder victims of drug dealers or biker gangs?

Forensic experts and police were busy eliminating individuals from their missing persons list of 243 males and 159 females when, to their amazement, a *fifth* foot was found floating in the water near Westham Island on June 16, less than a month after the discovery of the fourth foot. Spotted by two hikers, the left foot was partially submerged in water and, like the others, was still wearing an athletic shoe, a men's size eleven Nike. Through DNA testing, police were finally able to confirm a match: the fifth Westham Island foot and the third foot, found on Valdes Island, belonged to the same male. Although this foot, like the others, did not reveal any tool marks and appeared to have separated naturally from the rest of the body, police cautioned the public not to subscribe to any wild, unsubstantiated theories. Members of the RCMP and local B.C. police, overwhelmed with media calls from across Canada and around the world, addressed the many theories swirling around the discovery of the floating feet.

A RCMP spokesperson Constable Annie Linteau said:

> There has been a lot of speculation and public discussion surrounding the discovery of these human remains much of the discussion has referred to these feet as

having been "severed." This appears to have fuelled much public discussion surrounding various theories and an underlying theme the feet are being discovered as a result of some suspicious activities. Let me be clear, the forensic examination of the feet showed no evidence these feet were "severed" or mechanically removed from a human body. By that I mean, the evidence shows that the feet were separated from their bodies by a natural process of decomposition.

We have no information to suggest that, other than the third and fifth foot, these remains are connected.

The investigative team is aware of the numerous possibilities that have caused these remains to have been discovered in the area. We would like to assure the public that the police are approaching this issue with an open mind and are examining all possibilities. In doing so, investigators are applying science, technology, forensics and subject matter expertise to the issue.

While we have narrowed down the scope of our investigation thanks to forensic and scientific expertise — we will not rule out any possibilities.[3]

Investigating the feet, and trying to find matches, has become a collaborative process involving local police, the RCMP, forensic pathologists, anthropologists, DNA analysts, and the B.C. Coroner's Service, who have also stated: "In all cases, these remains appear to have naturally separated (disarticulated) from the body. There is no forensic evidence at this time to support anything other than disarticulation as there are no tool or trauma marks on the remains.[4]

Just two days after the RCMP held a major press conference to address the discoveries, the unthinkable happened: a sixth foot was discovered. A resident of Campbell River was walking along the Tyee Spit when the gruesome discovery was made. Stunned, the local immediately contacted a local trailer park manager, who went to see for herself. The remains of what looked like a rotting foot were clearly visible inside the shoe, bones poking out of the top. Police believed the footwear, a black men's Adidas size ten, could have come from the body of one of four sets of unrecovered remains from a plane crash three years earlier, or the body of a missing fisherman or a drowning victim.

Soon, yet another foot was found, this time not in Canada, but nearby in the United States. On August 1, 2008, a camper was walking along a remote Strait of Juan de Fuca beach in Pysht, Washington, when he made the gruesome find. The foot and shoe — a black size eleven high-top — was the first foot found outside of British Columbia, and was less than fourteen miles from the Canadian shoreline. The foot, found tangled in seaweed, didn't match any of those found in Canada, and could have been in the same spot for weeks, if not longer.

Considering the morbid nature of the discoveries, it seemed inevitable that someone would play a prank sooner or later. Upon further testing, the sixth human "foot" found inside a shoe along the Tyee Spit turned out to be a hoax, nothing more than a skeletonized animal paw stuffed into a sock and a shoe, along with some dried seaweed. While some people got a laugh out of the prank, calling it a "faux paw" or dismissing it as a sick joke, others didn't appreciate the dark humour. For the families of five men killed in a float plane crash off Quadra Island in February 2005, the fake foot served as a painful reminder that only one of the bodies has ever been recovered. The B.C. Coroner's Service (BCCS) described the hoax as "reprehensible," and the RCMP launched a new investigation into the hoax, which could result in a charge of public mischief.

"It is the position of BCCS that this type of hoax is reprehensible and very disrespectful to the families of missing persons," authorities said in a written statement. "It fuels inappropriate speculation and creates undue anxiety for families and communities while wasting valuable investigative time and resources that could be spent on the main investigations."[5]

Revealing that the sixth foot was a fake had a strange effect: instead of dampening interest from the media and the public, it actually increased curiosity about the case. Months passed. The next foot to be discovered was anything but bogus. On November 11, 2008, a left human foot was found inside a women's size seven, blue and white New Balance running shoe at Finn Slough near Richmond, B.C. Although DNA testing was unable to determine race or age, it revealed that the foot was a definitive match to the right foot found on Kirkland Island almost six months earlier, on May 22.

Almost a year went by with no other feet being discovered. Then, on October 27, 2009, another foot was found, the seventh in just over two years. Two men walking along Triangle Beach in the Vancouver suburb of Richmond noticed a white Nike athletic shoe, size eight and a half. This time, however, the coroner's office was able to state the foot came from a twenty-five-year-old man, missing since January 2008. Police did not believe the man was the victim of foul play, but someone who likely took his own life.

Human feet are marvelous things. While the foot doesn't possess the same dexterity as the hand, our feet are capable not only of locomotion, but supporting hundreds of pounds of pressure per square inch. Each foot possesses a matrix of muscles, ligaments, tendons, blood vessels, and nerves, along with twenty-six bones, accounting for a quarter of all the bones in our bodies. They are a perfect marriage of form and function, yet have taken on an unsavory quality in the past few years for anyone walking on British Columbia's picturesque beaches. Taking a leisurely stroll along the beach is anything but, as many of the province's residents are waiting to see if more remains will float to the surface in the future.

Are these disembodied feet found in the waters of British Columbia the product of a crime, or the remains of some unfortunate individuals who met with accidental deaths, or chose to take their own lives? Forensic pathologists, anthropologists, and police have been able to match several of the feet, but not all. Even though police state there is no evidence to support claims of foul play, such as cut marks, the question remains: how did the feet get into the water in the first place? Can they all come from the bodies of accident victims or suicides? Until police and forensic experts are able to conclusively link the feet to specific individuals, the rumours about how they washed up on B.C. beaches — murder victims, bodies dumped by motorcycle gangs or the mob, remains floating out to sea from the 2004 tsunami, dead or dying stowaways dumped overboard, or the product of a sick funeral home employee — will continue for years to come.

Notes

Chapter 1: Richard "Dickie" Hovey and Eric Jones

1. Martin Melhuish, *Heart of Gold: 30 Years of Canadian Pop Music,* (CBC Enterprises, 1983), 65.

2. Although these were the first two clay facial reconstructions he had ever done, Master Corporal Peter Thompson's fine work led to the identification of both Richard "Dickie" Hovey and Eric Jones, bringing a resolution to the families of both young men. Deservedly, Thompson received a Certificate of Recognition that states:

> For furthering awareness of the Canadian Forces Military Police and the Canadian Forces National Investigation Service through his technical expertise in forensic artistry and facial reconstruction. In November 2006, Master Corporal Thompson's skills assisted the Ontario Provincial Police in solving a forty year old homicide investigation. His outstanding reconstruction of two skulls directly led to the identification of one of the victims, garnering significant media attention. Master Corporal Thompson has represented the Military Police in a stellar manner and is commended for his efforts.

(Canadian Forces National Investigation Service [CFNIS] 2007 Annual Report).

3. Charles McCarry, *Citizen Nader*, (Toronto: Doubleday Canada Ltd., 1972), 9.

4. Robert K. Ressler and Tom Shachtman, *Whoever Fights Monsters: My Twenty Years Tracking Serial Killers for the FBI*, (New York: St. Martin's Paperbacks edition, 1993), 133–34.

5. *National Post* online, November 24, 2009.

6. *Globe and Mail* online, December 1, 2009.

7. *www.xtra.ca*, December 2, 2009.

8. Most of the stories in *Xtra!* on Hovey, Jones, and other unsolved murders of young gay men in Toronto were written by well-known Canadian mob expert, James Dubro.

Chapter 4: Wendy Tedford and Donna Stearne

1. *Toronto Sun*, February 22, 1982, 28.

2. On Friday May 31, 1974, seven-year-old Cheryl Hanson left her home on Bloomington Road in the town of Aurora, twenty-three kilometres north of Toronto. The child was going for a walk to her cousin's house, about 1.2 kilometres down the road. She never arrived. Despite massive searches of the area by police, the militia, and thousands of volunteers, no sign of the blonde, blue-eyed girl was ever found. At the time of her disappearance, Hanson was wearing a red jacket over matching dark brown sweater and pants, and white leather shoes. She was carrying a paper bag holding white pyjamas with a red floral pattern, which were never recovered. Her unsolved case is York Regional Police case Number 1974-10461.

On August 24, 1974, the remains of twenty-one-year-old Diana Singh, a resident of Toronto, were discovered off a laneway on the east side of Keele Street, north of the 15th Side Road in King Township. The Toronto waitress was last seen alive on Tuesday August 13, 1974, at 9:00 p.m. at a Becker's Milk Store at Jane Street and Woolner Avenue in Toronto. It is believed that Singh hitchhiked to the store. Reportedly pregnant at the time, Singh was stabbed to death. Her

murder remains unsolved, and is York Regional Police case Number
1974-13382.

On Thursday August 21, 1975, the body of Tracy Kundinger,
eighteen, was discovered by children in a field outside German
Mills Public School in Thornhill. She had been strangled to death
with a piece of twine, which was still wrapped around her throat
when she was found. Kundinger was lying on her back atop a
mound of topsoil, with sand in her eyes. She was only three blocks
from her parents' home. The evening before she was discovered,
Kundinger had been in downtown Toronto working as a part-time
lifeguard at the Ottawa Indoor Pool, at 650 Parliament Street. She
left work shortly after 10:00 p.m., and took public transit; police
believe she may have been on the same Steeles Avenue bus as her
killer. Still dressed in blue jeans and a denim jacket, she showed
no signs of sexual assault. Dead for at least twenty-four hours by
the time she was found, Kundinger had also been struck across the
face with a heavy object. At the time, police investigated a possible
link between Kundinger's murder and the October 1971 double
homicide of Catherine Edith Potter and Lee Rita Kirk, found in a
Pickering, Ontario, gravel pit. Kundinger's case is still unsolved,
York Regional Police Number 1975-12772.

3. Early newspaper reports erroneously stated Yvonne Leroux had
    been shot. She was beaten to death, and the object used to kill her
    has never been recovered.
4. *Toronto Star*, June 11, 1974, 1.

Chapter 5: Chrystal Elizabeth Van Huuksloot

1. Alternative spellings include Crystal Elizabeth Van Huuksloot, and
    VanHuuksloot.
2. In 1984 the name was changed to the Lester B. Pearson International
    Airport, in honour of Canada's fourteenth prime minister.
3. Ian Lester Rosenberg was a known enforcer for Paul Volpe, a
    Toronto-born mobster connected to Buffalo crime families. A drug
    user and drunk, known to regularly consume a forty-ounce bottle
    of whiskey a day, Rosenberg's behaviour had become increasingly

unpredictable, and some believe Volpe decreed that Rosenberg be killed to keep him quiet. "The hit was most likely ordered by Volpe because Rosenberg had become extremely erratic and unreliable and Volpe worried that he was co-operating with police after being charged with extortion," wrote Stephen Schneider in his book, *Iced: The Story of Organized Crime in Canada*, (Mississauga, ON: John Wiley & Sons Canada, Ltd., 2009), 331–32. Ultimately, Volpe would outlive Rosenberg by less than seven years. On Sunday, November 13, 1983, Paul Volpe — with his bodyguard away on vacation — went out by himself to the Toronto International Airport for a meeting with some unknown business associates. The next day he was found dead at the airport, in the trunk of the dark grey, four-door BMW sedan that was leased in his wife's name. Volpe had been shot at least twice in the back of the head with bullets from a small calibre handgun. Police believed he was murdered by a professional killer. The murder of Paul "the fox" Volpe was front page news across Canada for almost a week, and remains unsolved to this day.

4. *Globe and Mail*, March 7, 1978, 2.
5. *Globe and Mail*, March 21, 1978, 3.

Chapter 6: Veronica Kaye

1. *www.mississauga.com*, November 3, 2009.
2. *Toronto Star*, "Teen Hitched Ride to Death Police Say," October 15, 1981, A19.

Chapter 7: Susan Tice and Erin Gilmour

1. In response to calls from police agencies across Canada, the government assented the DNA Identification Act on December 10, 1998. As a result of the legislation, the Criminal Code was amended and a DNA data bank was created.

Chapter 8: Sharin' Morningstar Keenan

1. The spelling of Howe's name has also been published as Denis Melvin Howe.

2. *Toronto Star*, January 24, 1983, A7.
3. The name has been changed to Toronto Ambulance.
4. *Toronto Star*, January 31, 1983, A5.
5. The name of the officer has been changed.
6. Lynda Hurst, *Toronto Star*, February 20, 1983, D1.
7. The segment was produced in Toronto on July 6, 1984.
8. Name changed at request of the artist.
9. *Toronto Star*, June 2, 1984, A13.
10. This episode of *America's Most Wanted* was broadcast in Canada on July 29, 1990. The episode also featured the case of murderer Jerry Ronald Dowe, who turned himself in to authorities following the broadcast.
11. *Toronto Star*, October 1, 1999, A18.

Chapter 9: Nicole Louise Morin
1. *Toronto Star*, March 23, 1986, A6.
2. Name changed at request of the artist.
3. Aired in Canada on May 29, 2007.
4. *Guardian*, November 27, 2000.
5. *Toronto Star*, July 24, 1988, D01.
6. Alison, an aspiring young track star, was lured to Toronto's Varsity Stadium by a man claiming to be a photographer in July 1986. Raped and killed, her body was found in Kings Mill Park in the city's west end two days after she disappeared. Francis Carl Roy, a sex offender, was linked to Alison's murder through DNA evidence, and convicted of her murder in April 1999.

Chapter 10: Frank Roberts
1. *Toronto Star*, June 26, 1980 C2.
2. *Globe and Mail*, March 25, 1982, 15.
3. *Globe and Mail*, March 7, 1995, B14.
4. *Toronto Star*, August 14, 1998, A7.
5. *Canadian Business*, October 9, 1998, 81.
6. *Globe and Mail*, November 8, 1999, B1.

Chapter 11: Domenic and Nancy Ianiero

1. CTV News, February 26, 2006.
2. CBC News, March 31, 2006.
3. The website started by the two Thunder Bay women, *www. mexicoinjustice.ca*, is now defunct for reasons unknown.
4. *www.signonsandiego.com*, "Kidnappings of U.S. Citizens on Rise," February 6, 2008.

Chapter 12: Seven Feet Under

1. To date, the exact number of people who died in the catastrophic tsunami of 2004 is not known. Many countries were devastated, including Thailand and Malaysia, and it is believed some costal villages lost more than 70 percent of their population. Initial estimates stated between 250,000 and 300,000 people died as a result of the tsunami; later estimates were closer to 230,000 dead and missing.
2. RCMP B.C. press conference, Constable Annie Linteau, July 10, 2008.
3. RCMP B.C. press conference (same as above).
4. Ministry of Public Safety and Solicitor General, BC Coroners Service, July 10, 2008.
5. BBC News, "Canada Coroner Condemns Foot Hoax," June 19, 2008.

By the Same Author

The Last to Die
Ronald Turpin, Arthur Lucas,
and the End of Capital Punishment in Canada
by Robert Hoshowsky
978-1-55002-672-6
$24.99

Although they committed separate crimes, Arthur Lucas and Ronald Turpin met their deaths on the same scaffold at Toronto's Don Jail on December 11, 1962. They were the last two people executed in Canada, but surprisingly little was known about them until now. This is the first book to uncover the lives and deaths of Turpin, a Canadian criminal, and Lucas, a Detroit gangster. The result of more than five years of research, *The Last to Die* is based on original interviews, hidden documents, trial transcripts, and newspaper accounts.

Featuring crime scene photos and never-before-published documents, this riveting book also reveals the heroic efforts of lawyer Ross MacKay, who defended both men, and Chaplain Cyril Everitt, who remained with them to the end. What actually happened the night of the hangings is shrouded by myth and rumour. This book finally confirms the truth and reveals the gruesome mistake that cost Arthur Lucas not only his life but also his head.

Of Related Interest

Running With Dillinger
The Story of Red Hamilton and Other Forgotten Canadian Outlaws
Edward Butts
978-1-55002-683-2
$24.99

This book picks up where *The Desperate Ones: Canada's Forgotten Outlaws* left off. Here are more remarkable true stories about Canadian crimes and criminals — most of them tales that have been buried for years. The stories begin in colonial Newfoundland, with robbery and murder committed by the notorious Power Gang. As readers travel across the country and through time, they will meet the last two men to be hanged in Prince Edward Island, smugglers who made Lake Champlain a battleground, a counterfeiter whose bills were so good they fooled even bank managers, and teenage girls who committed murder in their escape from jail. They will meet the bandits who plundered banks and trains in eastern Canada and the west, and even the United States. Among them were Sam Behan, a robber whose harrowing testimony about the brutal conditions in the Kingston Penitentiary may have brought about his untimely death in "The Hole"; and John "Red" Hamilton, the Canadian-born member of the legendary Dillinger gang.

Available at your favourite bookseller.

What did you think of this book?
Visit *www.dundurn.com* for reviews, videos, updates, and more!

CPSIA information can be obtained at www.ICGtesting.com
Printed in the USA
LVOW12s0834210615

443183LV00002BA/109/P